REFLECTIONS ON

Mainland China and Taiwan

COMPILED AND EDITED BY MICHAEL A. STONE

對中國大陸和台灣的思考

Via Media — Via Media Publishing
www.viamediapublishing.com

對中國大陸和台灣的思考

Printed in the United States of America
The paper in this book meets the guidelines for permanence and durability of the Committee on Production Guidelines for Book Longevity of the Council on Library Resources.

Copyright © 2023
Via Media Publishing Company
941 Calle Mejia #822, Santa Fe, NM 87501 USA
E-mail: contact@viamediapublishing.com

Cover design by Via Media Publishing Company.
Background image: Map of East Asia (orthographic projection) by Ssolbergj.
The color was changed from green to putty. GNU Free Documentation License.

ISBN 9798218188122

Dedication

In gratitude to Professor Edwin Pak-wah Leung for his care and dedication to his students and for his profound influence in the field of Asian Studies.

**Professor
Edwin Pak-wah Leung**

Left: This antithetical couplet (對聯 *dui-lian*) is a special gift brushed and presented by Dr. Caroline Keung to Professor Leung in honor of his retirement. Using the two Chinese characters of Professor Leung's first name to begin, the rhyming couplet artistically summarizes his lifetime and out-standing achievements in producing fruitful and voluminous scholarly publications; in cultivating countless young minds; and in training so many young talents throughout his long teaching career in America and overseas.

Table of Contents

Preface

I am privileged to have assembled and edited these essays by colleagues and students of Dr. Edwin Pak-wah Leung as a tribute to his teaching and contributions to the field of Asian Studies. Dr. Leung was my mentor at Seton Hall and inspired me to pursue a career as an educator. I thank the contributors for sharing their writings and for their efforts. I especially wish to thank Michael DeMarco of Via Media for publishing and supporting this book. Mr. DeMarco was also a student of Dr. Leung, and he has made a significant and unique impact on Asian Studies by publishing and writing an array of books and articles in English and Chinese languages. Most notably, he published the academic *Journal of Asian Martial Arts* (1992 to 2012) and presently focuses on his own writings, such as *Wuxia America: The Emergence of a Chinese American Hero* (2023).

Michael A. Stone

Introduction

While a handful of large American universities, beginning with Yale University, created rudimentary Asian Studies programs in late 1800s, Seton Hall University was among the first of the smaller universities to create an extensive program in East Asian Studies. Seton Hall University was also among the first higher education institutions to focus on political, historical, economic, and cultural issues rather than just language and literature.

Seton Hall created its Institute of Far Eastern Studies in 1951 under the leadership of University President Monsignor John L. McNulty (1898-2005). The timing of this undertaking was a reaction to the devastation of World War II and the Korean War as well as the developing intensity of the Cold War between the Western bloc, led by the United States, and the Eastern bloc, led by the Soviet Union. The stated goal of the Institute was "to promote better understanding between the American people and the people of the Far East." It offered various courses in history, philosophy, and political science as well as language classes in Chinese, Japanese, Korean, and Vietnamese. The University cultivated exchanges with scholars in Beijing, Taiwan, Vietnam, and Seoul which included several Catholic universities in East Asia. The initial advisory board included many figures who would go on to become prominent figures in Asian politics and academics. The board included Paul Yu Pin (1901-1978) who served as the Cardinal of Nanjing; John Myon Chang (1899-1966), Prime Minister of South Korea; Kotaro Tanaka (1890-1974), Chief Justice of Japan and, subsequently, President of Sophia University; Ngo Dinh Diem (1901-1963), President of the First Republic of Vietnam; and John Ching-hsiung Wu (1899-1986), China's Ambassador to the Vatican as well as the chief author of the Republic of China's constitution and a professor at Seton Hall's Law School; among others.

In 1961, Seton Hall created the Department of Asian Studies to direct the University's classes while its Institute of Far Eastern Studies became the leading publisher of Asian language and history books which were used by universities and government programs. Fred Fang-yu Wang's dictionaries and John DeFrances's 12-volume series of Chinese books (published by the Yale University Press) became standard texts for English-speaking students learning Chinese. See Dr. Dongdong Chen's article in this volume for more information on the development of Chinese language programs in the United States including a detailed account of Seton Hall University's contribution to this Asian language instruction and the training of language educators.

It was in this dynamic period of growth and commitment to scholarship that Seton Hall recruited Dr. Edwin Pak-wah Leung to join the faculty as an Assistant Professor in its Asian Studies Department. Born in Hong Kong in 1950, Prof. Leung earned his first degree at The Chinese University of Hong Kong in 1972. Seeking to study diplomatic history under Immanuel C.Y. Hsu and Alexander DeConde, two notable scholars in the field, he attended the University of California on a scholarship where he received an MA degree in 1974 and PhD in History in 1978. His PhD thesis was titled "China's quasi-war with Japan: The dispute over the Ryukyu (Liu-ch'iu) Islands, 1871-1881." He was then recruited by Seton Hall University as an Assistant Professor in in 1978 and was promoted to Associate Professor in 1984 and full Professor in 1992. He was elected to three terms as Chair of the Asian Studies Department.

Prof. Leung brought a new perspective to the Department and advanced the University's programs in several ways. As a specialist in modern Asian history, he served as a bridge between the historical orientation of the Department and an understanding of modern Asia. He also developed a level of scholastic achievement that would raise the profile of Seton Hall and advance the field of Asian Studies by producing an extensive body of research and literature. Dr. Leung has written or edited over thirty books as well as dozens of academic articles in English and Chinese. His book, the *Historical Dictionary of Revolutionary China, 1839-1976* was cited as the Outstanding Academic Book in 1992 by the Association of College and Research Libraries. He also received the Research Publication Award and Creative Writing Award from the Association of Chinese Professors of Social Sciences in the U.S. in 2011, several Provost Publication Awards by Seton Hall as well as the Researcher of the Year Award in 2010. In addition, he was the recipient of many grants such as the National Endowment for the Humanities, and the National Endowment for the Arts.

A full bibliography of his work appears in the Appendix. In addition, he has lectured and presented at conferences and universities throughout the world. As Visiting Professor or Fellow, he has affiliated with many universities including UC Berkeley, UCLA, Michigan, Columbia, Princeton, Yale, Illinois, Peking, Wuhan and Zhejiang Universities, Hong Kong University, The Chinese University of Hong Kong, and Tokyo University.

In addition to his leadership within Seton Hall, Dr. Leung has served in an impressive variety of positions in academic and community organizations including serving as President of the Chinese American Professionals Association, U.S.-China Foundation for Medical Science and Technology, New Jersey Alliance for Learning and Preserving the History of World War II in Asia. He was also the Founding Chairman of the New Jersey Chinese Cultural Studies Foundation, among many other leadership positions.

As a result of his contributions to the field and to the community, Dr. Leung received numerous awards, most notably the Ellis Island Medal of Honor in 2007 and the Asian-American Achievement Award from the New Jersey Asian American Ethnic Council in 1996.

Dr. Leung retired in 2018 after 40 years of teaching at Seton Hall. Although he has continued to write and lecture, he remains involved in local organizations concerning Asian and Asian-American history and issues. He was granted *professor emeritus* status by Seton Hall University. In 2022, he was also presented with the Fahy Award to recognize his lifetime achievements and contributions to the University. We, his students and colleagues, are grateful to him for challenging us to strive for a standard of academic excellence and inspiring us to continue to learn and share what we have learned with our students and those who wish to better understand other cultures.

Michael A. Stone

Contributors

- **Michael C. Mascio** received his Ph.D. from New York University. His dissertation focused on the Roman poet Horace. His subsequent research has concentrated on the Stoic philosophers of the Roman period, i.e., Epictetus, Seneca, and Marcus Aurelius. He has published works on Horace, Aristotle, and the myth of Sisyphus. He is currently at work on a book on Stoic Moral Psychology in the realm of Addiction Recovery. Dr. Mascio is a Subject Expert Teacher in Classics and Philosophy at BASIS in Scottsdale, AZ.

- **Dongdong Chen** received her Ph.D. in Linguistics from McGill University. She is a Professor in Seton Hall University's Languages, Literatures, and Cultures Department where she teaches Chinese, linguistics, and Methods of Teaching Chinese and Japanese, among other courses. She is co-author of *50 Activities for the International Chinese Classroom*, *The Chopsticks-Fork Principle x 2: A Bilingual Reader*, *The Course for Cross-Cultural Communication*, and co-editor of and contributor to the volume *Linguistics*. Prof. Chen is the Director of the Chinese Program and Director of the Graduate Program in Asian Studies. She served as Chair for the Department of Languages, Literatures and Cultures at Seton Hall University and as President of the Chinese Language Teachers Association of Greater New York and has been the Chairperson for the New Jersey Chinese Culture Studies Foundation since 2012.

- **Michael A. Stone** received an M.B.A. from Boston University and an M.A. in Asian Studies from Seton Hall University. He served as the Director of Seton Hall's Global Learning Center and on the faculty of the Asian Studies Department. His most recent book is *Exploring China's Historic Heartland* published by the Shaanxi People Publishing House. He has written articles for a variety of magazines and newspapers. Recently, Prof. Stone was a consultant for the documentary: "China: Frame by Frame" and he has been a frequent presenter at academic conferences.

- **Daijuan Gao** has an M.S. in Counseling Psychology from West Chester University and an M.A. in Asian Studies from Seton Hall University. She currently serves as an Associate Professor at Brookdale Community College where she teaches Asian Studies and Psychology.

- **Ian Murphy** earned a B.S. at Seton Hall University's School of Diplomacy and an M.A. in National Security Studies from American Military University. He is completing a Global MBA from National Taiwan Normal

University. Mr. Murphy has written several articles on international relations, security and commerce, U.S. foreign policy, and cross-strait relations. He currently provides consulting services to companies with their U.S.-Taiwan business strategies.

- **Jiayi Zhang** received a B.S. in Diplomacy and International Relations at Seton Hall University. She also received a master's degree in International Affairs from George Washington University. She has worked at the Wilson Center and Eurasia Center in Washington, D.C. Currently, Ms. Zhang is serving as a Media Supervisor for the Public Affairs Department of the Grandview Institution, a civic think tank in Beijing sponsored by the CCP.

- **Gloria Shen** earned a Ph.D. in Comparative Literature and East Asian Languages and Cultures at Indiana University. She has taught various courses on literature, history, and Chinese at Seton Hall University. She has contributed several articles and translations to academic journals and anthologies. Prof. Shen's forthcoming book is *The Unity of Heaven and Man: Confucius' Poetics and the Book of Poetry*.

- **Wangyu Tang** earned an M.A. at Seton Hall University in Asian Studies with a concentration on Teaching Chinese Language and Culture. She currently teaches Chinese in New Jersey.

- **Wei Xiang** received an M.A. in Asian Studies at Seton Hall University. She is currently pursuing a Ph.D. at Temple University with a focus on Chinese Buddhist literature of the 11th and 12th centuries and digital humanities.

- **Paofong Cheng** received an M.A. from Asian Studies at Seton Hall University and a B.A. from the University of Maryland. She has taught at Seton Hall University, New Jersey City University, and Sanchong Community College.

- **Li Kang** received an M.A. in Asian Studies and a Ph.D. in Higher Education at Seton Hall University. He is currently working as a Mandarin teacher in Wallace Elementary School in Hoboken, NJ.

- **Michael DeMarco** received a M.A. in Asian Studies from Seton Hall University. For over twenty years, Mike published the *Journal of Asian Martial Arts* and continues with Via Media Publishing. He has also participated in television documentaries that were aired on the Discovery Channel, Arts and Entertainment, The History Channel & The Learning Channel.

Statue of Laozi
ID 31134630 www.123rf.com

Bust of Marcus Aurelius
Public domain. Wikimedia.com

Chapter 1

Observing Nature:
The Philosophical Imagery of
Marcus Aurelius' *Meditations* and the *Daodejing*

by Michael Mascio

Introduction

In recent years scholars have made fascinating contributions to the comparative philosophy of Daoism and Stoicism on the meaning and implications of philosophical tenets common to both philosophies, including the injunction to 'follow nature' (Yu, 2008), the ethic of emotional detachment (Wong, 2006; Machek, 2015), and conceptions of freedom (Machek, 2018). These valuable perspectives tend to focus on comparing and contrasting the 'what,' i.e., the ethical content, of the two philosophies on a macrocosmic level. In this analysis, I propose a different kind of approach, which will focus on the 'how' of the delivery of the philosophical message in a more specific manner and context, namely, the means by which the poetic imagery drawn from nature is utilized to illustrate the philosophies in the two texts I believe to have by far the most in common with each other within Daoism and Stoicism: the *Daodejing* and the *Meditations* of Marcus Aurelius. The novelty of Aurelius' approach to the elucidation of the relationship between *logos* and *phusis* in Stoicism will be revealed to have much in the common with the *Daodejing*'s innovative approach to defining *dao*. What the texts share as much as various philosophical perspectives is an approach to the illustration of philosophical concepts through the observance of nature and the implications which follow from such an approach. Delving into the poetic images of these texts themselves reveals striking similarities of expression that point the way for important philosophical implications.

I. A Structural Parallelism: *Logos* and *Phusis* in the *Meditations* and *Dao* and *Ziran* in the *Daodejing*

In Greco-Roman Stoicism the guiding principle of all things in the universe is the *logos*, reason, or the rational element of the universe. The *logos* pervades both human nature *qua* rational animal and nature as a whole. Two brief quotations from the *Meditations* sufficiently illustrate this:

One essence and one law, the *logos* common to all animals possessing intellect. (7.9)[1] All matter is soon made to disappear into the essence of the whole and everything responsible for its existence is taken back into the *logos* of the whole. (7.10)

The Greek term for nature is *phusis*, and Stoicism makes following *phusis* the central ethical injunction by which human beings, as the only rational animals in the universe, endeavor to be in alignment with their unique share of the *logos* and with the *logos* of *phusis* itself.[2] As a concrete elucidation of this philosophical conceptualization of the relationship between the human being, logos, and phusis, consider that at one point Aurelius defines a 'rebel' as one who 'withdraws from the *logos* of *phusis*'.[3] In the pages to follow, I hope to show that the originality of Aurelius' Stoicism is found in how he consistently characterizes man's relationship with the *logos* not just through the concept of *phusis* but through the imagery of the natural world itself. It is a procedure of philosophical illustration remarkably similar to that which is found throughout the *Daodejing*.

The fundamental similarity between the *logos* of Stoicism and the *dao* in Daoism is readily apparent to anyone familiar with both philosophies. Indeed, for Christians, the Stoic influence is felt in the famous prologue to the book of John where 'the word' that 'is the beginning and is with God and is God' is *logos* in Greek, a passage translated into Chinese not haphazardly and with deep understanding of the depth of shared philosophical perspective by John C. Wu by having *dao* replace *logos*![4] But the similarities go much deeper. Consider section 25 of the *Daodejing*:

> Man follows the ways of the earth,
> Earth follows the ways of Heaven;
> Heaven follows the ways of Dao;
> Dao follows the ways of itself.

'The ways of itself' at the close of this passage is a translation of *ziran*, a term also translated as nature.[5] *Phusis* in Greek likewise could be rendered as 'ways of itself' since it represents that which is inherently natural to a living being. In her analysis of this passage, Yu makes a very convincing

---

[1] All translations from Aurelius' Greek are my own.
[2] Schofield, 2003, p. 246.
[3] *Meditations*, 4.29. The Roman formulation was *ratio naturae*, the rational principle of the natural world.
[4] Thomas Merton points this out in his chapter on the *Daodejing* in *Mystics and Zen Masters*, 1967, p. 72
[5] See the very useful appendix to key terms in the *Daodejing* in Robert Eno's translation, pages 36ff. at http://www.fang.ece.ufl.edu/daodejing.pdf

argument about how to understand what the relationship is between *dao* and *ziran*:

> What Laozi (i.e., *Daodejing*), is saying is that *dao* is characterized by *ziran* and that this should be the right state of human beings, earth, and heaven. To characterize *dao* in terms of *ziran* is the novelty of Daoism. If one simply says that it is the best life to follow *dao*, this is a common premise of ancient Chinese philosophy. Yet, if one says that it is the best life to follow *dao* as *ziran* (nature or naturalness), then we have Daoism.[6]

The relation between *logos* and *phusis* in Stoicism and *dao* and *ziran* is not merely analogous then. It is essential to both philosophies that by observing and following nature, man may find the way to live in harmony with the guiding principle of the universe. While Stoic and Daoist definitions of the man's place within the natural world may not cohere in critical ways, they need not for the texts of the *Daodejing* and the *Meditations* to illustrate their respective philosophies through a language of poetic imagery derived from the natural world.[7]

II. An Obscure Path

Delving into the poetic images of these texts themselves reveals some striking similarities of expression which point the way for important philosophical implications. Aurelius writes in multiple places of the road or path of virtue which aligns with the *logos*:

> It (i.e., the motion of virtue) has free passage advancing on a path which is hard to understand. (*Meditations* 6.17)

At another point, Aurelius speaks of that which is without *logos* wandering at random, having lost the path. Now compare the imagery applied to the *dao* in Ch. 21:

> As to the *dao* itself, it is elusive and evasive, evasive, elusive.

As *dao* itself is a word with its root meaning in path or way (hence the most common English translation of 'The Way', both Aurelius' *Meditations* and the *Daodejing* present their philosophies as following a path which is not easily understood or comprehended. The language of obscurity and

---

[6] Yu, 2008, p. 4.
[7] See ibid p. 4, paragraph 3 and a fuller discussion below.

elusiveness applied to the path in both texts points to a coherence between image and philosophical message in the style of both texts: most people are lost on another road, one which they hope leads to riches, glory, pleasure, or the like. Few are willing to seek along the obscure, dim, and hard to comprehend path of true Stoic or Daoist enlightenment.

III. Water and the Flow of Life

Those familiar with the *Daodejing* even in a passing way may well recall just how prominent water imagery is within the text. Along with the ravine or valley, water is one of the primary symbols of Daoism, for it too is the soft or passive element which overcomes the hard and forcefully active. One particular passage is strikingly evocative of the role of water imagery in Aurelius' Stoicism:

> [The spontaneous working of] the *dao* in the world is
> like the flow of the valley brooks into a river or sea.
> (*Daodejing* 32)

Compare Aurelius' poetic simile for Stoic acceptance:

> A disposition welcoming every happening as necessary,
> as familiar, as *flowing* from just such a source and fount.
> (*Meditations* 4.33)

Notably the Stoics characterized those living a life aligned with the *logos* as 'having a good flow of life', *to euroun*.[8] In fact the dominant influence on Aurelius' own Stoicism, Epictetus, pairs *euroun* with *apathes* as the two primary goals of Stoicism.[9] *Apatheia* is the state of passionlessness, or elimination of the negative emotions which can overthrow rationality, which leads the Stoic to true serenity and tranquility in life. Aurelius chooses to expand the poetic imagery of nature around the concept of good flow in order to elucidate the doctrine. Alignment with the *logos* and elimination of the passions which threaten that alignment results in the good flow of life of the virtuous Stoic. The *Daodejing* likens the *dao* itself to water in Ch. 8.[10] The person of virtue in both Daoism and Stoicism is then one who lives a flow of life in harmony with the flow of the *dao* or the *logos*.

---

[8] In Diogenes Laertius' account of Zeno's doctrine at 7.88, we find the following formulation: εἶναι δ'αὐτὸ τοῦτο τὴν τοῦ εὐδαίμονος ἀρετὴν καὶ εὔροιαν βίου ('This is the virtue of the flourishing man and a good flow of life.")

[9] *Discourses*, 1.4.1

[10] "The highest good is like water. Water benefits all things generously and is without strife. It dwells in the lowly place that men disdain. Thus, it comes near to the Dao." *Daodejing*, Ch. 10.

In both texts water which is raging or torrential represents the opposite of the *dao* or the *logos*. Here the man living in accord with nature is pictured as the calm in the midst of storm, the separate, unaffected, still object in the raging sea of life:

> To be like the cape, against which the waves ceaselessly dash: it stands firm and the swollen waves are put to sleep around it. (*Meditations* 4.49)

Compare a similar image from the *Daodejing*:

> Sudden, like the sea, like a tempest, as though endless, the mass of people all have their means—I alone am obstinate, uncouth. I alone wish to be different from others, and value feeding from the mother. (Ch. 20)

Both passages exemplify the sage as a figure of stillness and calm separate and resistant to the surging mass of humanity, driven on as they are by their deluded desires for wealth and prestige, power and official authority, sexual pleasure and the pleasures of food, and the like.

IV. Purity and Cleanliness

Both Stoicism and Daoism emphasize the elimination of the unnecessary, the superfluous, the residue of distractions outside of oneself which hinder the still and gentle state being sought by both philosophies. The *Daodejing* formulates this goal as a question:

> In cleansing and purifying your mystic vision, can you be free from all dross? (Ch. 10)

Compare how Aurelius presents the Stoic goal of self-liberation by means of purification:

> How easily contented is the one who pushes back and wipes away every troublesome or inappropriate appearance and exists in an utterly tranquil sea. (5.2)

The shared language of cleansing here evokes a state of natural being, before the addition of all the accoutrement of civilization, in both texts and philosophies. This is clear in the *Daodejing* through as the question above immediately follows one about becoming 'as the new-born babe'. In a similar vein, Aurelius selects the adjective *eukolos* to describe the state resulting from pushing back and wiping away appearances. This adjective

5

has the root meaning of easily satisfied with one's food, thus evoking a very young child satisfied with nourishment prior to the develop of personal (dis)tastes.

V. Nature Over Art and the Uncarved Block

The specific language of cleansing and purifying as part of a return to the simplicity of an existence prior to the influence of conventional societal values is part of a larger thematic pattern recurrent in both the *Daodejing* and the *Meditations* centered on the superiority of the natural to the artificial. Here we can see how the microcosmic specifics of the choice of poetic language informs the macrocosmic level of the general ethical injunction 'to follow nature' central to both philosophies.[11] Aurelius lays this out in the clear terms of philosophical exegesis in contrast to some of the more poetic similes and metaphors we have seen him thus far employ:

> No natural creation is inferior to a work of art, since the arts
> indeed imitate nature. If this is the case, the most complete
> and comprehending nature of all other natures cannot
> be found wanting in comparison with well-crafted art.
> (*Meditations* 11.10)

The *Daodejing* continually emphasizes the same philosophical perspective through one of its most famous and dominant images, that of the uncarved block.

> He finds contentment in constant virtue,
> He returns to the uncarved block. (Ch. 28)

Several passages, such as the one below, address the danger inherent in carving or cutting the block:

> Once the block is cut, names appear. When names begin
> to appear, know then that there is a time to stop. It is by
> this knowledge that danger may be avoided. (Ch. 32)

The uncarved block is the dominant image of nature prior to the application of craft. In contemplating it, one sees how simple yet complete it is. One might think of how statues of Laozi were themselves made to resemble natural formations in harmony with their topographical surroundings, as if part of the natural world rather than works of art made to stand out.

---

[11] See Yu (2008) for a careful analysis of what is and isn't shared in ethical perspective by this shared injunction.

The Stoics weren't the Cynics with their extreme ethic of the abandonment of civilized custom and return to animal nature; but they were born as a kind of hybrid child of Socrates and Diogenes.[12] This is especially true of Epictetus, Aurelius' chief influence.[13] They are highly distrustful of much of the artifice of society, high society in particular. Epictetus did not abandon his drinking cup, seeing that a child was utilizing his cupped hands, as Diogenes did. But he did find a simple clay vessel superior to vessels of greater artifice. Aurelius and the other Roman Stoics would certainly have embraced the philosophical implications of the uncarved block, for its shared ideal of a simplicity closest to nature and most devoid of the artifice of man.

The *Dao*'s greater proximity to the natural, as opposed to that created by art or craft, and Aurelius' corresponding evaluation of the superiority of nature to art, point to a shared ethic of simplicity which manifests itself within both of these texts, and in Daoism and Stoicism more generally. Acting and doing are not inherently valuable in either philosophy, since contemplating the uncarved block is superior to carving it. Both point rather to the excess of doing and action in most lives. Aurelius turns to an aphorism from the pre-Socratic philosopher Democritus:[14]

> 'If you are to be of cheerful disposition, do less.' Or perhaps
> better, do what is necessary and just so many things as
> the *logos* of an animal social by nature demands and as
> it demands; indeed this brings a cheerful disposition not
> only from doing things well but also from doing the few
> essential things (*Meditations* 4.24).

Here, Aurelius interprets a well-known ethical maxim in more specifically Stoic terms. This is another instance in which Aurelius defines the *logos* in terms of *phusis*, in this case the specific *phusis* of human beings as social animals, a core tenet of the Stoic ethical foundation. For Aurelius, men spend much of their time doing and acting outside of the requirements of the *logos*, putting themselves at odds with their natural selves. A desire to earn money to buy luxury items is a suitable example. Here, a man does more, but because he is driven by a desire for unnatural pleasures, his actions do not harmonize with his nature, and thus, the *logos*. Aurelius' injunction here is not dissimilar to the Daoist ethic of *wuwei*, one of the more difficult concepts of the *Daodejing* for many to comprehend:

---

[12] The patron saint of the Cynic extreme of rejection of civilized custom, as he rejected clothing, money, and, most infamously, facilities for bodily evacuations.

[13] Yu, 2017/1877.

[14] Democritus, along with Leucippus, is one of the original formulators of atomic theory.

Dao invariably does nothing (*wuwei*)
And yet there is nothing that is not done.

And further:

> To win the world one must attend to nothing,
> When one attends to this and that,
> He will not win the world. (Ch. 37)

Wuwei, often translated as above as 'doing nothing' or 'inaction' is not an ethic of the absence of action, but rather one of the eliminations of unnecessary action along the lines Aurelius speaks of above. The man in harmony with the *dao* will not seek to do *something*, but rather naturally do what is essential. Machek (2015) has convincingly elucidated the perspectives on freedom shared by Daoism and Stoicism in just these terms, namely the freedom that comes from doing only necessary things.

VI. The Unity of Opposites in the Man of Virtue

In accord with the simplicity and naturalness of the man of virtue is his unification in one person of qualities which are dichotomous in others, qualities which may make of one man either one thing or another, like the block after it is carved, rather than a whole which embraces multiple potentialities like the uncarved block. Both Aurelius' *Meditations* and the *Daodejing* formulate this state of potentiality through a unification of opposites in the description of the man of virtue:

> Who can be turbid, yet settling slowly clear?
> Who can be at rest, yet moving slowly come to life?
> (*Daodejing*, Ch. 15)

Again, the *Daodejing* opts for an illustration of personality through an image from nature, a pool of water disturbed but settling into clarity, thus, in essence, being neither one state nor another. Aurelius chooses to put the unity of opposites in more direct terms:

> The man following the *logos* in every way is both leisurely
> slow and quickly agile simultaneously, both cheery and
> grave at the same time. (*Meditations,* 10.12a)

The man in harmony with the *logos* possesses the dichotomous unity of the *logos* just as the man of virtue has those qualities of the *dao* represented by the simultaneity of turbidity and clarity. The lack of commitment to one state or another, the full acceptance of the potentiality of both, is

8

closely tied to two ethical concepts centered on indifference and transformation in both Stoicism and Daoism. Another key Daoist text, the *Zhuangzi*, illustrates the close relation between the unity of opposites and the indifference or lack of preference born of understanding transformation as the fundamental law of nature and *Dao*,

> 'He does not prefer the one or the other. He lets himself
> be transformed into whatever it may be.' (*Zhuangzi*, Ch. 6)

The acceptance of all things outside of virtue as indifferent, or *adiaphora* in the language of the Stoics, neither good nor bad in their essential nature, is one of the most fundamental tenets of Stoic moral doctrine. Aurelius himself shows a near obsession with the theme of constant transformation revealed to him through his observation of natural phenomena:

> Contemplate continuously how everything comes into
> being through change and habituate yourself to consider
> that the nature of all things cherishes nothing so much as
> to change existing things and to make new things similar
> to them. (*Meditations*, 4.36)

The shared approach to the expression of the unity of opposites in Aurelius' *Meditations* and the *Daodejing* is a foundational link in the larger set of connections of ethical perspective between Stoicism and Daoism.

Conclusion

I want to be clear in my concluding remarks that it is in no way reasonable to reductively consider Stoicism as Western Daoism or Daoism as Eastern Stoicism. Though they share much in terms of both ethical and metaphysical content as well as structure of thought, there are also huge gaps between these philosophies of life. The aim of my analysis here is to have elucidated how the centrality of the observance of the natural world is an inextricable part of how two central texts of these philosophies poetically express their ethical aims. The value of such a comparative philosophical approach is not so much in providing new insights on *what* these philosophies are as in offering perspectives on *how* these philosophies are illustrated in the mind of the student of philosophy.

Bibliography

DE BARY, W.M. Theodore and Bloo, I. (1999). *Sources of Chinese tradition*: Vol. 1. Columbia University Press.

HAINES, C. (1930) Marcus Aurelius. Cambridge, MA: Harvard University Press.

Hays, G. (Trans.). (2003). *Meditations.* New York: Random House Publishing Group.

INWOOD, B. (Ed.) (2003). *The Cambridge companion to Stoic philosophy.* Cambridge: Cambridge University Press.

LAERTIUS, D. (2018). *Lives of eminent philosophers.* Oxford: Oxford University Press.

LONG, A. (2004). *Epictetus: A Stoic and Socratic guide to life.* Oxford University Press.

LAOZI (n.d). *Daodejing.* (R. Eno, Trans.). Bloomington, Indiana: Robert Eno. http://www.fang.ece.ufl.edu/daodejing.pdf

MACHEK, D. (2018). Stoics and Daoists on freedom as doing necessary things. In Philosophy East and West, 68(1). (referenced in Intro)

MACHEK, D. (2015) "'Emotions that do not move': Zhuangzhi and Stoics on self-emerging feelings' in Dao. In *A Journal of Comparative Philosophy*, Volume 14. (referenced in Intro)

MERTON, T. (1967). *Mystics and Zen masters.* New York: Farrar, Straus and Giroux.

OLDFATHER, W. (1995). *Epictetus: The Discourses.* Cambridge, MA: Harvard University Press.

SCHOFIELD, M. (2003). Stoic ethics. In B. Inwood (Ed.), *The Cambridge Companion to the Stoics* (pp. 233-256). Cambridge, MA: Cambridge University Press.

WONG, D. (2006). The meaning of detachment in Daoism, Buddhism, and Stoicism. In *Dao: A Journal of Comparative Philosophy*, Vol. 5. (referenced in Intro)

YU, JIYUAN (2008). Living with nature: Stoicism and Daoism. In *History of Philosophy Quarterly, 25*(1). (referenced in fn. 6 and fn. 11)

西東大學
亞洲研究

Chinese Program at Seton Hall University, 1952-2012: A Case Study of Teaching Chinese as a Foreign Language in America[1]

by Dongdong Chen

Introduction

Teaching Chinese as a Foreign Language (TCFL) in America was inaugurated at Yale University, where Addison Van Name was recorded in the Yale University Catalogue of 1871 as the first instructor of Chinese and Japanese.[2] In 1887, Samuel Wells Williams served as the first professor of Chinese after retiring from twenty plus years of working in China.[3] Similarly, Harvard University launched its Chinese lecture in 1879 by inviting the first native Chinese, Ge Kunghua, to teach his native language.[4] Thereafter, the University of California at Berkeley in 1896, Columbia University in 1901, University of Chicago in 1936, and Stanford University in 1937 initiated their Chinese courses respectively. With these universities in the lead, the teaching and learning of Chinese slowly progressed in the United Sates because, in those days, only a limited number of serious-minded persons were attracted to the language, mainly for missionary purpose.[5]

When World War Two broke out in 1942, Yale University, at the request of the United States Air Force, started to offer intensive Chinese instruction to military personnel who were required to utilize Chinese to do their jobs.[6] In order to help pilots converse in Chinese as soon as

---

[1] I wish to thank Paul Chao, Associate Dean of Walsh Library of Seton Hall University, Alan Delozier, Director and University Archivist, and Kate Dodds, Archival Assistant of Archives and Special Collections Center from Walsh Library. Their professional help made my research effective and enjoyable. I would also like to acknowledge Dr. Yea-Fen Chen, former Executive Director of Chinese Language Teachers Association, Dr. Minru Li, Assistant Director, and Lauren Barrett from National East Asian Languages Resource Center at The Ohio State University, who readily offered their support when I turned to them for help. This article was completed in 2012. All errors are mine. A brief version of this chapter in Chinese appears in Ling, 2018, pp. 107-113.
[2] Tsu, 1970, pp. 562-578.
[3] Chao, 2007, pp. 1-25.
[4] Chen, 2011, pp. 30-42.
[5] Zhou, 2011, pp. 131-149.

possible, audio-lingual techniques, also known as "army methods," were used. In contrast to grammar translation, a traditional method that emphasized the instruction of grammatical rules with an aim to help learners achieve reading literacy, the audio-lingual method concentrated on the acquisition of oral language via intensive practices with pattern drills.[7] In addition, to facilitate the learning of Chinese pronunciation, a "Yale System" was specially developed to target English-speaking learners' difficulty with the Wade-Giles romanization system, which had been widely employed in the West to teach Chinese before *pinyin* was developed in 1958 by the People's Republic of China.

The outbreak of the Korean War in 1951 alerted many Americans to the critical importance of learning about Asia and understanding it, particularly the Chinese people and their culture. Among these was the president of Seton Hall University (SHU), who established the Institute of Far Eastern Studies (IFES), offering a wide variety of courses on Chinese language and culture.[8]

After the former Soviet Union successfully launched its first satellite in 1957, the American Congress passed the National Defense Education Act (NDEA) in 1958, with the hope of promoting the learning of Chinese as well as four other "critical" foreign languages (i.e., Japanese, Russian, Arabic, and Hindi). Universities like Seton Hall, which already had a Chinese Program, received federal grants and financial support from private foundations to enhance the teaching of Chinese. Other colleges and universities that expressed interest in offering Chinese were financially supported to launch a Chinese curriculum.

After President Nixon visited China in 1972 there was a surge in Chinese language students. As documented by an American Modern Language Association (MLA) survey, in 1974 a total of 10,576 students were studying Chinese in various American colleges and universities, with an increase of 70% in enrollment from 1970 to 1974.[9] According to another study,[10] in the late 1940s, only 25 American institutions of higher education offered degree programs in Chinese language studies, but 40 such programs were listed in the *1975 College Blue Book* and by 1978 about 180 U.S. colleges and universities were teaching Chinese. Towards the end of 1980s, approximately 250 colleges/universities, and 80 high schools offered Chinese courses.[11]

In early 1991, David Boren, a U.S. senator from Oklahoma, proposed

---

[6] Tsu, 1970, p. 564.
[7] Richards & Rodgers, 2001, pp. 50-69.
[8] *The Setonian*, November 2, 1951.
[9] Furman, et al., December 2010.
[10] Chi, 1989, pp. 109-122.
[11] Ibid., p. 110.

a National Security Education Act (NSEA) that authorized a program known as the National Security Education Program (NSEP) to address international education, i.e., the study of those foreign languages and world area that were regarded as critical to the U.S. competitiveness and security. Chinese was included in this group. The attack on the World Trade Center on September 11, 2001 spurred a renewed focus on critical languages that resulted in the National Security Language Initiative in 2006. As part of this Initiative, a Critical Language Scholarship Program was created to specially support college and university students interested in the study of foreign languages to go to the regions where the languages are spoken. With an inclusion of Chinese, there are now thirteen critical languages.[12]

Today the Chinese language has become one of the favorite foreign languages among American students. Two recent MLA survey reports indicated that by 2006 there were 661 Chinese programs in institutions of higher education, with 60,976 enrollments in 2009.[13] At the K-12 level, the latest estimates from the American Council on the Teaching of Foreign Languages (ACTFL) show a 200 percent increase from 2005 to 2008.[14] However, for a long time, Chinese was regarded as a "Less Commonly Taught Language" (LCTL) in contrast to Spanish, French, and German, which are "Commonly Taught Languages" (CTL). It was not until recently that the Chinese language began to lose its LCTL status.[15] Livaccari projected that 2012 will be the year when Mandarin Chinese becomes a CTL and "enters the mainstream" because of the "cognitive and academic benefits of the Chinese language learning" such as its "character-based writing system, tones, and long continuous cultural history."[16]

Examining the history of TCFL in the U.S., one can see that the status of Chinese has only been recently transformed substantially.[17] Some external factors, such as globalization, the rise of China as an international power, and the growing population of Chinese Americans, have directly led to this transformation.[18] On the other hand, there must be institutional causes for such a progression. In terms of advancing Chinese programming, little has been studied about the relative impact of administrative

---

[12] For details about the NSEP Program, see http://www.nsep.gov/about/ administration/; for the Critical Language Scholarship Program, see http://clscholarship.org.

[13] Furman et al., Fall 2006; Fall 2009.

[14] Livaccari, December 2011.

[15] Chen, 2011, p. 33.

[16] Livaccari, December 2011.

[17] Zhou (2011), in his article "Globalization and Language Order," discusses the development of TCFL in the U.S. within the conceptual framework of multilingualism as language ideology and order.

[18] Chen Dongdong (2011) analyzes the development of TCFL from the perspective of American policies, while Shuhan C. Wang (2007, pp. 27-52), addresses, among other issues, how Chinese-Americans' efforts in keeping their Chinese heritage affect TCFL.

leadership, curriculum design, and the quality of instructors reacting to the development of TCFL. What are the crucial elements that a Chinese program must possess in order to ensure the success of teaching and learning the language? What are the fundamental contributions that a Chinese program can make to the field of TCFL? In this article we will address these two questions by examining how the Chinese Program at Seton Hall University (CPSHU) evolved in the past sixty years. To be more precise, we will focus on CPSHU's contributions to the overall development of TCFL in the nation. Our discussion of the CPSHU will start with the establishment of the Institute of Far Eastern Studies.

Establishing the Institute of Far Eastern Studies

On October 29, 1951, during the midst of Korean War, Monsignor John L. McNulty, then president of Seton Hall University (SHU), hosted a historic luncheon at which he announced the University's establishment of the Institute of Far Eastern Studies (IFES).[19] The founding advisory board of IFES included a number of prominent figures from several Asian countries including China, Japan, the Republic of Korea, and Vietnam.[20] IFES was established to promote better understanding between the American people and people of Far East. To that end, the institute made every effort to use all means available to encourage the exchange of Eastern and Western cultures. Classroom teaching, public lecturing, research and publication were the three major activities of the Institute in its earlier years.

IFES opened on February 4, 1952, offering to the Seton Hall community a variety of courses in Far Eastern Studies.[21] The China-related courses gave students an opportunity to learn about China from many perspectives, i.e., the linguistic, cultural, historical, political, economic, religious, and social. From the beginning, the IFES courses were conducted based on students' needs and schedules. A number of programs were directed at students in journalism, business, and government services. A Certificate of Completion was issued to a student who successfully passed

---

[19] *The Setonian,* November 2, 1951.
[20] Recorded in Seton Hall University's *General Bulletin* (1952), those dignities included the Most Reverend Paul Yu-Pin, Archbishop of Nanking, China, and later a Cardinal and President of China's Fu Jen Catholic University; John Myon Chang, former Prime Minister of Korea, later Vice President of the Republic of Korea; Kotaro Tanaka, Chief Justice of the Supreme Court of Japan, later President of Tokyo University; Ngo Dinh Diem, former Minister of Interior, and later president of the Republic of Vietnam; and John C. H. Wu, former Chinese minister to the Vatican, later appointed as professor of law at Seton Hall's School of Law. As reported in a *World Journal* article by Meiling Liu about the celebration of the 50th anniversary of the Asia Center, President McNulty founded IFES at the suggestions of the Most Reverend Paul Yu-Pin, and Dr. John C. H. Wu.
[21] *The Setonian,* January 17, 1952.

a comprehensive examination on the whole area of study. A few years later, IFES started to offer M.A. degrees as part of its academic curriculum. Students could work for an M.A. in Asian Studies with a concentration in Chinese/Japanese, or in General Professional Education with a focus in Far Eastern Languages and/or Area Studies. In 1961 the Department of Asian Studies was created, which took charge of all academic matters, and a B.A. in Asian Studies was added to the curriculum in 1969. In addition to instructional activities, IFES offered a series of lectures on Chinese culture and history throughout the academic year. Among the regular lecturers were the world-renowned scholars Dr. Hu Shih, former Chinese ambassador to the U.S. and later president of National University, Beijing, and John C. H. Wu, former Chinese minister to the Vatican.[22]

In research and publication, IFES was the first publisher in the nation to produce Asian language and history textbooks, which became widely used by schools and government agencies.[23] As far as China Studies were concerned, earlier research included a wide range of projects covering political, social, economic, and cultural aspects of China. Starting in the late 1960's, publications made possible by Seton Hall University Press began to focus on the study of language, literature, linguistics, and teaching pedagogy. Some well-known works include Fred Fang-yu Wang's *Mandarin Chinese Dictionaries* (Chinese-English and English-Chinese versions), *Introduction to Literary Chinese Volume I & II*, and *Readings in Teaching Chinese* by Li Ying-che and Blanche Speer.

In the spring of 1989, the Asia Center was established. Assuming responsibility for the functions formerly carried out by IFES, the Center remained "faithful to its core mission of spanning the cultural and political divide between Asia and the West."[24] The founding of IFES, with its offering of Chinese language courses and lectures, marked the beginning of grass-roots-level teaching and learning of Chinese in America. It is at IFES that Chinese courses were opened to high school and college students, who could register on a matriculated or non-matriculated basis. It is at IFES that many key projects were established, implemented, and brought to fruition, to which we will turn one by one in the following.

Training Language Teachers

In 1958 John B. Tsu joined SHU as the second director of IFES. Two years later, Dr. Tsu founded the Department of Asian Studies and served as its chair. During Dr. Tsu's 19-year tenure at SHU, he helped CPSHU contribute tremendously to the development of TCFL in America, including

---

[22] Seton Hall University's *General Bulletin,* 1952.
[23] Kay, 2002, pp. 26-28.
[24] Ibid., p. 26.

(i) the introduction of instruction in Chinese to American secondary and elementary schools; (ii) the training of English-Chinese bilingual and bicultural educators and administrators; (iii) the compilation of Chinese teaching materials; and (iv) the creation of the Chinese Language Teachers Association and its academic journal. This section will focus on the first and the second contributions, leaving the third and fourth for the sections that follow.

After arriving at Seton Hall, Dr. Tsu soon noticed an interesting phenomenon: while the number of Chinese programs in American colleges and universities increased drastically, yet the student enrollment in Chinese did not grow at a similar rate. He concluded that to promote the Chinese language among Americans, language instruction should be brought to secondary schools so that students could start their linguistic journey at an earlier age. When the federal government and private foundations decided to provide funding to promote "critical languages" like Chinese, Dr. Tsu immediately took advantage of the opportunity to pioneer the teaching of Chinese in secondary schools. Towards that end, Dr. Tsu did three things simultaneously. First, he wrote to high school principals in New Jersey and New York proposing the offering of Chinese courses. Second, he sought financial funding to support his endeavor. Third, he looked for partners from both the East and the West Coasts to launch a nationwide movement to bring Chinese to secondary schools. Through joint efforts from principals of high schools and colleagues at Seton Hall, the project took off.

Along with two other schools, Seton Hall was awarded a grant from Carnegie Foundation in 1960, with which it established the NDEA Summer Chinese Language Institute on Seton Hall's campus to provide the most up-to-date professional training for elementary and high school teachers.[25] As recorded in an internal document of 1981 retrieved from the Archives of Asian Studies, between 1962 and 1970, Seton Hall received a total of 12 NDEA grants, some for the summer programs, while others were for programs held during the regular school year. In addition, Seton Hall received funds from the U.S. Office of Education (USOE). All these enabled various programs to be conducted with different foci and features, upgrading not only teachers' proficiency in Chinese, but also their hands-on teaching experience. For instance, during the seven-week NDEA Summer Institute in 1967, special attention was given to the question of media and methodology; students had the first opportunity to learn how to teach Chinese using a new computer-aided program, as designed and conducted by Prof. Fred Fang-yu Wang.[26] In the fall of 1967,

---

[25] *The Setonian,* November 2, 1960.
[26] CLTA, 1967, pp. 116-129.

with a grant from USOE, a full-time program was developed leading to an M.A. degree in Secondary Education for the teaching of Chinese in grades six to twelve. Each of these programs attracted many participants. For instance, the 1966 Summer Program had an enrollment of 178 students, of whom 145 were undergraduates, and 33 graduates.[27] By 1970, 95% of high school Chinese language teachers in the U.S. were graduates of either SHU or San Francisco State College programs.[28]

These developments immediately established Seton Hall as a national leader in training quality teachers of Chinese and fulfilled Dr. Tsu's vision whereby Seton Hall could compete with the formidable Asian Studies programs at Columbia University and Princeton University. In 1967, Senator Ralph Yarborough of Texas introduced a bill to provide assistance to school districts that would establish educational programs specifically for students with limited English-speaking ability (initially this program was only for Spanish-speaking students). A year later, merging with other bills that had been introduced as a result of the first, Title VII of the Elementary and Secondary Act or the Bilingual Education Act was enacted. This created bilingual programs for students whose native language was not English.[29] Under Title VII, immigrant children having limited English proficiency were taught English and other skills in their native tongue, with which, together with ESL programs, they were gradually prepared academically for receiving instruction only in English. Given that a growing number of Asian immigrants were settling in the United States, Dr. Tsu realized that bilingual education for these children provided a great opportunity for the Department of Asian Studies to train educators and administrators for educating Chinese, Japanese, and/or Korean students. By successfully training K-12 Asian language teachers, the leadership at CPSHU initiated further measures which led to the establishment of the following two prestigious bilingual programs in 1975:

> Title VII Bilingual Education Fellowship Program (Ed.S. and Ed.D.), designed to "prepare Chinese, Japanese, Korean, and Spanish bilingual education administration and teacher trainers;"

> Title VII Bilingual Education Teacher Training Program (B.A. and M.A.), designed to "train Chinese, Japanese, Spanish and Korean bilingual education teachers."

---

[27] CLTA, 1966, pp. 115-124.
[28] Tsu, 1970, pp. 574.
[29] Stewner-Manzanares, 1988.

Jointly sponsored by Seton Hall's School of Education and the College of Arts and Sciences, these programs were built to prepare bilingual administrators and teacher trainers for school districts, colleges, and universities in New Jersey, as well as other states, with an aim to developing participants' competencies in bilingual education and educational administration and supervision. More specifically, participants were trained through an interdisciplinary approach to be able to (i) develop professional knowledge of bilingual and bicultural education, including its historical, philosophical and social value; (ii) design bilingual and bicultural curricula; (iii) organize and administer bilingual programs; and (iv) teach Chinese as a first language and English as a second language. Furthermore, the programs were constructed to be flexible so that participants could individualize their course of study based on their self-selected specialization. While linguistics and teaching English as a second language were the most important components in the programs, cross-cultural studies were also stressed to insure and facilitate the acquisition of appropriate understanding and appreciation of the students' target culture. The programs were teaching-oriented, supported by practical research. Students were required to serve as teaching or administrative interns in colleges or districts after completing the methodology courses.

These two comprehensive programs soon met the national standards for accreditation established by the National Association of State Directors of Teacher Education and Certification and National Council for Accreditation of Teacher Education. An internal document of 1982 from the Archives of Asian Studies indicates that, from 1975 to the late 1980s, Seton Hall was annually assured of 15 to 20 bilingual fellowships for Chinese and Japanese doctoral students, and some 20 traineeships in Asian languages. In 1976, the Title VII Asian Bilingual Curriculum Development Center was established at Seton Hall to compile Chinese, Japanese, and Korean bilingual education curriculum materials, thus making SHU the only university in the nation to receive the Department of Education support to conduct all three bilingual programs. By 1980, the Department of Asian Studies had the following programs in place: a B.A. in Asian Studies, an M.A. in teaching Chinese, Japanese, and Asian studies, an Ed.S. in Bilingual Education, and an Ed.D. in Bilingual Education. These programs trained numerous English-Chinese speaking trainers and administrators, most of whom are now leaders in the field of TCFL. The M.A. and Ed.D. in Bilingual Education programs continued until around the early 1990s, when the federal funding stopped because of a change of government policy towards bilingual education.

Following the announcement of the American College Board in 2003 to create an Advanced Placement (AP) test in Chinese language and culture, 2,400 high schools expressed an interest in offering Chinese courses to prepare students for the exam.[30] In response to this "Chinese Fever" and a demand for qualified Chinese language teachers, a new graduate component culminating in an M.A. in Asian Studies with a Concentration in Teaching Chinese Language and Culture, was proposed in 2006, which was soon endorsed by the New Jersey Department of Education. Immediately seven students enrolled in the program, followed by many more students in the following academic years. To SHU's credit, like those graduating from the NDEA programs and bilingual/bicultural education fellowship/training programs, these new graduates are performing well in various K-16 schools.[31]

Compiling Teaching Materials

As high school and college students started to learn Chinese throughout the U.S., an urgent need for up-to-date teaching materials followed. CPSHU, with the financial support from the USOE, responded to this need, with the result that a good number of textbooks, dictionaries, and other teaching materials were published starting in the early 1960's. For instance, the aforementioned two-volume *Mandarin Chinese Dictionaries* by Fred Fang-yu Wang became popular among beginning learners throughout the United States right after they were published; the two dictionaries were reprinted by another publisher in 2002. John DeFrancis completed a 12-volume set of Chinese textbooks, known as the "DeFrancis series." These textbooks were the most widely used resources for learning Chinese in the 1970s and 80s, educating a generation of China studies scholars. In this section, we will only examine the "DeFrancis series."

In 1961, Dr. John B. Tsu reached out to Dr. John DeFrancis, offering him a six-month contract to compile a Chinese textbook for beginners. After Dr. DeFrancis completed the book on time, Dr. Tsu used the success to obtain more federal grants which eventually enabled Dr. DeFrancis to produce 12 volumes.[32] The series, published by Yale University Press for SHU are in three sets: (i) 3 conversation textbooks in transcription for the levels of beginning, intermediate and advanced proficiency; (ii) 3 parallel character versions of the conversation textbooks with identical text; and (iii) 5 companion readers, with two at the beginning level (Part I & Part II), two for the intermediate level (Part I and Part II), and one for the advanced level. The 12th volume serves as a comprehensive index to the above 11 books.

---

[30] Asia Society, 2005.

[31] This track was initiated and implemented under the leadership of Dr. Edwin Pak-wah Leung, then chair of the Department of Asian Studies, and Dr. Dongdong Chen, director of CPSHU. The program was the only kind in New Jersey in 2006.

[32] DeFrancis completed a Chinese textbook entitled *Beginning Chinese*, written in Yale's Romanization, when he was working at Columbia University in 1945.

Before discussing the essence of this series, it may help to first review DeFrancis' idea about improving learners' reading skills. Such a review would help us to understand his approach to compiling his work. In the 1960s, Chinese programs in the institutions of higher education contained two major components: one targeting learners' speaking skills and one for reading skills. Each learner could choose to focus on one or both areas. In some universities, learners could decide when to work at each, though usually the order was to speak first, then read. At that time, Chinese textbooks were published in two versions. Although both had the same content, one was in the format of transcription—either in the Wade-Giles or Yuan Ren Chao's National Language romanization system, or the Yale system—and one in the format of characters. The intent was to use the transcription version for developing learners' conversational skills while using the character version for building reading skills. In this way, students, when using the transcription version, could concentrate on pronunciation in speaking without being distracted from the difficulty in studying characters. Moreover, when learning Chinese characters, students could feel familiar with vocabulary and grammar as those had already been encountered.

This approach had, according to DeFrancis, two major problems: a rigid connection between speaking and reading and an excessive emphasis on learning characters.[33] In DeFrancis' opinion, whether a user is a native speaker or a foreign language learner, his/her vocabularies of speech and reading do not match. In some cases, spoken proficiency is dominant, and in other cases reading proficiency is dominant. The learning situation is complicated by the fact that Chinese dialectical pronunciation can differ greatly although the written characters remain the same. DeFrancis, therefore, proposed a 3-part-content program for beginners learning Chinese, as shown in Diagram 1. In this program, each part has its own major vocabulary and grammar. In the *Speaking Only* part, learners would study the vocabulary that is not likely to occur in the *Speaking & Reading* part. Consequently, when learners come to the *Reading Only* part, they would encounter the vocabulary and syntactic structures mostly reserved for written Chinese. In the overlapping *Speaking & Reading* part, basic structure patterns and vocabulary occur. DeFrancis thus suggested that in addition to having transcription and character versions of the conversation textbooks with identical text, a separate companion reader should be developed to raise learners' reading literacy.

Regarding the problem of too much emphasis on learning characters, DeFrancis pointed out that for students to learn to read Chinese, it was not merely the size of vocabulary that played a role. Since Chinese is rich in compounding, any text would contain many compounds. As Chinese compounding structure is complicated—with many different ways of

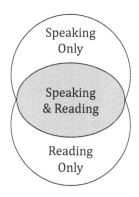

Diagram 1:
Three-Part-Content
Chinese Program
Source: DeFrancis, 1966a, p, 4.

producing compounds—merely identifying, reading, and writing the component characters of a compound would not help figure out the meaning of the whole. Thus, what is crucial in becoming fluent readers, is to study the structural combinations of Chinese characters and to read more to become familiar with different possible combinations of those component characters. Given that understanding the relationship between characters, recognizing special idioms, becoming familiar with the subject matter under discussion are more important than identifying each character to read something in Chinese, the key to teaching reading is a two-step process. First, have students learn a limited number of characters that are most frequently used vocabulary, and that occur with higher frequency in compounds. Second, expose students to more reading materials that contain numerous occurrences of compounds formed from these component characters. In this way, time spent on learning less useful, infrequently occurring characters is shifted to a more productive use of characters and compounds. Only when learners have developed an "intuitive" familiarity with Chinese compounding structures by greater exposure to reading materials would they be able to improve their ability to read fluently. To illustrate, let us look at Table 1 (see next page), which lists the number of characters, combinations, and characters of running text, and the ratios among these elements as they occur in three different sets of textbooks.

One set is comprised of the three readers in DeFrancis' series, i.e., *Beginning Chinese Reader* (BCR), *Intermediate Chinese Reader* (ICR), *Advanced Chinese Reader* (ACR). One set is comprised of the three books compiled and published by Yale University in the early 1960's, i.e., *Read Chinese Book I* (RC I) by Fred Fang-yu Wang; *Read Chinese Book II* (RC II) by Richard I. Chang; *Read Chinese Book III* (RC III) by Fred Fang-yu Wang and Richard Chang. The third one is *Mandarin Primer* (MP) compiled by Yuan Ren Chao published by Cambridge University Press in 1948. A comparison of these figures across three sets of textbooks indicates that DeFrancis' *Readers* are the only textbooks that contain fewer individual new characters—only 400 for each reader—but these characters are

23

Table 1: Characters Used in Three Different Textbooks

	MP	RC I	RC II	RC III	BCR	ICR	ACR
Number of Characters	1,372	300	300	400	400	400	400
Number of Combinations	2,200	390	620	500	1,250	2,400	2,400
Characters of Running Text	25,000	24,000	23,000	120,000	120,000	120,000	120,000
Combinations per Character	1.6	1.3	2.1	1.3	3.1	6.0	6.0
Running Text per Character	19	80	77	50	300	300	300
Running Text per combination	12	61	37	40	95	50	50

Source: DeFrancis, (1966a), p. 15.

maximally utilized in numerous combinations, as suggested by the following ratios of different elements: (i) the 400 new characters lead to 2,400 combinations for *ICR* and *ACR*, and 1,250 combinations for *BC*; (ii) each character has at least three different combinations for *BCR*, but six combinations for *ICR* and *ACR*; (iii) the occurrence of each of the 400 characters for all the three *Readers* reaches as high as 300 times; (iv) each combination occurs at least 50 times for *ICR* and *ACR*, but 95 times for BCR; (v) the number of characters in the running text reaches as many as 120,000 for all the three *Readers*. All these figures suggest a higher occurrence of characters and a richer use of combinations. In this lies the strength of the DeFrancis *Readers*, since learners are exposed to a variety of combinations of frequently occurring component characters and are thus more likely to lessen the time needed to acquire that "intuitive" familiarity which is the basis for reading fluency.

The above discussion of DeFrancis' ideas on the teaching of written Chinese helps us understand why five *Readers* are included in his 12-volume series and what role they should play. Let us now turn to his conversation set. Again, the principle of using limited but high-frequency new characters which are richly involved in compounds is evident in the three conversation books. There are 494 characters used in *Beginning Chinese*, 696 in *Intermediate Chinese*, and 904 in *Advanced Chinese*, with

25 to 47 characters for each lesson. All these are frequently-used characters, taken from the dictionary *Yutiwen Yingyong Zihui* (Frequent Vocabulary of Modern Chinese). In *Advanced Chinese*, only transcription is used for the sixty-nine relatively rare characters thereby reducing the anxiety that might otherwise arise when encountering these relatively more difficult characters. To ensure more occurrences of each individual character, several measures were taken. First, the use of characters is illustrated in words and sentences immediately following the vocabulary list so that learners will know how to use the characters. Second, dialogues and narratives containing those characters are provided to show how the characters are used in different contexts. Third, sentences containing the combinations of these new characters are repeated time and again to reinforce learners' attention to the characters in their myriad variations. Fourth, frequent reviews of vocabulary and of grammatical structures appear throughout lessons and volume units. The reminders are an effective means of delivering a lot of materials to promote fluency.

A deeper analysis of the DeFrancis series is beyond the scope of this article. However, three points are worth mentioning: (i) *Pinyin* was used as romanization when the revised edition of the series was published in 1966; (ii) *Beginning Chinese* is still in print and used in some schools in the United States; (iii) teachers and learners still contact the Language Resources Center of SHU requesting the audio files which were specially designed and developed for this series.

Creating a Profession of TCFL

For any academic discipline to develop and expand, professional networking is needed. Such is the case of the Teaching Chinese as a Foreign Language (TCFL). Since its inception, TCFL in America was only loosely scattered until 1962 when the Chinese Language Teachers Association (CLTA) was established and 1966 when an academic journal was launched. Below is a review of these momentous beginnings per the CPSHU.

As previously discussed, after John B. Tsu joined SHU in 1961, he started working to promote Chinese so that it would become a part of the foreign language curriculum in American schools. To Tsu, a crucial step was to mobilize Chinese language teachers into a means for disseminating his ideas to the educational mainstream. To do this, a small group of Chinese teachers organized a Chinese Conference within the MLA in 1961 by forming an Advisory Committee on the Chinese Language to promote its inclusion in curricula. The next year, the Committee founded the CLTA with the following objectives: (i) to actively promote the teaching and learning of Chinese as a foreign language in American elementary and secondary schools as well as colleges and universities; (ii) to develop relevant teaching materials for learners at different proficiency levels; (iii) to produce competent Chinese language teachers. Dr. Allyan Rickett, Professor of Chinese Studies in the University of Pennsylvania's Department of Oriental Studies chaired the Executive Board of the Association, while Dr. John B. Tsu chaired the Membership Committee.

In 1962, apart from encouraging more teachers to organize panels for the Chinese Conference within the MLA, Tsu and his colleagues launched the *Newsletter of the Chinese Language Teachers Association* (NCLTA). With Dr. Kai-yu Hsu, Professor of Chinese at San Francisco State College's Modern Language Department as its first editor, there was now a means to keep CLTA members informed of news in the field, including information about department changes, new programs, projects, publications, and professional meetings. Published twice yearly, *NCLTA* carried the information that was collected from a liaison at each school where Chinese was taught. By 1966, responding to the increased interest in teaching and learning Chinese in the United States, *NCLTA* was replaced by the *Journal of the Chinese Language Teachers Association* (*JCLTA*) with the main task of encouraging research on linguistic and pedagogical concerns. Adele Rickett, Professor of Chinese Studies at University of Pennsylvania's Department of Oriental Studies, was *JCLTA*'s first editor. Published thrice annually, the new emphasis on technical and research feature articles complemented the continuing need for newsletter information.

For many years, Seton Hall University was a sponsor of both CLTA and *JCLTA*. SHU's Institute of Far Eastern Studies provided all the administrative support required for running a professional organization and an academic journal, from answering inquiries about the Association to typing, packaging, and mailing the Journal, and from advancing funds to changing typeface. At the beginning, it even repeatedly assumed some of the expenses, being reimbursed only later when CLTA received some funding.[34] Seton Hall maintained the function of distributing the Journal until in February 1981, when Ohio State University took over the responsibilities. In February 1990, Seton Hall's sponsoring function for the Association was taken over by Princeton University, which turned it over shortly to another institution.

With CLTA established, and *JCLTA* launched, TCFL in the U.S. was able to grow as a profession. CPSHU not only played an instrumental role in the process of conceiving the project, implementing the idea, making it a reality, and assuring its healthy growth, but also provided leadership, with CPSHU faculty serving on CLTA's Executive Board for several years.

---

[34] In the early days, membership dues were only $3 per person yearly. CLTA was largely operated with funding from Asia Foundation, which provided $1,000 yearly to help improve the teaching of the Chinese language in American K-16 schools. The information about CLTA and JCLTA can be found in first three issues of *Journal of the Chinese Language Teachers Association*, i.e., *1*(1) (1966): 48; *1*(2) (1966): 80; *1*(3) (1966): 130.

Succeeding John DeFrancis' two terms as chair from 1964 to 1966, John B. Tsu led CLTA from 1966 to 1968, and he facilitated an affiliation with the Association for Asian Studies, ACTFL, and the MLA, thereby providing access to their professional resources.

Similarly, CPSHU was a source of leadership for *JCLTA*, insofar as John DeFrancis was editor from 1969 to 1979, while Winston Yang worked as its Review Editor from 1976 to 1984, and William Lin served as Associate Review Editor in 1984.[35]

CLTA has become the largest and longest-lived professional association for Chinese language educators outside China. Over its fifty-year existence, its character has greatly expanded in order to meet the requirements of global engagement with multiple languages and cultures. Nevertheless, promoting the Chinese language, providing professional supports to language teachers, and supporting quality Chinese programs remain CLTA's core mission. *JCLTA*, now a major publication for Chinese language teachers worldwide, has become a valuable medium for exchanging information and discussing issues in the field of TCFL. These early pioneers paved the way to today's success.

Conclusion

In this article, we reviewed the past sixty-year history of CPSHU with a focus on how it has evolved in response to the overall development of TCFL in the United States. We described five major CPSHU accomplishments which laid the groundwork for the TCFL. First, as one of the earliest pioneers in the nation to offer a wide variety of Chinese courses, CPSHU started an era of teaching Chinese at a grassroots level. Second, CPSHU introduced the teaching and learning Chinese to American secondary and elementary schools, thereby expanding TCFL from institutions of higher education to the pre-college settings. Third, CPSHU developed a series of well-known Chinese language teaching materials, some of which have become widely used over many years in Western schools of various levels. Fourth, CPSHU led the nation in teacher training and education by producing a large number of bilingual (English-Chinese) educators and administrators for the K-16 setting. Finally, CPSHU played an instrumental role in organizing CLTA, and launching its academic journal, thereby making TCFL a recognized profession in the United States.

In examining the evolution of CPSHU and its various roles in the development of TCFL, we noted two important attributes: leadership and

---

[35] As indicated in *Journal of the Chinese Language Teachers Association* 1(3) (1966): 137, DeFrancis was on leave of absence from Seton Hall University during the academic year of 1966-1967 to teach Chinese and do research at University of Hawaii. While serving as the JCLTA editor, DeFrancis was already relocated to University of Hawaii, but still affiliated with Seton Hall University as research professor.

scholarship. These two attributes have, on one hand, ensured the success of CPSHU and, on the other hand, impacted TCFL significantly. The importance of a strong leader with the vision to be far-sighted and the talent to devise effective strategies cannot be understated. Dr. John B. Tsu was not trained as a specialist in Chinese linguistics or literature or teaching pedagogy, yet he had the acumen and courage to implement what he conceived.[36] By founding the Department of Asian Studies at SHU to better promote Chinese Studies, and focusing on teacher education, this first such department in the U.S. became the first bilingual and bicultural training center in the nation. By creating a professional organization for Chinese language teachers, Dr. Tsu made it possible for them to enter the mainstream of foreign language education. Moreover, Dr. Tsu wisely recommended the use of *pinyin* to DeFrancis, who then adopted it in 1966 when revising his *Beginning Chinese*.[37] This was the first use of *pinyin* in Chinese textbooks in the United States. Similarly, Dr. Tsu's advocacy of instruction in simplified Chinese characters was instrumental in preparing American students to communicate more effectively with people in mainland China. Not just a visionary, Dr. Tsu was a true servant leader who tirelessly dedicated his time and energy to all his projects, great and small. He did this by writing almost a thousand letters to principals proposing that Chinese be taught in their high schools, by applying for various grants to obtain support for teacher training programs, by helping students do the same, by visiting Chinese classes taught by SHU graduates, and even by collecting CLTA membership dues. Such a servant leader with vision and strategy is hard to find nowadays.[38]

Upon Dr. Tsu's solid institutional foundation, scholarship flourished with the establishment of the Institute of Far Eastern Studies and the Department of Asian Studies. Commitment to research and publishing results has been a strong tradition at CPSHU. DeFrancis' series and Fred Fang-yu Wang's bilingual dictionaries are just two exemplary works.

In conclusion, CPSHU has a national reputation for its many endeavors—from institutionalizing China Studies to formalizing teacher preparation, from developing teaching materials to enhancing professional development. In its wake, the TCFL in America was able to gain momentum

---

[36] It was reported in a TV program that Dr. John B. Tsu was a true linguist, able to speak Chinese, English, Japanese, Korean, Russian, and Spanish (http://www.dingding.tv/bencandy.php?fid=38&id=359).

[37] Zhou, 2011, p. 144.

[38] Dr. John B. Tsu was glorious in the field of TCFL. However, he was much more well-known in the political arena. Appointed by five different American Presidents (i.e., Presidents Nixon, Region, Ford, George H. W. Bush, and George W. Bush) to many high-level boards and commissions, Dr. Tsu served, among many positions, as Chairman of Presidential Advisory Commission on Asian Americans and Pacific Islanders.

and succeed. Such a legacy is an inspiration for all educators, especially the Chinese language teachers and students who have benefitted.

Bibliography

ASIA SOCIETY (2005). *Expanding Chinese language capacity in the United States: What would it take to have 5 percent of high school students learning Chinese by 2015?* New York: Asia Society.

ASIAN STUDIES (1981). Department memo. Archives on the Department of Asian Studies, Walsh Library of Seton Hall University.

ASIAN STUDIES (1982). *Exchanges with China.* Archives on the Department of Asian Studies, Walsh Library of Seton Hall University.

CHANG, R. (1962). *Read Chinese book II.* New Heaven: Yale University Press.

CHAO, DER-LIN (2007). Samuel Wells Williams (1812-1884): A pioneer student and a scholar of Chinese. *Journal of the Chinese Language Teachers Association 42*(1): 1-26.

CHAO, YUAN REN (1948). *Mandarin primer.* Cambridge, MA: Cambridge University Press.

CHEN, DONGDONG (2011). Teaching Chinese in America: From less commonly taught language to critical language. *Journal of Chinese Language Globalization Studies 2*: 30-42.

CHEN, DONGDONG (2018). The effect of U.S. government initiatives on the development of Chinse language education–the Seton Hall story. In V. Ling (Ed.), *The field of Chinese language education in the U.S.: A retrospective of the 20th century* (pp. 107-113). Abingdon, UK: Routledge.

CHEN, HEQIN (1928). *Yutiwen yingyong zihui* (Frequent vocabulary of modern Chinese). Shanghai: Commercial Press.

CHI, R. (1989). Observations on the past, present, and future of teaching Mandarin Chinese as a foreign language. *Journal of the Chinese Language Teachers Association 24*(2): 109-122.

CLTA (1966). News of the Association. *Journal of the Chinese Language Teachers Association 1*(1): 47-49.

CLTA (1966). News of the Association. *Journal of the Chinese Language Teachers Association 1*(2): 80-82.

CLTA (1966). Report on summer Chinese language programs. *Journal of the Chinese Language Teachers Association 1*(3): 115-124.

CLTA (1967). News of the field. *Journal of the Chinese Language Teachers Association 2*(3): 116-129.

DEFRANCIS, J. (1963). *Beginning Chinese.* New Haven: Yale University Press.

DEFRANCIS, J. (1965). *Intermediate Chinese.* New Haven: Yale University

Press.

DeFrancis, J. (1965). *Character text for beginning Chinese*. New Haven: Yale University Press.

DeFrancis, J. (1965). *Beginning Chinese reader I*. New Haven: Yale University Press.

DeFrancis, J. (1965). *Beginning Chinese reader II*. New Haven: Yale University Press.

DeFrancis, J. (1965). *Character text for intermediate Chinese*. New Haven: Yale University Press.

DeFrancis, J. (1965). *Intermediate Chinese reader I*. New Haven: Yale University Press.

DeFrancis, J. (1965). *Intermediate Chinese reader II*. New Haven: Yale University Press.

DeFrancis, J. (1966a). Why Johnny can't read Chinese. *Journal of the Chinese Language Teachers Association 1*(1): 1-20.

DeFrancis, J. (1966). *Advanced Chinese*. New Haven: Yale University Press.

DeFrancis, J. (1966). *Character text for advanced Chinese*. New Haven: Yale University Press.

DeFrancis, J. (1967). *Advanced Chinese reader*. New Haven: Yale University Press.

Furman, N., Goldberg, D., & Lusin, N. (2007 November). Enrollments in languages other than English in United States institutions of higher education, Fall 2006. MLA Web publication, http://www. mla.org/pdf /06enrollmentsurvey_final.pdf.

Furman, N., Goldberg, D., & Lusin, N. (2010 December). Enrollments in languages other than English in United States institutions of higher education, Fall 2009. MLA Web publication, http://www. mla.org/pdf /2009_enrollment_survey.pdf.

Kay, C. (2002 Winter/Spring). Pathway across the Pacific. *Seton Hall Magazine*: 26-28, http://blogs.shu.edu/magazine/files/2011/02/winter-spring2002.pdf.

Li, Ying-che, & Speer, B. (1976). *Readings in teaching Chinese*. South Orange, NJ: Seton Hall University Press.

Ling, V. (Ed.), (2018). *The field of Chinese language education in the U.S.: A retrospective of the 20th century*. Abingdon, UK: Routledge.

Liu, Meiling (April 30, 2002). John Tsu received the life achievement in East-West Education Award. New York: *The World Journal*, news section.

Livaccari, C. (2011 December). Will 2012 be the year Chinese becomes a 'commonly taught language'. *Newsletter of Asia Society: Asia Society's Year in Review*. Asia Society Web publication, http://asiasociety.org/ blog/asia/2012-year-mandarin-chinese-becomes-commonly-taught-language.

Richards, J., & Rodgers, T. (2001). *Approaches and methods in language teaching*. Cambridge, MA: Cambridge University Press.

SETON HALL UNIVERSITY (1952). *The general bulletin: Announcement of Courses for 1952-1953*. Walsh Library of Seton Hall University.

STEWNER-MANZANARES, G. (1988 Fall No. 6). The bilingual education act: Twenty years later. *New Focus*, The National Clearinghouse for Bilingual Education, Occasional Papers in Bilingual Education, ED337031, https://files.eric.ed.gov/fulltext/ED337031.pdf.

THE SETONIAN (1951 November 2). Seton Hall inaugurates Far Eastern Studies. Official Undergraduate Newspaper of Seton Hall University, Walsh Library of Seton Hall University.

THE SETONIAN (1952 January 17). Institute of Far Eastern Studies opens on February 4. Official Undergraduate Newspaper of Seton Hall University, Walsh Library of Seton Hall University.

THE SETONIAN (1960 December 2). Far Eastern Institutes receives aid. Official Undergraduate Newspaper of Seton Hall University, Walsh Library of Seton Hall University.

TSU, J. (1970). The teaching of Chinese in colleges and schools of the United States. *The Modern Language Journal 54*(8): 562–579.

WANG, FRED FANG-YU (1961). *Read Chinese book I*. New Haven: Yale University Press.

WANG, FRED FANG-YU, & CHANG, R. (1961). *Read Chinese book III*. New Haven: Yale University Press.

WANG, FRED FANG-YU (1967). *Mandarin Chinese dictionary: Chinese-English*. South Orange, NJ: Seton Hall University Press.

WANG, FRED FANG-YU (1971). *Mandarin Chinese dictionary: English-Chinese*. South Orange, NJ: Seton Hall University Press.

WANG, FRED FANG-YU (1971). *Introduction to literary Chinese volumes I & II*, South Orange, NJ: Seton Hall University Press.

WANG, SHUHAN C. (2007). Building societal capital: Chinese in the U.S. *Language Policy 6*: 27–52.

ZHOU, MINGLANG (2011). Globalization and language order: Teaching Chinese as a foreign language in the United States. In L. Tsung & K. Cruickshank (Eds.), *Teaching and learning Chinese in global contexts* (pp. 131-149). London: Continuum.

"Qiu Jin" – oil painting by Wang Xin (王忻)

Chapter 3

The Merging of Modern Nationalism and Modern Feminism During China's Late Qing and the Role of Qiu Jin

by Michael A. Stone

Introduction

This paper explores the intersection of modern nationalism and modern feminism during China's late Qing dynasty and focuses on the life of Qiu Jin[1] (秋瑾 1875-1907)[2] as a significant figure and symbol of both movements. In the last decades of the Qing, when the Manchu court was under pressure from foreign aggression, internal rebellions, and natural disasters, China's intellectuals vigorously sought ways to modernize and strengthen China. Seeing that Japan and the Western powers had become militarily powerful and technologically advanced, many of China's scholarly elites turned to Western ideas of science, politics, economics, and social systems as a means to defend and renew China. They also noted how Europe and America had largely relegated or ousted their monarchies and feudalism. These desperate times engendered a new sense of nationalism with the goal of saving the country, expelling foreigners and, ultimately, overthrowing the Manchu rulers.[3] This concept would redefine the nation as not just one of shared culture or geography, but rather as a modern nation-state with a strong central government that would ensure the rights and welfare of its people.

References to women's issues date back centuries in China but the first appeals for women's rights in the modern sense began to appear in the late nineteenth century made by a small number of Chinese intellectuals. Some nationalists would suggest how women could contribute to revitalizing China. While the importance of raising strong and healthy children was still a common theme, there were also calls for women to contribute in more public ways to Chinese society. It was argued that by restricting Chinese women solely to the home, China was wasting one of the country's most valuable resources. Hence freeing women from their cloistered domestic existence and transforming them into productive

---

[1] Her courtesy names were Xuanqing 璿卿 and Jingxiong 競雄.
[2] Some sources give Qiu Jin's year of birth as 1877, e.g., Chan, 1992, p. 84.
[3] Wright, 1968, p. 6-7.

citizens would strengthen the national economy. This dovetailed with the ideas of proponents of women's rights who wanted equality in education, inheritance rights and an end to footbinding, concubinage and other oppressive traditions. Reform-minded intellectuals, including the country's leading reformer and philosopher, Liang Qichao (1873-1929)[4], spoke of fairness and the potential value of women serving as equal partners in revitalizing China at the beginning of the twentieth century. Modern feminism was among the Western concepts that circulated among the educated Chinese elite at the end of the nineteenth century.

Qiu Jin, a revolutionary and feminist activist, was among the first to call upon women to actively participate in the overthrow of the Manchus and the need for females to be educated to gain independence from men and contribute to society. She devoted her life to these dual causes of saving China and freeing women because she believed that the fate of China and the future of women were inevitably connected.

Modern Feminism

Patriarchy pervades the history of most cultures but in China it was formally institutionalized for millennia by Confucianism with its clearly articulated relationships that relegated women to perpetually subservient roles. Chinese history has had its share of female heroes, scholars, writers, and artists. Their numbers began to increase during the late Ming and Qing dynasties,[5,6] although the overall rate of women's literacy was low.[7] Had any talented women writers been men, they would have parleyed their skills to obtain official positions (a common career path for men), but such access to positions of power were not open to women.

The basic principles of Confucianism defined relationships known as the *san-cong* ("three obediences"), whereby girls were subordinate to their fathers, and wives to their husbands. If a woman's husband pre-deceased her, she would then be subordinate to her oldest son. Females were subjected to footbinding, concubinage, arranged marriages and an oppressive emphasis on chastity. Females who were born or married into families of means and therefore not needed to work the family farm or in the family business were cloistered in the home, isolating them from interaction with society. Women were trained to be obedient daughters and wives and good mothers. Formal education of girls was rare in imperial China but when it existed, the purpose was to reinforce female Confucian roles and not to contribute to society on a broader scale.[8] Even the brilliant

---

[4] Sudo, 2006, p. 472.
[5] Rankin, 1975, p. 41.
[6] Ropp, 1993, p. 107.
[7] Hong, 1997, p. 33.
[8] Liu, et al., 2013, p. 212.

female historian of the Han dynasty, Ban Zhao (c. 48-116 CE), in her book *Nü jie* ("Admonitions of Women") written c. 106 CE, advised girls that they should be gentle, quiet, chaste, and act in accordance with the prevailing social conventions. As one modern historian said, the goal of these texts was "perfect submission, not personal development".[9]

Calls for abolishing footbinding, which were sporadic before the late Qing, coalesced into anti-footbinding societies. This movement gained greater legitimacy when notable scholars such as Kang Youwei and Liang Qichao took firm stands against the practice. Kang Youwei organized one of the first societies in 1883 and he submitted a "Memorial Requesting a Ban on the Binding of Women's Feet" to the court in 1898.[10] More general discussions of women's rights appeared in a few journals around the beginning of the twentieth century, but the first major published articulation advocating women's rights was *Nüjie zhong* ("The Women's Bell") (1903) by the male scholar and poet Jin Tianhe (1873-1947).[11]

Essays of the famous scholar Liang Qichao provided a powerful and influential voice advocating for educating women and integrating them into Chinese society. Liang Qichao said ". . . when I seek the root causes of national weakness, I find that they inevitably lie in women's lack of education".[12]

His principal reasons centered not only on fairness but also on practical reasoning, i.e., that women should contribute to the economy through gainful employment rather than rely upon men. He said:

> For true progress of nations to occur, only such occupations
> as agriculture, commercial business, medicine, law, science,
> and manufacture are to be encouraged. No matter whether
> one is a man or a woman, all people in a nation should engage
> in their own line of work and be able to support themselves,
> eliminating the division between those who can provide for
> themselves and those who cannot. Toward this end, men and
> women must receive comparable education."[13]

Like Jin Tianhe, Liang Qichao linked motherhood to the nation's future albeit in a more pragmatic way: "Educated women can better educate the country's children. If a mother understands the fundamentals of education . . . her children . . . will already have established their ambitions and aspirations".[14] Unlike the traditional notion that lauded ignorance in

---

[9] Hong, 1997, p. 52.
[10] Ono, 1978, pp. 32, 211.
[11] Sudo, 2006, p. 476.
[12] Liu et al., 2013, p. 190.
[13] Liu et al., 2013, p. 201-202.

woman as a virtue, Liang Qichao spoke of the innate injustice of a system whereby women's "minds are frozen, their path toward learning is blocked, their livelihood is cut off, and so they have no choice but to be totally subservient to those with power". [15]

Not all the early feminists were content with the liberal reforms proposed by Liang Qichao and others. One important feminist writer, Chen Xiefen (1883-1923) said in a 1903 article in the journal *Nübao* (which she founded at age 16 in 1899[16] and edited) that women should not rely on men despite their stated support for women's rights because men will only support these rights when it is convenient for them.[17] Women, she believed, should only rely on themselves to advance women's education and rights.[18]

The anarchist He Zhen (c. 1884-c.1920) presented a more radical view of feminism in her essay "On the Question of Women's Liberation" and her articles in the journal she edited, *Tianyi* ("Natural Justice"), which was a voice for anarchism during its brief period of publication between 1907-1908. It was *Tianyi* which introduced Marxist communism to China by publishing the first translation of a section of the *Communist Manifesto*.[19] He Zhen believed it was insufficient to focus on women's rights and advocated deposing the country's entire social and economic structure. Men could oppress women, she believed, because of the inequities in the social and economic systems. "You women," he said, "do not hate the man: hate that you don't have food to eat. Why don't you have food to eat? Because you can't buy food without money. Why don't you have money? Because the rich have stolen our property and walk all over the majority of the people".[20]

The terms of the treaties that were signed after the First Opium War (1839-1842) allowed Christian missionaries to expand their evangelical efforts in China. As a result, Western missionaries founded China's first schools for girls beginning with the Girls' School in Ningbo, Zhejiang in 1844, founded by Mary Ann Aldersey (1797-1868). The curriculum included Bible studies, Chinese, mathematics, and embroidery. Because the Chinese mistrusted foreigners, most of the early students were recruited from the desperately poor or abandoned. But as Western learning gained credibility, the number of schools increased, and more well-to-do families sent their daughters to be educated. By 1898, there were 7,000 girls enrolled in 300 mission schools.

---

[14] Liu et al., 2013, p. 193.

[15] Liu et al., 2013, p. 300.

[16] Lee et al., 1998, p. 22. *Nübao* was only the second magazine published in China intended for a female readership.

[17] Sudo, 2006, p. 478.

[18] Ono, 1978, p. 57.

[19] Liu et al., 2013, pp. 2-4, 7.

[20] Quoted in Zarrow, 1988, p. 801.

The first Chinese-sponsored schools for girls started around fifty years after the first mission school with the founding of the Jingzheng Girls' School in Shanghai in 1898. Initially, the Empress Dowager and reactionary court officials forced the school to close but when pressure to institute reforms became overwhelming, the Qing officials passed reforms in 1907 which finally permitted and regulated girls' schools. Revolutionaries opened their own girls' school in 1902 in Shanghai called the Patriotic Girls' School which was established through the efforts of Cai Yuanpei (1868-1940)[21] who would later serve as President of Peking University, among others. Even with these new schools, only 13,000 Chinese girls were enrolled in school in 1909.[22]

Chinese women went to college in Western countries on church-sponsored or government scholarships. In 1915, a few missionary colleges for women opened in China and women were admitted to Peking University for the first time in 1920 and to the University of Hong Kong in 1921. Women's colleges were established in every province to train teachers as part of the 1907 reforms.

Although the number of girls and women who achieved an education was relatively small, the impact of female education started to have a profound effect on society. Besides receiving an education, girls and women were finally being seen in public instead of cloistered in the house. Once they obtained their education, some women became professionals, such as physicians working in China's most modern hospitals. Girls' schools also provided a platform for those advocating and organizing on behalf of women's issues such as suffrage, anti-footbinding, the outlawing of selling girls as concubines, inheritance rights and equal education.

The people most active in the movement for women's rights were part of the elite gentry because they had the education and freedom from social and financial constraints to pursue their activism. Women of the upper class would take advantage of the first opening of girls' and women's schools. They went on to start their own schools, publish journals for women and organize against footbinding.[23] Publications addressing women's issues proliferated beginning in 1898. By 1911, over thirty periodicals were published including *Nüxue bao* (first introduced in 1898 and appeared in at least two iterations thereafter), *Dong'ou nübaijie*, *Nüzi shiji*, Qiu Jin's *Zhongguo Nübao*, *Beijing nübao*, *Tianyi*, *Zhongguo xinnüji zazhi*, *Ershi shiji zhi Zhongguo nüzi* and *Nüexuesheng* in 1910, among others.

Later, women's rights would become one of the demands of the New Culture and May 4th Movements (1915-1919). At this point, references to

---

[21] Liu, 2010, p. 103.
[22] Spence, 1990, p. 241.
[23] Rankin, 1975, p. 39.

women's issues began to appear in more mainstream publications.[24] In 1926, the Second National Conference of the Guomindang passed the *Funü yundong jueyi an* ("Resolution on the Women's Movement") giving women equal rights in inheritance and the freedom to marry and divorce as they pleased. The Guomindang endorsed equal pay for equal work.[25] Ultimately, the Chinese Communist Party adopted the concept of equality that emerged from these early efforts on behalf of women's rights.

The Short Life and Revolutionary Career of Qiu Jin

Introduction: Qiu Jin was a skilled poet and essayist and a feminist activist who passionately campaigned for women's rights and against the Qing government. She advocated that women join the battle to overthrow the Manchu court not just as supportive wives, diligent mothers, or even productive contributors to society, but as warriors. In essays, lectures, and her efforts as an educator, she campaigned for girls and women to develop the skills necessary to become independent of men, politically and financially. Like He Zhen, Qiu Jin challenged women not to rely on men to give them their rights, but to seize their liberation on their own. For Qiu Jin, education, whether in a trade or profession, was the key with which women could free themselves of their reliance on men and thereby win their freedom. Although her work for women and girls is still celebrated by the Chinese to this day, she was mostly known as a martyr since she was beheaded by the court in 1907 for being anti-Qing revolutionary five years before the fall of the dynastic system.

Family Background: Like many of the highly literate women who questioned the traditional role of men and women in China, Qiu Jin was from a gentry family. She was born in 1875 in the treaty port[26] of Amoy (modern-day Xiamen) in southern Fujian and later moved to Shaoxing in Zhejiang. Her grandfather and great-grandfather Qiu Jiahe, had both achieved the eminent rank of prefect in the Qing bureaucracy. Her father, Qiu Shounan (1850-1901), was also a degree holder but did not attain a prestigious position and generally served as a secretary to other officials in various locations. Qiu Jin's mother (née Shan) (1845-1906) was highly literate and wrote poetry is believed that she inspired Qiu Jin to read and love poetry. She had two brothers (one older, Qiu Yuchang, and one younger) and a younger sister.

From an early age, Qiu Jin demonstrated an affinity and love for

---

[24] Wang, 1999, p. xvi.

[25] Ling, 1997, p. 223.

[26] Treaty ports were those which China was forced to open in accordance with terms of the "unequal" treaties signed after China's defeats in the Opium Wars. Xiamen was opened to the British in 1842.

literature. While families rarely invested any resources in educating their daughters, scholarly families would occasionally justify educating their daughters to enhance their value when it came time to negotiate for husbands on the girls' behalf. The motivation was that a literate wife would be able to assist with the education of the couples' future sons.[27] Qiu Jin's parents indulged her interest and talent for scholarship and saw to it that she received a classical education[28] conducted within the family's home. This education included traditional Chinese *shi* and *ci* poetry. Qiu Jin would become a prolific writer of poems, letters, song lyrics and essays. Two hundred and fifty-two of her poems have survived.[29] She began writing poems at age thirteen.[30] Her first ones were about traditional subjects of flowers, history, the seasons, and her home life.[31]

Qiu Jin was a passionate girl who loved Chinese history and literature, especially the stories of military heroines of China's past including legendary Hua Mulan and female generals Qin Liangyu (1574?-1648?) of the Ming, Liang Hongyu (1102-1135) of the Song, and Shen Yunying (1624-1661) of the Ming.[32] She also loved the stories of Jing Ke (?-227 BCE) who died while attempting to assassinate the King of Qin, Ying Zheng (260-210 BCE), who went on to become China's first emperor. Qiu Jin enjoyed reading about Li Shimin (598-649) who founded the Tang dynasty (618-907) and became the Emperor Taizong (598-649) as well as figures from the Three Kingdoms Period (220-280). Her favorite poets included Du Fu (712-770) and Xin Qiji (1140-1207) of the Tang and Song dynasties.[33] Qiu Jin's mother stopped trying to teach her the skills a young girl of Qiu Jin's station was typically expected to learn such as embroidery.[34] Qiu Jin also enjoyed sports including horseback riding and archery,[35] and later martial arts and swordsmanship.[36]

When Qiu Jin's father was offered a position in Taiwan in 1887, her entire family relocated to the island for three years. Her contact with the Taiwanese people and region was limited because the family kept her within the family compound for protection from what was considered an unstable region. The family returned to the family home in Shaoxing in 1889 until her father found another assignment in Changde, Hunan.[37] The rest of the family joined him in 1892. Later, Qiu Jin's father found a position in Xiangxiang, Hunan. It was here that her father arranged for her to marry Wang Zifang (1879-1909) the son of a wealthy Hunan merchant and friend of her father, Wang Fuchen. The Qiu family was concerned that their daugh-

[27] Wu, 2011, pp. 8-9.
[28] Rankin, 1971, p. 40.
[29] Chang & Huan Saussy, 1999, p. 632.
[30] Hsu, 1994, p. 76.
[31] Wang, 2004, p. 30.
[32] Chang, 2009, "Autumn Gem."
[33] Mangan & Hong, 2001, p. 30.
[34] Dooling, 2005, p. 40.
[35] Rankin, 1971, p. 40.
[36] Judkins, 2012.
[37] Hsu, 1994, p. 76.

ter, now twenty-one, was old by Chinese standards for an unmarried woman. Both families considered the match as preserving their social standing since the scholarship of the Qiu family was matched by the wealth and success of the Wang family. "The marriage was my father's wish, not mine," Qiu Jin said.[38] The couple were married in April 1897 and although they had two children: a boy, Wang Yuande (1897-1955) and a girl, Wang Guifen (1901-1967, also called Canzhi), Qiu Jin often expressed contempt for her husband's conventionality and lack of ambition. She was unhappy in her marriage and felt mistreated by her husband which she expressed in a letter to her older brother "That person's behavior is worse than an animal's . . . He treats me as less than nothing. . . My treatment in that household was worse than a slave's; the poison of hatred has eaten deeply into me".[39] She devoted much of her time to writing poetry which often reflected her loneliness as in her poem Pusa Man: Sent to a Woman Friend:

> Moonlight in front of the screen, radiant, lovely,
> a sight to be cherished.
> More's the pity that the moon
> shines on our separation,
> our joyous meetings a thing of the past.
> My nostalgia: the mist-imbued, river-bank trees,
> stretching far into the distance —
> While the river itself rushes on,
> pitiless and uncaring.
> Kept apart by a range of mountains and vast,
> unbridgeable space,
> Despite our wish, we have no way to see each other.
> When I write to you, I struggle for words.
> My sorrow, like the clepsydra, drips on and on,
> never a pause, or an end.[40]

Married Life, Move to Beijing and Radicalization: Qiu Jin's life changed dramatically when her husband purchased a governmental position with the Ministry of Revenue in Beijing in 1903. They purchased a house at Chunshu Hutung in an area of Beijing known as West City. Initially, Qiu Jin enjoyed exploring the capital by hiring a horse-drawn carriage. It was the custom for women to keep the carriage shades drawn when traveling in public, but Qiu Jin was more interested in investigating the city than in decorum.

In Beijing, she befriended a group of women who were wives of

---

[38] Mangan & Hong, 2001, p. 30.
[39] Wang, 2004, p. 39.
[40] Quoted in Chang and Saussy, 1999, pp. 635-636.

other government officials. Their status as gentry and the cosmopolitan atmosphere of the capital gave the women a measure of freedom.[41] Among the women intellectuals Qiu Jin met was the noted calligrapher and poet Wu Zhiying (1868-1934) who became her life-long friend. Qiu Jin and Wu Zhiying pledged to become sworn sisters in February 1903.[42] The women formed study groups in which they shared journals and books and discussed politics. This was Qiu Jin's first exposure to the Chinese fledgling women's movement including the anti-footbinding campaign. The group read *Xin xiaoshuo* ("New Fiction"), edited by Liang Qichao, which presented politically-based fiction.[43, 44] They also read newly translated biographies of Western heroines and martyrs including Joan of Arc, Madame Anita Roland of the French Revolution, and Sophia Perovskaya (1853-1881), an early Russian revolutionary who participated in the assassination of Czar Alexander II (1818-1881).[45] Another woman with whom Qiu Jin became close was Hattori Shigeko, wife of the Japanese professor Hattori Unokichi (1867-1939), who taught at *Jingshi Daxuetang* (Metropolitan Academy, the precursor to Peking University).

It was around this time that Qiu Jin began occasionally dressing in men's clothing. Shigeko described her first encounter with her friend:

"Was this person before me a man or a woman?
A tall slender body bent slightly forward in Western male
dress with a full head of trimmed black hair. A blue hunting
cap sitting sideways on her head covered half her ears.
A dark blue, secondhand business suit didn't fit her at all.
The sleeves were too long and from her cuffs one could
see just her white, delicate hands. She carried a slender
walking stick. Beneath her baggy trousers, worn-out
brown shoes peeped through. A green necktie hung
loosely over her chest."[46]

Shigeko asked why she dressed like a Western man and Qiu Jin responded: "My aim is to dress like a man! As your husband well knows, in China men are strong, and women are oppressed because they're supposed to be weak. I want somehow to have a mind as strong as a man's. If I first take on the form of a man, then I think my mind too will eventually become that of a man."[47]

---

[41] Mangan & Hong, 2001, p. 33.
[42] Hsu, 1994, p. 77.
[43] Dooling, 2005, p. 40.
[44] Wong, 1998, p. 105.
[45] Mangan & Hong, 2001, p. 24.
[46] Ono, 1978, p. 60.
[47] Ono, 1978, p. 60.

*Qiu Jin as a man
in Western clothes,
circa 1906. Photo is
on various websites
without date or credit.*

Qiu Jin wrote a poem that she labeled: *Inscribed on a Photograph of Myself Dressed as a Man*:

> This image I see, so dignified, so grave, who in fact, could
> it be? — Knight-errant bones of an earlier incarnation
> trapped, regrettably, in a female body. Dead and buried
> is my previous form: it was nothing but an illusion.
> My future vista, on the other hand, promises possibilities
> for authenticity. Too much time has elapsed; still my selves
> have finally met, generating naturally a mixture of emotions
> When once again I lament the times, it will be with
> unprecedented boldness. At future meetings with old friends,
> They'll be told — I've swept away all that's trivial,
> All that's just Surface dust.[48]

The poem reveals her dream of being one of the warriors in the swashbuckling tales she read a child and her intention and apprehension about her future. It also illustrates the singlemindedness of Qiu Jin who would soon embark on a new phase in her revolutionary quest.

Qiu Jin was living in Beijing during the foreign occupation that followed the Boxer Rebellion (1898-1900) which, like many of her compatriots, she found deeply humiliating. She had written earlier about her anguish over China's loss to the Japanese during the First Sino-Japanese War in 1895. Seeing how the Manchu court was unable to protect the country, Qiu Jin developed a fierce hatred for the Qing court, which she saw as corrupt and weak. That her husband was a governmental employee who was more interested in Beijing's nightlife[49] and did not share her indignation poisoned her feelings toward him.

---

[48] Quoted in Chang & Saussy, 1999, p. 648.
[49] Tao, Winter 2000-2001, p. 5.

One incident seemed to have set the couple on a course of permanent separation. In 1903, during the Mid-Autumn Festival, Qiu Jin attended a theater performance alone disguised as a man while her husband was not at home. When he found out, her husband was furious and reportedly struck her. Qiu Jin left home and stayed at a hostel. Her husband tried to convince her to return home and when she refused, he asked Wu Zhiying to take Qiu Jin to her house. Qiu Jin stayed with Wu Zhiying and then another friend. During this period of being away from home, she read issues of *Xin Min Cong Bao* ("New Citizen"),[50] a bi-weekly journal published by Liang Qichao between 1902 and 1903 in Japan, and the anti-Manchu *Su-bao* journal.[51] Qiu Jin was said to tell her husband, "Our ideas are different, it is as if we live in [hell]. I do not desire to live in hell, nor do I wish you to be there. We will part".[52]

Studying in Japan, Becoming a Professional Revolutionary: Qiu Jin considered leaving China to study law in America but lacked the funds and sponsorship. Shigeko urged her to study in Japan and Qiu Jin made the appropriate arrangements to do so with the assistance of Hattori Unokichi.[53] Japan had become a haven for radicals fleeing China, some for their support of the Hundred Days' Reforms and later those who criticized the Qing government.

In April 1904, Qiu Jin took the astounding step of leaving her children and husband to travel to Japan, an unusual decision in most cultures, but especially in imperial China. Her mother-in-law would take charge of the children's upbringing. Thus, Qiu Jin became the embodiment of the character Nora in Ibsen's play, *A Doll House*, who also left her husband and children. The play was widely read and discussed among scholars in China when it was translated in 1918.[54]

Qiu Jin's husband reluctantly decided to share the family's income with her even though he had lost money by investing in a relative's failed business. Qiu Jin sold her jewelry[55] for funds but anonymously gave much of the proceeds to a fellow member of the Reform Party. She expressed her feelings about leaving China and her frustration over money in a poem which was said to be written on the boat she took to Japan.

---

[50] The journal title has also been translated as "A New People" or "People Made New."

[51] Hsu, 1994, p. 77.

[52] Ayscough, 1937), p. 144.

[53] Ono, 1978, p. 60.

[54] Spence, 1990, p. 317. For more on this subject, see Li, Xia (2008), pp. 217-35.

[55] Including her "hair ornaments" which may have been part of her dowry.

Sun and moon have no light left, earth is dark;
Our women's world is sunk so deep, who can help us?
Jewelry sold to pay this trip across the seas,
Cut off from my family I leave my native land.
Unbinding my feet I clean out a thousand years of poison.
With heated heart arouse all women's spirits.
Alas, this delicate kerchief here
Is half stained with blood, and half with tears.[56]

There were already around 1,500 Chinese students studying in Japan when Qiu Jin arrived. Although the number of Chinese women were few, important female radicals were there including He Zhen, Li Ziping (?-1949), and Chen Xiefen. After briefly studying at a Japanese language school in Surugadai, Qiu Jin attended the Aoyama Vocational Girls' School in Kojimachi, Tokyo which had become a popular choice of Chinese female students. She was known to spend more time on revolutionary activities than attending class[57] and stopped attending classes in 1905. She joined a variety of organizations such as the Yokohama branch of the Triads composed of revolutionary students whose goal was to overthrow the Qing.[58] She also joined the *Gong Ai Hui* ("Mutual Love Society," sometimes translated as the "Humanitarian Society"), founded by Chinese students at the Aoyama School in April 1903 to "rescue the 200,000,000 Chinese women, to restore their basic and fundamental rights, to enable them to possess the idea of nationhood, so that they may ultimately perform their duties as women citizens".[59] She would go on to assume a leadership role in the *Gong Ai Hui* in 1904. She also joined the organizations associated with students from the provinces of Zhejiang and Hunan and helped found the *Yanshou Lianxi Hui* ("Society for the Study of Oratory") and the *Shi Ren Tuan* ("Ten Person Corps").[60] In 1904, she contacted the Yokohama branch of the Triads Society[61] led by Feng Ziyou (1882-1958). She met Sun Yat-sen in August 1905 in Tokyo.[62]

Qiu Jin also helped form a Chinese debating club called the *Yenshou Lien Xi Hui* whose members shared rooms in a student hostel. This is where Qiu Jin would hone her skills as an orator.[63] She also studied swordsmanship and archery at the Martial Arts Society in Tokyo and exercised regularly.[64] The theme of Qiu Jin's poetry at this point was primarily political with themes of feminism and saving her country. In her poem, *Zhequ tian*, she refers to her potential martyrdom:

[56] Hong & Mangan, 2001, pp. 35-6.
[57] Rankin, 1971, p. 41.
[58] Rankin, 1971, p. 41.
[59] Ng, 1997, p. 200.
[60] Rankin, 1975, p. 51.
[61] Rankin, 1971, p. 51.
[62] Giles, 1917, p. 6.
[63] Chan, 1992, p. 85.
[64] Hong, 1997, p. 91.

The motherland almost submerged —
I can't suppress my feelings.
When free I seek true friends across the sea.
A gold jug chipped must be repaired;
For my country I dare to be a sacrificial lamb.
Alas! Dangers and obstacles! I sigh at my floating life.
Across ten thousand *li* of mountains
and passes I make the intrepid journey.
Don't say that women are not heroic figures —
Night after night my Dragon Spring Sword sings on the wall![65]

Between 1904 and 1905, while in Japan, she edited and wrote six essays for *Baihua bao* ("Vernacular Journal")[66] which published anti-Manchu and women's rights articles. One essay printed in *Baihua bao*, "A Respectful Proclamation to China's 200 Million Women Comrades," contained her famous call-to-arms: "Oh, the most unfairly treated people in the world are we 200 million fellow women. Once born, it's better to have a good father; but if your father is a hot-tempered obstinate sort, when you open your mouth and shout, 'You good-for-nothing,' it will seem as though he's sorry he can't grab and kill you".[67] After outlining the abuses Chinese women had suffered and the role women of every age should play in their individual and collective liberation, she urged women to take up the nationalistic cause of their country: "Everyone, the nation is on the verge of collapse. Men can no longer protect, so how can we depend on them? If we fail to rouse ourselves, it will be too late after the nation perishes."[68]

While in Japan, she adopted the sobriquet, "The Woman Knight of Mirror Lake," *Jianhu Nüxia*, a name by which she is still known. The title refers to a lake near her home and appeared on a stele that stood in front of her first tomb which read "Alas, here lies Qiu Jin, female night-errant from Mirror Lake".[69] Mirror Lake was located near her Shaoxing home. She also used another name, Jin Xiong, which translates as "rival to men".[70]

Qiu Jin was able to write in the arcane classical literary style that had hereto been used for all official documents and serious literature. This style required years of education to understand, therefore, the pool of potential readers was small, especially among women. So she, among others, began producing works written in the style of everyday speech called *baihua*. Less than two decades later, the conversion to *baihua* became a principal tenet of the New Culture and May 4th Movements to modernize written Chinese

---

[65] Quoted in Chang & Saussy, 1999, p. 650.   [68] Ono, 1978, p. 63.
[66] Rankin, 1955, p. 51.   [69] Hu, 2007, p. 150.
[67] Ono, 1978, p. 62-63.   [70] Hong, 1997, p. 91.

and spread ideas to a greater portion of the population. The transition from the classical style to *baihua* would ultimately change China's literary tradition.

Armed with her solid literary background, Qiu Jin also undertook a more challenging medium. *Tanci* ("plucking rhymes") was a traditional art form which combined singing and recited words. During the Qing, this genre was especially popular with female audiences and several women writers used it to express social criticism on women's lot in society.[71] Qiu Jin wanted to use this form to create a revolutionary work that would speak to the masses. She began writing this semi-autobiographical work in 1905 which was called *Jingwei shi* ("Stones of the Jingwei Bird"). The title was based on a well-known Chinese legend of a bird who tried to fill up the ocean one pebble at a time. The story tells of five women whose lives illustrate the suffering and indignities of Chinese females. True to Qiu Jin's mission, it merges the liberation of women with the salvation of the nation. She completed twenty-one chapters of the piece but did not live long enough to finish it. The following excerpts show Qiu Jin at her most eloquent and radical. She starts by commenting on the inequality of the system:

> "Poor women, we're considered less than human.
> If a daughter is born, people say she is bad luck and
> that she will belong to another family once she is
> married. Enlightened parents will still love her, but
> those who aren't will hate her the instant they see her.
> They always say that girls are useless and do nothing
> more than cost them a lot of dowry money. But when
> a son is born, everybody loves and treasures him. They
> let him go to school to study the *Five Classics*, while
> girls aren't even permitted to get near books. On the
> contrary, they claim that talented girls will suffer a bad
> fate. . . We are equal to men in talent and intelligence
> and if we were able to get an education, we too could
> earn money to support our parents."[72]

Qiu Jin gradually asks the audience to relate their own circumstance to that of the plight of the characters she has created in *Jingwei shi*.

> "What woman doesn't suffer? We are confined to the
> inner chambers our whole lives; we have our own
> opinions but can do nothing on our own initiative;

---

[71] Ropp, 1993, pp. 127-131.   [72] Dooling, 2005, pp. 63-64.

we are completely restricted and haven't an ounce
of power, as if we were orphans who must obey our
master's every word. At home, our parents won't teach
us and forbid us to leave our chambers. All day long
they watch over us and demand that we learn to sew,
to the point where our hunched-over backs ache.[73]

Qiu Jin then offers hope in the form of an alternative already in existence
rather than just a theoretical one.

"But I'll have you know, I will not submit. Recently,
I've had the chance to read many books from Europe
and America that discuss the right to liberty, and
how women and men are created equal. Heaven was
impartial in endowing us with rights and privileges."[74]

In the *tanci*, she also offers an image of heroic and glorious freedom to
inspire women to seek their own liberation.

"We never consider escaping this slave trap, or becoming
women heroes. . . Nor do we think about the thousands
of ways in which we suffer, or about escaping this living
hell. But today, I have awoken from this former dream,
and therefore I am confident that I can achieve my goals.
When a phoenix is inside a cage, who can appreciate its
brilliant colors? But one day it will fly to heaven, breaking
out of its stupor to seek independence."[75]

Qiu Jin began to make speeches and continued to write lyrics to popular
tunes to communicate to a larger audience, since literacy among women
was especially low. Another example of the many lyrics she wrote is the
revolutionary "Song of Women: Four Stanzas," two stanzas of which were:

We women are equal to ants and ephemera;
Trapped in the inner chambers, we don't have freedom
We are the dignified and noble female descendants of our ancestors
Yet we have been insulted and shamed by men.
Muddling away our prime years,
Women are equal to ants and ephemera.

---

[73] Dooling, 2005, p. 66.
[74] Dooling, 2005, pp. 71-2.
[75] Dooling, 2005, p. 73.

We women are also citizens;
Myriads of our compatriots are sinking into degradation.
Alas, my compatriots,
How can we still follow the old pattern?
Society has evolved, and our rights should be asserted.
We women are also citizens.[76]

She wrote an essay in which she said speech had the advantage of being able to occur at any time and place and address any subject. It could be understood by anyone of any age and without cost. She also believed that it had the power to inspire the people into concerted action. Qiu Jin's own oral eloquence and passionate speeches were said to move her listeners to tears and could whip the audience into a frenzy for her cause. At this point, Qiu Jin had evolved from being a radical student to a revolutionary leader.

She returned to China for a few months in the Spring of 1905 to ask her mother for funds. Before leaving she met with Tao Chengzhang (1878-1912), a leader of the *Guangfu Hui* ("Restoration Society", also translated as the "Recovery Society"), an anti-Qing revolutionary group formed in Shanghai in 1904 by Cai Yuanpei, Gong Baoqu, Xu Xilin (1873-1907) and Tao Chengzhang.[77] Qiu Jin requested a letter of introduction to meet other revolutionaries while she was in China. With some initial hesitation, Tao Chengzhang provided the letters of introduction to five revolutionary groups which Qiu Jin used to meet Xu Xilin[78] and Cai Yuanpei during a visit to her hometown of Shaoxing in the Spring of 1905.[79] Like Qiu Jin, Xu Xilin was from a wealthy family from Shaoxing, Zhejiang. The two would later conspire to plan uprisings in Zhejiang and Anhui.[80]

Qiu returned to Japan in July 1905. That same month, Sun Yat-sen arrived in Japan to form the *Tongmeng Hui* ("Revolutionary Alliance") which Qiu Jin soon joined as one of its first female members. The Tongmeng Hui was an umbrella organization for several revolutionary organizations, and after the Revolution, it would form the basis of the Guomindang Party in August 1912. At the Tongmeng Hui's meeting on August 20, 1905, Sun Yat-sen was elected its President and Qiu Jin was elected to head its Zhejiang branch.

Qiu studied bomb-making at the Revolutionary Alliance's facility in Yokohama where Russian anarchists trained the Chinese radicals in

---

[76] Li, 2013, pp. 162-3.
[77] Most of these men were from Zhejiang; another example of its strong revolutionary tradition.
[78] Giles, 1917, p. 7.
[79] Rankin, 1975, p. 51.
[80] Rankin, 1975, p. 51.

explosives. Qiu Jin was joined there by other female revolutionaries. While in Tokyo she posed for what would become an iconic photo of her wearing a man's kimono and holding a dagger she had purchased.

Return to China: Her time in Japan ended in early 1906 when she and many other students left in protest of the Japanese Ministry for Education's crackdown on Chinese students' revolutionary activities. Cheng Tianhua (1875-1905), another Chinese revolutionary and poet living in Japan, committed suicide to protest the Japanese government's action.[81] She gave a passionate speech at a meeting of the Zhejiang students saying: "If I return to the motherland, surrender to the Manchu barbarian, and deceive the Han people, stab me with this dagger!" and then jabbed the dagger into the podium.[82]

Upon her return to China in February 1906, Qiu Jin planned to devote herself to the revolution. In a letter to a friend, Wang Shize, she wrote:

> After my return to China, I will exert my greatest efforts
> for the restoration of my country. I hope to meet you
> on the Central Plan. Though my success or failure is
> unpredictable, I won't spare any effort toward this goal
> for the rest of my life. Since 1900, I have not minded
> much my own life. If I should fail and die, I won't regret.
> The great exploit of Restoration brooks no delay, not
> even one day. Many men have died for the cause of the
> Restoration . . . but no woman has yet sacrificed her life
> for it. This is a disgrace to us women."[83]

Qiu Jin began her career as an educator and joined the *Guangfu Hui* ("Restoration Society") in March 1906. Initially, she joined the teaching staff of a revolutionary school in Nanxun, Zhejiang, called the Xunxi Girls' School where she taught Japanese, hygiene and science.[84] Her tenure at the school, however, was brief because she was deemed too radical[85] by a member of the school's Board of Directors and she left the school after the Spring term and went to Shanghai.

Qiu Jin translated a book from Japanese to Chinese on nursing techniques in 1906 called "A Course in the Science of Nursing." To Qiu Jin, nursing was an example of how the role of women was undervalued

---

[81] Hong & Mangan, 2001, p. 39.
[82] Ono, 1978, pp. 61-62.
[83] Hsu, 1994, p. 84. Tang Caichang (唐才常 1867-1900), Shen Jin (沈荩 1872-1903), Shi Jianru (史坚如 1879-1900) and Wu Yue (吴樾 1878-1905).
[84] Rankin, 1975, p. 55.
[85] Rankin, 1971, p. 44.

by patriarchal society but also a means for women to contribute to the revolution. In the introduction to the book, Qiu Jin wrote: "However, restrained by social custom, it is common to regard nursing as a 'base occupation'—this is a very grave error. . . . since [we] are able to protect the tranquility of society in peacetime and add to the nation's advantage in wartime, it would be no exaggeration to call [nursing] a profession of advantage to the nation and convenience to the people."

Qiu Jin in 1905 posing for a portrait wearing a man's Japanese kimono and holding a dagger. Public domain.

Qiu Jin also raised funds for the *Zhongquo Gongxue* ("Public Institute School") which was started by radical students who had returned from Japan.[86] She and her revolutionary associates were making dynamite in 1906 and nearly blew up the house they were renting. She then relocated to Shaoxing to organize the local revolutionary groups and recruit new members for the Revolutionary Alliance.

She also helped plan a rebellion in Zhejiang in support of the Ping-Liu-Li Uprising (so called because it was centered in Pingxiang, Liuyang and Liling Counties in Hunan) which eventually involved 30,000 rebels. Despite initial success against the local government troops, the rebels were unable to coordinate the many groups participating in the rebellion and therefore could not hold on to their gains. The Qing Government then responded in force. To Qiu Jin's disappointment, the Zhejiang uprising she was planning to assist the Ping-Liu-Uprising was cancelled.[87, 88]

Qiu Jin founded the journal *Zhongguo nübao* ("Chinese Women's Journal") in 1906 which published its first issue in January 1907. It stated that its goal was "to enlighten the customs and advocate education for women and to unite those with like feelings and organize a group as a basis for a women's cooperative society".[89] Xu Zihua, her friend from the Xunxi Girls' School, had come to Shanghai to help her with the journal. In her

---

[86] Rankin, 1971, pp. 111-115.
[87] Rankin, 1975, p. 53.
[88] Hsu, 1994, p. 85.
[89] Beahan, October 1975, p. 399.

articles, Qiu Jin continued to criticize women for accepting their role as "slave" as well as men for creating an oppressive patriarchal society. She often spoke of the struggle for women's rights as beginning in the home. For example, by allowing women to develop the skills for gainful employment, women would not only contribute to society as Liang Qichao had proposed but would also raise their status within the family and set the stage for their own liberation. However, due to lack of funds, only one other issue of the journal appeared although Qiu Jin written most of a third issue.

Qiu visited Sun Yat-sen onboard his steamship when he secretly visited Shanghai and she helped raise money for his trip to Southeast Asia.[90] Sun, who was constantly short of funds to support his trips abroad, was traveling under a false Japanese identity. Qiu Jin delivered several thousand dollars to him which she had helped solicit.

In 1907, Qiu Jin became director of the Mingdao Girls' School in her hometown of Shaoxing, Zhejiang, and she also accepted a supervisory position with the nearby Datong School, a revolutionary school founded by Xu Xilin. Qiu Jin focused on physical education with a military orientation including fencing and horseback riding. Qiu Jin met her friend, Xu Zihua in Hangzhou on March 17, 1907. Xu Zihua gave Qiu Jin her jewelry to help fund the rebellion. Together they visited the tomb of General Yue Fei (1103-1142) on the shore of *Xi Hu* ("West Lake"). General Yue defended the Southern Song dynasty against the Jurchens. It was then that Qiu Jin told Xu Zihua that she wanted to be buried near Yue Fei's tomb if she should die in the uprising. Qiu Jin's mother died on December 29, 1906, and Qiu Jin returned to Shaoxing to conduct the funeral.[91]

It was during this time that Qiu Jin and Xu Xilin[92] planned to stage simultaneous uprisings in Hangzhou, Zhejiang, and Anqing, Anhui. Xu Xilin had used his connections to purchase a position as head of the police academy in Anqing in 1906, thereby giving him an opportunity to assassinate the ethnic Manchu governor, Enming (1873-1907) in an uprising. The plan was that Qiu Jin would then lead a simultaneous uprising in Hangzhou with the Restoration Army she had organized. It was planned for July 19, 1907.[93] Xu Xilin had contacts with an army unit and members of the police academy who were to execute the attacks. Qiu Jin would lead her own students in a separate attack in the adjacent province with local revolutionary groups she had tried to organize into the *Guangfu Jun* ("Recovery Army"). They seemed to have naïvely believed they could garner sufficient forces

---

[90] Hsu, 1994, pp. 84-5.
[91] Hsu, 1994, p. 85.
[92] Some sources say that Xi Xilin was a cousin of Qiu Jin although, in a 2014 interview between the author and the Director Wei Xiao Jin of the Qiu Jin Museum in Shaoxing, she Wei could not confirm this hypothesis.
[93] Hong & Mangan, 2001, p. 44.

to realistically execute their plans. Perhaps, they were inspired by the local peasants of the area who had staged two food riots that year.[94] Instead, the leader of the local rebel group started the uprising prematurely, thereby alerting the authorities who also found incriminating documents that listed the names of revolutionaries including those associated with the Datong School.

Xu Xilin was ultimately unable to coordinate his plan with that of Qiu Jin's intended uprising and he took the initiative to assassinate Governor Enming on July 8, 1907, during a graduation ceremony at the police academy. Many of the recruits who had pledged to join the attack fled the scene and Xu Xilin and twenty to thirty of his supporters were only able to capture an armory. Government troops apprehended Xu Xilin and nineteen of his surviving supporters. During his interrogation, he said his goal was to free China of a Manchu oppressor. He was executed shortly thereafter.

The Death of Qiu Jin: Although Xu Xilin did not reveal any information about his relationship with Qiu Jin, Xu Xilin's brother implicated her. Two companies of soldiers were sent to Shaoxing. Qiu Jin had warnings that the school would soon be attacked. Most of the students had left for the summer. Those that remained at the school begged her to flee but she refused. When the assault came, Qiu Jin and a few students resisted but were quickly overwhelmed. Two students were killed, and Qiu Jin was arrested along with seventeen others.[95]

Qiu Jin was interrogated three times and tortured but refused to reveal any information. Legend says that instead of confessing, she wrote a last, brief poem which read: "The autumn wind and the autumn rain will make me die of sorrow."[96] Based on evidence found at the school and various testimony, the local prefect, Guifu, recommended that she be put to death. The sentence was quickly approved by Governor Zhang Zengyang (1843-1921). The swiftness of the proceedings was intended to discourage another uprising or prevent an attempted rescue. Qiu Jin was beheaded on July 15, 1907. She was only thirty-one years old. In an untitled poem written three days before her death, Qiu Jin wrote:

> In the blink of an eye, the most opportune moment is over,
> My bold ambition is not fulfilled, to my bitterest regret.
> We dropped our whips into the sea to check its ruthless inundation.
> We raised our swords to the sky to sharpen them on the moon.
> No clay to seal up Hangu — imperiling armored horses.
> Copious tears in Luoyang — Shed by bronze camels.

---

[94] Hong & Mangan, 2001, p. 44.
[95] Wright, 1968, p. 355.
[96] Wright, 1968, p. 356.

Having my flesh reduced to dust, my bones ground to powder,
such fate is now a banality.

I only hope my sacrifice will help us to preserve our country.[97]

The Fight Goes On: Women were directly involved in the 1911 Xinhai Revolution that ended China's imperial system. Perhaps inspired by Qiu Jin's call to arms, some served in a military capacity. Among the most famous of the revolutionary warriors were two sisters who were former students and followers of Qiu Jin. Yin Ruizhi (1890-1948) and Yin Weijun (1894-1919) were affiliated with the Restoration Society at an early age. When they were only eighteen and thirteen years of age, the Yin Sisters were involved with bomb-making and the assassinations of two Qing officials[98] and also fought in Shanghai, Hangzhou, and Nanjing.[99] They also operated the Riujun Academy which was a front for the Restoration Society. After the Wuchang Uprising, the Riujun Academy served as "the command center" in 1911.[100] Yin Ruizhi was injured in an explosion in Shanghai and Yin Weijun joined one of several women's armies called the Northern Expeditionary Women's "Dare to Die" Corps.[101]

Qiu Jin's essays may have also inspired others to publish feminist-oriented journals such as *Women's News in the Heavenly State* (*Shenzhou nübao*) by Chen Boping (1882-1907)[102] which, like most of the radical journals, was published in Shanghai.

Qiu Jin as a Symbol: Qiu Jin immediately became a symbol upon her death. But the nature of that symbol changed depending on who appropriated her legacy. Initially, the public sympathized with the brave woman who many thought was convicted on flimsy evidence. The blow to the Manchu government's prestige may have been greater than the actual damage of Qiu Jin's revolutionary activities.

Regarding her burial, Qiu Jin told a friend "I do not want to be placed in any burial site, for China does not have one inch of territory which is clean and unpolluted"[103] although, as previously indicated, she also told her friend Xu Zhihua that she wanted to be buried on the shore of Xi Hu (West Lake) in Hangzhou. After her execution, her body was dumped into the street. A laundry woman from the Datong School wrapped her body in a mat and the Tongshan Tang, a local charity, buried her in a modest grave at the base of Wolong Hill where the criminals and the poor were buried. Qiu Jin's family immediately went into hiding and some of her associates were persecuted. Qiu Jin's elder brother, Qiu Yuzhang (1873-

---

[97] Qiu Jin quoted in Chang & Saussy, 1999, p. 648.
[98] Edwards, 2008, p. 48.
[99] Tao, Zheng, & Mow, 2004, p. 59.
[100] Ono, 1978, p. 78.
[101] Tao, Zheng, & Mow, 2004, p. 60.
[102] Chen, 2011, p. 38.
[103] Ip, 2005, p. 103.

1909) arranged to have the body moved to a mortuary.

On December 31, 1907, Qiu Jin's devoted friends, Xu Zihua and Wu Zhiying, moved the body to Hangzhou. Xu Zihua financed and built a dome-shaped tomb for her on West Lake where she was reburied on February 25, 1908. Xu Zhihua wrote an epitaph for Qiu Jin and had it carved into a large stele which stood in front of the tomb and read, in part: "This epitaph is engraved here so that later generations may know that 'death by calumniation' did not cease with the Southern Song; so that they may imagine [Qiu Jin's] extraordinary heroism; so that they may shed tears and find it hard to tear themselves away. Thus, may her tomb stand imperishable just like the tomb of the princely Yue".[104] Her devoted friends, led by Wu Zhiying and Xu Zihua, held a public memorial service for Qiu Jin in February 1908 which was attended by hundreds as an act of defiance against the Manchu government.[105] The Manchu government sent soldiers to raze the tomb later that year. A friend of the family had alerted Qiu Jin's brother, Qiu Yuzhang, of the tomb's eminent destruction and he arranged for her body to be put in storage until she was buried with her husband, Wang Zifang, in his family's graveyard in Changsha, Hunan in 1909.

After Qiu Jin's death, Wu Zhiying published poems and five essays on Qiu Jin. Three of the essays were published during the Qing. By this time Wu Zhiying was already on the government's "watch list" but she was staying in a German hospital in the foreign ligation of Shanghai and, therefore, beyond the reach of the Qing.[106] Her two other essays appeared after the founding of the Republic of China in 1912. The initial essays attempt to contradict Qiu Jin's official status as a criminal and threat to the state. Wu Zhiying's later essays (published after the overthrow of the Qing), would celebrate Qiu Jin's life and the poems Wu Zhiying wrote about Qiu Jin emphasized their personal relationship. Xu Zihua defended Qiu Jin's character in an essay written in February 1908:

> "In closely examining [Qiu Jin's] conduct, [we see that] she
> was careless of details, tended to give free expression to her
> emotions, and loved wine and swords—all as if she were
> not reined in by convention. Yet, in her true essence, she was
> exceptionally upright and prudent . . . Although she loved freedom,
> in matters concerning propriety, she never transgressed."[107]

Qiu Jin's supporters, led by Xu Zihua, created two schools in her honor including the Jiangxiong Women's School in Shanghai and founded the *Qiushe* ("Qiu Society") to promote commemoration of Qiu Jin's

---

[104] Guo (Ed)., 1987, pp. 149-50.   [106] Hong, 1997, p. 52.
[105] Hu, 2004, p. 119.   [107] Hu, 2004, p. 130.

legacy.[108] Xu Zihua served as principal of the school for sixteen years until Qiu Jin's daughter took over the position in 1927. In 1912, the Republican government built a memorial to Qiu Jin in Changsha, Hunan and Sun Yat-sen delivered her eulogy. But Sun Yat-sen did not support building a major memorial to her possibly because of ill feeling that came out of an earlier split between Sun's Revolutionary Alliance and the Restoration Society, with which Qiu Jin had planned uprisings, even though Qiu Jin was a member of both organizations and the major rift between the organizations occurred after her death.[109]

Qiu Jin's friends had prepared a new mausoleum for her on West Lake. In the meantime, Qiu Jin's body had been moved from Xiangtan, Hunan to Changsha, Hunan. Yuan Shikai (1859-1916), the general who ruled China from 1912 to 1916, wanted to minimize her legacy because of her affiliation with Sun Yat-sen and ordered the plans for the mausoleum be reduced. Following an emotional struggle between her husband's family and revolutionaries from Hunan and those of Zhejiang along with her closest friends, she was again buried at West Lake in October 1912. The Restoration Society led the effort to construct a monument on the site of her execution in Shaoxing that was completed in 1930. It was vigorously championed by Cai Yuanpei who had said, "The founding of the Republic was largely dependent on the sacrifice of earlier martyrs: and Qiu Jin as the first female martyr should be made known to later generations."[110]

In 1939, Zhou Enlai (1898-1976), visited Qiu Jin's tomb ten years before the Communist era when he would become China's Premier. Zhou Enlai was also a Shaoxing native but had another connection to Qiu Jin, his uncle, Wang Ziyu, had helped organize support for a pavilion and stele honoring Qiu Jin. During a visit to Shaoxing in 1929, Zhou Enlai wrote a short verse in his calligraphy which he presented to Wang Ziyu's daughter:

Do not forget the legacy of Qiu Jin
Strive to add glory to the daughters of Eastern Zhejiang.[111]

Wang Ziyu's son worked to convert Qiu Jin's family home into a museum in the 1980s and 90s when he became Deputy Mayor of Shaoxing.[112]

Although Mao Zedong (1893-1976) seems to have never mentioned Qiu Jin specifically, he lauded the martyrs of Zhejiang. However, Mao certainly approved of the concept of women soldiers. In 1961, over fifty years after Qiu Jin's death, Mao composed the following poem which he

---

[108] Chang & Saussy, 1999, p. 658.
[109] Gilmartin, 1995, pp. 155-156.
[110] Ho, 2007, p. 164.
[111] Hu, 2007, 168.
[112] Hu, 2007, 168.

wrote on a photograph of militia women:

> How bright and brave they look, shouldering five-foot rifles
> On the parade ground lit up by the first gleams of day.
> China's daughters have high-aspiring minds,
> They love their battle array, not silks and satins.[113]

Qiu Jin was defamed during the Cultural Revolution because she preceded the Mao era, and her body was moved back and forth between West Lake and the surrounding hills. But her legacy was later restored during the period of Deng Xiaoping's (1904-1997) reforms.[114] Throughout the twentieth century, Qiu Jin's physical remains were buried, discarded, and reburied numerous times in an eerie dance that reflected China's tumultuous twentieth century history. In September 1981, a new memorial with a 2.7-meter (8 feet, 10 inches) sculpture of Qiu Jin carved from a block of white marble was placed on the shore of Xi Hu along with her remains. It is located near the site of the Xiling Bridge on the shore of Xi Hu where she once requested to be buried. An image of Sun Yat-sen's tribute proclaiming her as a heroine appears on the front in gold characters.

Above: Site of Qiu Jin's execution in Shaoxing, Zhejiang built by the Restoration Society in 1931.

Left: Memorial to Qiu Jin on the shore of West Lake in Hangzhou, Zhejiang. Source: Wikipedia, Creative Commons.

---

[113] Mao, 1976, p. 38.

[114] Hu, 2007, passim.

Qiu Jin's grandfather's home in Shaoxing, Zhejiang, where she lived for many years, has been converted to a museum with extensive displays on her life.

Qiu Jin in Popular Culture: It has been said that Qiu Jin is the best-known figure of the Revolution of 1911, second only to Sun Yat-sen. The image of her martyrdom has resonated in the hearts of the Chinese people throughout the turmoil of the twentieth century and until today. Above all, she represents patriotism, but her tireless advocacy of women's rights has inspired feminists of subsequent generations both within and outside China. However, the dramatic story of her life has been portrayed in a wide variety of media including books, plays, an opera, television series, and comic books. She was also the subject of at least six films, which often exaggerate and sensationalize the violence of her capture and her martial art.

Conclusion

From an early age, Qiu Jin was captivated by the military heroes of Chinese history and literature and was particularly enthralled by the stories of women warriors. They fought injustice, often against a greater foe, and generally died for their cause. They also shaped her sense of nationalism. While such romantic stories usually inspire young readers, they permanently imprinted onto Qiu Jin's character. Qiu Jin would come to associate these heroes and their feats of patriotism with her own destiny. Her desire to emulate their military achievements and sacrifices on behalf of China increased as she witnessed the country's exploitation and humiliation by Westerners. She blamed the corrupt Manchu Qing government for holding its own interests above those of the people and failing to protect the country.

When Qiu Jin relocated to the capital, she met other educated women who introduced her to a wider world which included Western ideas of democracy, rebellion, social issues, and women's rights. Thereafter, women's rights became her lifelong cause. Her own unhappiness with the restraints of married life and the traditional obligations and constraints imposed by conservative Chinese society on Chinese wives and mothers further deepened her convictions. In one of her poems she wrote, "I want to go to the battlefield to die for my country, but as a woman I have to stay home."[115] Her time in Japan furthered her commitment to fight the Manchu court and for women's rights. It was where she became a professional revolutionary and developed connections with other revolutionaries and organizations.

---

[115] Mangan & Hong, 2001, p. 33.

For Qiu Jin, nationalism and women's rights were inexorably linked. Revolution would liberate China so it could become a strong nation again and greater freedom for women would naturally result. There is little evidence that she had a clear understanding as to how China would govern itself once the imperial system was overthrown. But she saw a clear path for how women would achieve their independence and respect—through education. When women learned a skill or trade, they could support themselves and not be dependent upon men. Qiu was not the first to propose this concept, but she set an early example by becoming a teacher upon her return to China from Japan.

She scolded women for accepting their second-rate status in society. She exhorted them to be a part of the revolution. This was the path to individual liberation, emancipation of all Chinese and, ultimately, deliverance of the entire country. She often bemoaned how there were no females among the many martyrs of revolution against the Qing. She succeeded in not only being the first but in becoming the best known.

There is another theme in Qiu Jin's life—a respect for the beauty and the power of the word. She loved the written word and showed talent in writing from childhood. Literate girls were rare, but Qiu Jin developed skill in the difficult style of classical Chinese called *guwen* and was on the vanguard of writing in the vernacular called *baihua*. Publishing in the vernacular would become one of the central themes of the May 4th and New Culture Movements in the mid-1910s and 1920s. Her poetry and essays were impressive, but she also saw the value of the spoken word and developed into an effective orator.

While her military contributions to the 1911 Revolution may not have been significant, Qiu Jin was one of the first modern feminist activists in China to urge women to become part of history and fight for their country. She tirelessly devoted herself to the cause with her writing, speaking, organizing, teaching and, most of all, she served as a model in the way she conducted her life. She challenged women to create their destiny and not wait for men to decide their fate.

As an icon, however, she has been appropriated by various constituencies for their own purposes, often with only tangential connection to her actual life. The leaders of the Republic of China and the Chinese Communist Party alternatively embraced her as a model revolutionary and distanced themselves from her when they felt her prestige detracted from their own prominence. But the dramatic story of life and the passion with which she embraced her causes have ensured her a permanent place in Chinese history and legend.

Bibliography

ANDREWS, B. (2001). From bedpan to revolution: Qin Jin and Western nursing, *Clio Medica: Acta Academiae Internationalis Historiae Medicinae, 61*: 53-71.

AYSCOUGH, F. (1937). *Chinese women: Yesterday and today.* Boston: Houghton Mifflin.

BEAHAN, C. (October 1975). Feminism and nationalism in the Chinese women's press: 1902-1911. *Modern China, 1*(4): 379-416.

CHAN, HENRY Y.S. (1992). Ch'iu Chin. In Edwin Pak-wah Leung, (Ed.), *Historical dictionary of revolutionary China, 1839-1976* (pp. 84-86). Westport, CT: Greenwood Press.

CHANG, RAE (2009). *Autumn Gem* [Film]. San Francisco: San Francisco Film Society. A 53-minute documentary feature about Qiu Jin. Written by Rae Chang. Directed by Rae Chang and Adam Tow.

CHANG, KANG-I SUN & SAUSSY, H. (Eds.) (1999). *Women writers of traditional China: An anthology of poetry and criticism.* Stanford: Stanford University Press.

CHEN, YA-CHEN (2011). *The many dimensions of Chinese feminism.* New York: Palgave Macmillan.

CHENG, CHUNG-YING & BUNNIN, N. (Eds.). (2002). *Contemporary Chinese philosophy.* Malden, MA: Blackwell Publishing.

DOOLING, A. (2005). *Women's literary feminism in twentieth century China.* London: Palgrave Macmillan.

DOOLING, A., & TORGESON, K. (1998). *Writing women in modern China: An anthology of women's literature from the early twentieth century.* New York: Columbia University Press.

EAST CHINA NORMAL UNIVERSITY.https://english.ecnu.edu.cn/_t89/51/95/c 1703a20885/page.htm

EDGERTON-TARPLEY, K. (2004 Winter). Family and gender in famine: Cultural responses to disaster in north China, 1876-1879. *Journal of Women's History 16*(4): 119-147, 235.

EDWARDS, L. (2008). *Gender, politics, and democracy: Women's suffrage in China.* Stanford, CA: Stanford University Press.

FENBY, J. (2011 October). The birth of China's tragedy. *History Today 61*(10): 29-35. https://www.historytoday.com/archive/birth-chinas-tragedy.

FRANCIS, M. (2014). *Herbert Spencer and the invention of modern life.* New York: Routledge.

GILES, L. (1917). Ch'iu Chin: A Chinese heroine. Originally, a paper read before the China Society at Caxton Hall Westminster on March 29, 1917. Later published in London by East & West, Ltd.

GILMARTIN, C. (1995). *Engendering the Chinese Revolution: Radical women, communist politics, and mass movements in the 1920s.* Berkeley: University of California Press.

Guo, Yanli (Ed.) (1987). *Qiu Jin yanjiu ziliao* [Research material on Qiu Jin]. Two Volumes. Jinan: Shandong jiaoyu.

Harrison, J. (1969). *Modern Chinese nationalism.* New York: Hunter College of the City University of New York.

Hong, Fan (1997). *Footbinding, feminism and freedom: The liberation of women's bodies in modern China.* Portland: Frank Cass.

Hong, Fan, & Mangan, J. (2001). A martyr for modernity: Qiu Jin—Feminist, warrior and revolutionary. *The International Journal of the History of Sport 18*(1): 27-54.

Hsu, C.Y. (1994 Summer). Ch'un Chin – Revolutionary martyr. *Asian Culture Quarterly 22*(2): 75-94.

Hu, Ying (2007 Spring). Qiu Jin's nine burials: The making of historical monuments and public memory. *Modern Chinese Literature and Culture 19*(1): 138-191.

Hu, Ying (2004 December). Writing Qiu Jin's life: Wu Zhiying and her family learning. *Late Imperial China 25*(2): 119-160.

Ip, Hong-yok (2005). *Intellectuals in revolutionary China 1921-1949: Leaders, heroes and sophisticates.* Abington, Oregon: Routledge.

Judkins, B. (2012 September 14). Lives of Chinese martial artists: Qiu Jin—The last sword maiden, part II. *Kungfu Tea.* http://chinesemartial-studies.com/2012/09/14/lives-of-chinese-martial-artists-qiu-jin-the-last-sword-maiden-part-ii/.

Lee, L., et al. (Eds.) (1998). *Biographical dictionary of Chinese women, vol. 1: The Qing period 1644-1911.* New York: Routledge.

Li, Xia (2008). Nora and her sisters: Lu Xun's reflections on the role of women in Chinese society with particular reference to Elfriede Jelinke's 'What happened after Nora left her husband or pillars of society (1979)'. *Neohelion 2*: 217-35.

Li, Xiaorong (2013). *Women's poetry of late imperial China: Transforming the inner chambers.* Seattle: University of Washington Press.

Ling, Huping (1997 Spring). A history of Chinese female students in the United States, 1880s-1990s. *Journal of American Ethnic History 16*(3): 81-109.

Liu, L., Karl, R., & Ko, D. (Eds.). (2013). *The birth of Chinese feminism: Essential texts in transnational theory.* New York: Columbia University Press.

Liu, Xiaoyi (2010 Summer-Winter). The rise of women's modern schooling in late Qing China (1840-1911). *Education Journal 37*(1-2): 89-117.

Ma, Yuxin (2010). *Women journalists and feminism in China, 1989-1927.* Amherst: Cambria Press.

Mangan, J., & Hong, Fan (2001). *Freeing the female body: Inspirational icons.* New York: Frank Cass.

Mao, Zedong (1976). *Mao Tsetung poems.* Peking: Foreign Languages Press.

Ng, V. (1997). Looking for lesbians in Chinese history. In M. Duberman,

(Ed.), *A queer world: The center for lesbian and gay studies reader*. New York: New York University Press.

ONO, KAZUKO (1978). *Chinese women in a century of revolution, 1850-1950*. J. Fogel (Trans. & Ed.). Stanford, CA: Stanford University Press.

QIU, JIN (2011). *Qiu Jin Shi Wen Xuan Zhu* (Anthology of Qiu Jin's poetry). Beijing: China Publishing House.

RANKIN, M. (1971). *Early Chinese revolutionaries: Radical intellectuals in Shanghai and Chekiang, 1902-1911*. Cambridge, MA: Harvard University Press.

RANKIN, M. (1975). The emergence of women at the end of the Ch'ing: The case of Ch'iu Chin. In M. Wolf & R. Witke (Eds.), *Women in Chinese society*. Stanford: Stanford University Press.

ROPP, P. (1993). Love, literacy, and laments: Themes of women writers in late imperial China. *Women's History Review 2*(1): 107-141.

SCHIFFRIN, H. (1980). *Reluctant revolutionary*. Boston: Little Brown.

SPENCE, J. (1990). *In search of modern China*. New York: W. W. Norton.

SUDO, MIZUYO (2006 November). Concepts of women's rights in modern China. *Gender & History 18*(3): 472-489.

TAO CHIA-LIN PAO (2000-2001 Winter). Historical introduction. *Chinese Studies in History 34*(2): 5-9.

TAO JIE, ZHENG BIJUAN, & MOW, S. (2004). *Holding up half the sky: Chinese women past, present and future*. New York: Feminist Press.

TAIPEI TIMES (2011 March 29). Granddaughter to attend Chiu Chin commemoration. http://www.taipeitimes.com/News/taiwan/archives/2011/03/29/2003499390.

TOWNSEND, J. (1992 January). Chinese nationalism. *The Australian Journal of Chinese Affairs 27*: 97-130.

TSOU, RONG (1968). *The revolutionary army*. John Lust, (Trans. and Ed.). Paris: Mouton & Co.

WANG, LINGZHEN (2004). Woman, writer, martyr: Qiu Jin's life and autobiographical work at the end of the Qing dynasty. In L. Wang (Ed.), *Personal matters: Women's autobiographical practice in twentieth century China*. Stanford, CA: Stanford University Press.

WANG, Y.C. (1966). *Chinese intellectuals and the West*. Chapel Hill: University of North Carolina Press.

WANG, ZHENG (1999). *Women in the Chinese enlightenment: Oral and textual histories*. Berkeley: University of California Press.

WONG, WANG-CHI, L. (1998). 'The sole purpose is to express my political views': Liang Qichao and the translation and writing of the political novels in the late Qing. In D. Pollard (Ed.), *Translation and creation: Readings of western literature in early modern China, 1840-1918* (pp. 21-39). Philadelphia: John Benjamins.

WRIGHT, M. (1968). *China in revolution: The first phase – 1900-1913*. New

Haven: Yale University Press.

Wu, Xianning (2011). *Xu Xilin Qiu Jin*. Beijing: Tuan Jie Chubanshe.

Xiao, Xiao et al. (Eds.). (2015). *Biographical dictionary of Chinese women: Vol. 1: The Qing period, 1644-1911*. New York: Routledge.

Yan, Haiping (2006). *Chinese writers and the feminist imagination, 1905-1948*. Abington: Routledge.

Zarrow, P. (1988 November). He Zhen and anarcho-feminism in China. *The Journal of Asian Studies 47*(4): 796-813.

Zhao, Gang (2006 January). Reinventing China: Imperial Qing ideology and the rise of modern Chinese national identity in the early twentieth century. *Modern China 32*(1): 3-30.

Zheng, Su (1997 Winter). Female heroes and Moonish lovers: Women's paradoxical identities in modern Chinese songs. *Journal of Women's History 8*(4): 91-125.

Shanghai Jewish Refugees Museum - Sculpture created by artist He Ning
Photography by Paulo Leong, CC BY-SA 4.0

Chapter 4

European Jewish Refugees
in Shanghai During World War II

by Daijuan Gao

From 1938 to 1941, approximately 20,000 European Jews fled the Nazi terror and found a refuge in Shanghai during World War II. Stripped of their citizenship and assets by the Nazis, life for the Jewish refugees in the war-torn Shanghai was harsh as most of them were destitute and depended upon the aid of international and local Jewish relief committees to survive. Their living condition worsened after the Japanese forced all stateless refugees to relocate to the Hongkou quarter in 1943. Living amongst impoverished Chinese, who commiserated with the plight of European Jews, the refugees found tolerance they did not experience in their home countries. About 17,000 Jewish refugees survived the war in Shanghai (Blumenthal, 2005: 15), and nearly all of them left China for other countries after the war. The Shanghai Jews did more than survive. They created a culturally rich community in Hongkou that not only sustained their own lives, but also enriched the culture of Shanghai. Their survival and creation of a vibrant community in Shanghai represents a significant chapter in modern history and triumph of the human spirit.

As part of the research for this paper, I conducted original primary source interviews with former Shanghai Jewish refugee, Henry Meisel (1930-2017). Meisel resided in Shanghai from 1939 to 1949. The interviews were conducted on November 6 and 20, 2015 at his residence in Matawan, New Jersey.

The Jewish Plight under the Nazi Rule

After Adolf Hitler assumed power in Germany in 1933, he launched an anti-Semitic campaign that progressed from harassment to planned genocide. Before 1941, the Nazis were determined to create a Jews-free German Reich by coerced emigration. Jews in Germany and annexed Austria hoped that the persecution would eventually subside, and their lives would return to normal, but their situation steadily deteriorated instead. The notorious *Kristallnacht* ("Night of Broken Glass"), a Nazis orchestrated pogrom against Jews took place in Germany, Austria, and the

Sudetenland on November 9 and 10, 1938, dashed their hopes. The intensified persecution convinced many Jewish families to emigrate. Meisel's family was one of the first families in Vienna who took action to flee the Nazi terror. During *Kristallnacht*, Meisel and his parents were hiding in the house of another Jewish family, since the husband of that family was already arrested, it was unlikely that the Gestapo would come to the house to search for men again. The family had planned to go to Shanghai before the arrest of the husband. Not wanting to leave her husband behind, his wife offered their ship tickets to Shanghai to Meisel's family. During the night of *Kristallnacht*, Meisel's father left Vienna for Italy where Meisel's maternal grandfather resided. A month later, Meisel who was eight years old, and his mother joined his father in Italy. From Genoa, they embarked on an Italian liner and sailed to Shanghai.

Earlier in July 1938, in an attempt to resolve the European Jewish refugee crisis, thirty-two countries including Great Britain, France, Australia, and the United States convened a conference in Evian, France. While most of the countries were sympathetic to the Jewish plight, none of the Western countries were willing to accept Jewish refugees without stringent restrictions. Even the events of *Kristallnacht* did not change their position. While many Jews were eager to escape the Nazi horror after *Kristallnacht*, it became increasingly difficult to obtain entry visas from other countries since most of the nations had closed their doors to Jewish refugees.

While many foreign diplomats chose to follow their country's orders to not issue visas to Jews, one Chinese diplomat, Dr. Fengshan Ho (1901-1997), who served as China's Consul General from 1938 to 1940 in Vienna extended help to Austrian Jews by issuing them visas to Shanghai. He did this despite his immediate supervisor's stated opposition. The number of visas granted by Dr. Ho was estimated in the thousands (Ho, 1999: 8). Another Asian diplomat, Chiune Sugihara (1900-1986) was also instrumental in helping the European Jews' escape to Shanghai. While serving as the Japanese Consul in Kaunas, Lithuania, in the summer of 1940, Sugihara issued thousands of transit visas to Japan to Jewish refugees who had just fled the Nazis from Poland (Sakamoto, 1998: 6). More than two thousand refugees landed in Japan and stayed in Kobe until they were forcibly relocated to Shanghai by the Japanese government in August 1941 (Gao, 2013: 118).

Shanghai: The Last Resort

A strange city located in exotic Far East Asia, Shanghai was accessible for the European Jews due to its unique status as a city under the control of Western powers and the Japanese occupation. Shanghai was a treaty port city opened to Western countries since the First Opium War in 1842 and the resultant "unequal treaties." Before the first arrival of the Jewish refugees, Shanghai was ruled by both foreign powers and the Chinese Nationalist government. While in the Foreign Concessions, the Hongkou District was occupied by the Japanese, the French Concession by the French Council, and the International Settlement by the Shanghai Municipal Council represented by eleven Western powers, the "old Chinese city" was ruled by the Nationalist government. The Nationalist directed passport control in Shanghai until the outbreak of the war between China and Japan in July 1937. After the Japanese expelled the Nationalist government in the city, there was no immigration control in the port of Shanghai. Therefore, for a brief period, one could step off the ship and land in China without a visa or passport. This chaotic situation created by the war in China offered a unique opportunity for European Jews to flee Nazi persecution.

Arrival in Shanghai: The Cultural Shock

Many Jewish refugees enjoyed their voyage from Mediterranean to the Far East. The experience on the European luxury liners hardly prepared them for the life that awaited them in Shanghai. Even though Meisel and his family did not have a first-class cabin on the ship, Meisel recalled it as a pleasant experience—the crew was friendly, the food was great, and they stopped in many places such as Mumbai, Suez Canal, Singapore, and Hong Kong. However, "[Our] arrival in Shanghai was a shock," he said. His experience was the same as that of other Jewish refugees. Upon their arrival, they were loaded into trucks which drove them across the Garden Bridge to the Embankment Building, an apartment building in Shanghai's Hongkou District. It was owned by a Jewish real estate magnate, Vitor Sasson, who converted the building into a relief camp outfitted with bunk beds for the refugees until they could be resettled.

Historian Steven Hochstadt recounted the cultural shock for these middle-class European Jews upon their arrival in Shanghai, "Two hallmarks of European domestic life, privacy and cleanliness, were suddenly replaced by tropical heat, bedbugs, and shared toilets. The Nazis had stolen their possessions in Europe, but the reality of refugee poverty struck them first in China" (2012: 75). Meisel's family was well-off before the Nazis' persecution. His father had an established business and owned apartment buildings in Vienna, and his mother had a maid. Meisel described their initial experience in Shanghai as a disaster. When they arrived in Shanghai in January 1939, they were shocked by the poverty in Hongkou. Although it was winter, there was no heat. Like many refugees' reminiscences, he remembers seeing the corpses of beggars who were frozen to death during the night lying in the streets of Shanghai.

In August 1938, the Sephardic Jewish community, represented by the prominent Sassoon, Kadoorie, and Hardoon families, created the Committee for the Assistance of European Jewish Refugees in Shanghai

(CAEJR) to provide the refugees with temporary housing and assist them with integrating into the Shanghai economy. The American Joint Distribution Committee (JDC) provided funds from the U.S. The less affluent Russian Jewish community also offered assistant though on a smaller scale (Hochstadt, 2012: 77). A few of the first refugees with adequate financial means or technical skills could quickly integrate into the Shanghai economy and therefore could afford an apartment or a house in the upscale French Concession and the International Settlement. Most of the refugees settled in Hongkou, the Japanese-occupied northeastern part of the International Settlement.

The initial adjustment was difficult for Meisel's family. After staying in the relief camp, the *heime*[1] for a short while, his family started to look for a place to live. The first place they saw was infested by bedbugs. Finally, his family settled in a single room in a building on Wayside Road in Hongkou. Meisel said they were lucky that they had a toilet, though they had to share it with two other families. His mother learned to cook on a kerosene stove, and sometimes she mixed sand coal with water to make coal balls for the fuel. To provide for the family, his father started a second-hand clothing business. As Meisel described, his father would bring Chinese customers up to their room where he had racks of clothes. His mother worked as a waitress in a Russian restaurant for a while. Back in Austria, Meisel's grandfather on his father's side was arrested and died in the infamous Dachau concentration camp. But his grandmother later embarked on the same journey as Meisel's family by herself and joined them in Shanghai. His father's sister also ended up in Shanghai from Austria. In Italy, Meisel's maternal grandfather went into hiding on a farm and survived the Holocaust.

The Creation of the Jewish Refugee Community

Much of Hongkou had been ravaged by the battle between the Japanese and the Nationalist force in 1937. With the financial support of Victor Sassoon, the refugees rebuilt entire streets in Hongkou. The appearance of European style stores, restaurants, open-air cafes, bars, and nightclubs turned the streets into "Little Vienna." The Jewish community founded hospitals and formed sports teams to provide an outlet for the energetic youth. Even to this day, Meisel talks fondly about his soccer team and the time he spent in playing sports after school.

German-Austrian refugee journalists established a Yiddish-German-language press which published several newspapers and journals. Zionism thrived among various groups such as the Revisionist Zionists which had been active in Europe (Kranzler, 1976: 376-9). Yeshiva students who fled

---

[1] A term commonly used by the Jewish refugees in Shanghai.

Nazi occupied Poland initially went to Japan using Sugihara's transit visas and then landed in Shanghai in 1941 were determined to continue their study in Hongkou. Steve Hochstadt remarked that many Jewish families had not related their Jewish identities in Europe, especially the highly assimilated German and Austrian Jews. For instance, Meisel's father, Moses Meisel, immigrated to Vienna from Poland after World War I, and he worked diligently to assimilate himself into the Austrian culture by learning and practicing the proper German. However, as Hochstadt pointed out, "the Nazis forced them to consider their Jewishness" (2012: 77). In Shanghai, these European Jews rediscovered and revived their Jewish heritage.

One of the most colossal achievements in Hongkou was the creation of the Shanghai Jewish Youth Association School, informally referred to as the Kadoorie School after the name of the financial provider, Horace Kadoorie. The school was modeled after Jewish schools in Germany and offered a mixture of religious and secular courses taught in English by refugees and had an enrollment of approximately 600 students (Hochstadt, 2012: 78). Meisel was initially sent to study in a Jesuit school in Shanghai, and he was transferred to the Kadoorie School after he finished his studies in the Jesuit school.

Another cultural aspect that sustained or even brightened the refugees' spirit was the theater and music they created. The achievements in theater by the refugees rivaled their European counterparts (Kranzler, 1976: 368). Over sixty German-Language plays were produced by the refugees and Yiddish plays were performed mostly by the Polish refugees (1976: 379); Refugee families also cherished a puppet theater (1976: 369-70).

There were many musicians among the arrival of 20,000 refugees who not only enhanced the cultural life in the refugee community, but also improved the musical scene of Shanghai. These musicians often taught in the schools and thereby raised the professional standard of their respective institutions. Among these professors, the most prominent were Wolfgang Fraenke, Julius Schloss, and Karl Steiner, members of the "Second Viennese School" and students of Arnold Schoenberg, Alban Berg, and Anton Webern (Rosenson, 1999: 249). Rosenson proposed that contemporary Chinese music was strongly influenced by these three prominent musicians (1999: 246). The Chinese music students, Sang Tong, Ding Shande, Xu Xixian, and Tang Zhengfang who were trained by Fraenke and Schloss all became musical grandmasters in China (Pan & Wang, 2010: 231).

Hongkou: The Designated District for Stateless Jews

The Pacific War that started with the Pearl Harbor attack in December 1941 had direct impact on the refugees' lives. The Japanese military, which had controlled Hongkou and the Chinese portions of Shanghai seized the entire city including the French Concessions and the International Settlement. After the Tripartite Pact (1940), the Nazis representatives began to pressure their allies to take a more drastic measure to solve "the Jewish issue." Rumors ran wild that the Nazis had encouraged the Japanese to exterminate the Shanghai Jews including stories that the Japanese would put all the Jews onto deserted boats and sink them to the sea. Although the Japanese did not embrace the German-plan of genocide, they did take an action targeted at the Jewish refugees. On February 18, in 1943, the Japanese authority decreed a proclamation forcing all "stateless refugees" who came after 1937 to move into the Hongkou District (Hochstadt, 2012: 127) which the refugees referred to as the Hongkou Ghetto.

This ghettoization changed many refugees' lives drastically. Some refugee families who lived in better parts of city had to give up their comfortable housing and moved to the crammed Hongkou quarter. Many refugees who worked outside of Hongkou lost their jobs as they could not obtain a permit to leave the ghetto from the Japanese authorities. The Secretary of Treasury under President Jimmy Carter, Michael Blumenthal is a former Shanghai Jewish refugee. Before the Japanese edict, his family stayed at a home near Weihai Road in downtown Shanghai, a more upscale area of Shanghai (Chen, 2011). But after his family moved into a single room in Hongkou which he called "a shed," the 16-year-old Blumenthal had to quit school and work various jobs including delivering bread to support his family (Yan, 2015). The refugee community also lost the aid from two major relief committees, the Committee for the Assistance of European Jewish Refugees in Shanghai (CAEJR) and the American Jewish Joint Distribution Committee(JDC). The Japanese occupation authorities had interned the Sephardic Jews who had created the CAEJR as they were British subjects. The Japanese also blocked the distribution of the relief funds sent to Shanghai by the JDC.

In the confinement of the Hongkou ghetto, the refugees lived at a "bare subsistence level" and struggled with hunger, sanitation problems, rampant disease, and the Japanese harassment and cruelty (Falbaum, 2005: 15). Thousands of refugees were kept alive by a community organization called Kitchen Found which only offered "one hot meal a day with nine ounces of bread" (Kranzler, 1976: 546). It was run by the community leadership and supported by the Russian Jews in Shanghai since their freedom, unlike the Sephardic Jews, was not restricted by the Japanese yet. About ten percent of the refugees died in Shanghai, mostly during the difficult years of 1943 to 1945 (Hochstadt, 2012: 129).

Before the proclamation, Meisel's family had moved from Wayside Road to another single room in a building on Chushan Road. Meisel said that the segregation did not affect his family significantly since they had already settled in Hongkou, and he had no trouble getting a pass to go to school. His father continued his second-hand clothing business; his mother sold hats for a Jewish woman because she was trilingual: she spoke German, Italian, and English. His parents worked hard to provide for the family and to continue Meisel's education. With limited aid from some international relief committees and his parents' diligence, his family managed to survive the difficult years during the war.

Surviving the War

The war in Europe ended in May 1945, and the Japanese surrendered officially on August 15, 1945. As some former refugees described, all of sudden, the Japanese soldiers had disappeared from Hongkou (Yan, 2015). Meisel said that they were ecstatic when the news broke out that the war had ended. They rejoiced with a sense of freedom that the refugees had not experienced for years, celebrating by "singing, dancing, kissing everybody," as recollected by Shanghai refugees, Betty Grebenschikoff and Blumenthal (Yan, 2015). They had survived the war! The arrival of the American military provided job opportunities for the refugees who spoke English. Meisel who was seventeen years old and had graduated from high school in 1947 was hired to run the office of the clothing department by the U.S. army.

Many Shanghai Jewish survivors believed that the Japanese had spared them. "It was the Japanese who saved us," Meisel expressed the same belief in the interview. In order to determine whether the Japanese actually saved the Jews in Shanghai, it is essential to understand Japan's policies toward the Jewish refugees during World War II. In her book, *Shanghai Sanctuary: Chinese and Japanese Policy toward European Jewish Refugees during World War II*, Gao Bei stated that in the Japanese-occupied Shanghai the Japanese did not restrict the influx of the European Jews for a pragmatic reason. Their policies as formulated by the Japanese "Jewish experts," Colonel Norihiro Yasue and Captain Koreshige Inuzuka, intended to exploit the Jews' alleged financial and political power in order to serve Japan's war in East Asia. According to their plan, the more European Jews that landed in the Japanese-occupied areas, the more opportunities the Japanese had to exploit them (Gao, 2013: 6). Gao concluded that Yasue and Inuzuka's plan to exploit the Jewish wealth ironically saved the Jewish refugees even though the Japanese never intended to rescue them in Shanghai. The "Jewish experts" controlled the fate of the Shanghai Jews, and they regularly threatened the refugees enforcing them to believe that their survival solely depended on their cooperation with Japan (2013: 137).

The assumption that the Japanese saved the Shanghai Jews was based on the premise that in the summer of 1942, Josef Meisinger, the Gestapo representative in Tokyo, was sent to Shanghai to discuss the "Jewish issue" with the Japanese. It was said that Meisinger, known as the

"Butcher of Warsaw," was responsible for the murder of tens of thousands of Jews in Warsaw, proposed to exterminate the Jews in Shanghai. The Japanese, however, were unwilling to be part of Germany's "final solution." James Ross, one of the early authors who did research on Jewish refugees in Shanghai, argued that "there is no credible evidence among the thousands of documents" proving that the Nazi German had pressured Japan to kill the Jews in Shanghai. He contended that a recently [1994] released report from the Office of Naval Intelligence suggested that "the plot may have been fabricated by a Japanese official to extort money from the wealthier Russian Jews who had resisted Japanese requests for funds to assist the European refugees." Ross' research on Japan's motive confirms Gao Bei's conclusion that the Japanese did not save the Jews for humanitarian reasons, but rather they intended to utilize alleged Jewish wealth and influence for the benefit of Japan.

Whether the Nazis ever officially urged the Japanese to participate in their "final solution" remains a mystery. The Japanese government has been unwilling to share information about it. When serving as the Secretary of Treasury in the 1970s, Michael Blumenthal approached the Japanese officials many times about the "final solution" hoping to uncover the truth. However, the Japanese reply was that "They do not remember it anymore, and they have no records; they have no papers, no archives, no information about that" (Yan, 2015). Blumenthal also commented that unlike the Germans who have taken ownership for the atrocities they inflicted upon the world by apologizing and making amends, the Japanese have not taken any responsibility for the crimes they committed during World War II (Yan, 2015).

Another reason as to why the Japanese did not annihilate the Shanghai Jews is that anti-Semitism was not part of Japanese culture. Unlike the European culture, Japanese culture was not built on Christianity, and therefore, the hatred created by the religious conflicts did not exist in Japan. Moreover, since Japan did not have much interaction with Jews until the early 20th-century, there was no ground for the tension, jealousy, and resentment held by gentiles toward Jews as a result of Jewish prosperity and intellectual achievements in Europe. Therefore, one can conclude that although the Japanese did not go out their way to save the Jews, they had no desire to kill them either.

The Jewish refugees who had made a courageous choice to flee the Nazis for Shanghai eventually found a refuge. Many former Shanghai Jewish refugees today expressed their gratitude toward China and its people. Frey Sidel said, "Nobody invited us. We didn't ask anybody for permission. But the Chinese people tolerated us. Nobody said 'Listen, we don't have enough to eat, get out. You've taken away from us.' And eventually it became good symbiosis. One lived off the other and benefited from the other.

And the Chinese tried to befriend of us" (Ying, 2010). Joseph Ganj recalled his memory of Shanghai, "We were very happy that we found a haven here when we came from Europe . . . People [the Chinese] were very nice to us, and we remember it very kindly. We thank them for what they did for us" (Zhou & Du Cane, 2004, slightly paraphrased). Mak Tak Wah shared his gratitude with poignant emotion, "I had very kind memories of Shanghai and Chinese people. I can never forget, and I get choked up inside when somebody asks me about China. Shanghai to me was my life" (Zhou & Du Cane, 2004). Meisel reported that the Chinese had deep respect for the Jews who brought their rich culture into Shanghai. He also recalled that his father did business with the Chinese, and they got along very well. As the former Jewish refugees expressed, the tolerance and kindness from the local Chinese had made the European Jews' survival possible in Shanghai.

The CAEJR, the JDC, the local Russian Jewish relief committee, and other relief aid from overseas played a pivotal role in the refugees' survival. They provided food and shelter for new arrivals and funds for the families without a financial means. Another factor that sustained these Jews was a strong sense of community. Jews help Jews around the world no matter where they are. As one of the former Shanghai Jews, Ruth Sumner remarked, "Jews always look after each other . . . that's one thing you can give them credit for" (Hochstadt, 2012: 186).

It is hard to imagine what it was like for the European Jews to leave behind their familiar life and culture to exile to an unknown part of the world. However, they left their homes in Europe filled with courage and hope, and they brought their cultural heritage with them to the Far East. Their resilient spirit allowed them to build a vibrant Jewish community in war-ravaged Hongkou. In his speech for the occasion of the Rickshaw Reunion in 2002,[2] Blumenthal remarked, "Our parents created a little community there with a remarkable intellectual component that reflected the culture of German-speaking Jewry while retaining their dignity, showing immense courage and raw capacity and will to survive" (2005: 16). He also recalled that it was in the crowded single room he shared with his father and sister in Hongkou that he first heard the music of Beethoven and Tchaikovsky and read Goethe, Heine, and Shakespeare (2005: 16). The rich cultural life that the refugees created not only provided them with entertainment but also a spiritual strength that assisted them to endure the hardship during the war. Sino scholar Vera Schwarz said, "Jewish refugees in Shanghai are living proof of the will to survive as a distinctive community" (1999: 291). She remarked that the life they created in the midst of adversity was a "miracle" (1999: 295).

---

[2] One of the former Shanghai Jewish refugee reunions.

Leaving Shanghai

Nearly 21,000 Jewish refugees survived the war in China (Sakamoto 1998: 7). They looked forward to starting a new life, which for them meant either repatriation to Europe or immigration to a new country. The JDC established an emigration program to assist the refugees to settle in their new homes (Hochstadt, 2012: 188). From 1946 to the late 1950s, the JDC arranged for nearly 16,000 Jews to leave China. Among them, 1,500 refugees returned to Germany and Austria; over 5,000 left for the United States; 2,500 immigrated to Australia; and more than 5,000 landed in the newly established Israel in 1948 (quoted in Gao, 2013: 134). Most of the Jewish refugees had already left Shanghai by the time Mao's Communists took control of Shanghai in May 1949 (quoted in Gao, 2013: 134).

Meisel and his family also survived the war in Shanghai, though his grandmother passed away either in 1947 or 1948. By 1949, Meisel had applied to immigrate to the U.S. with the support from his aunt in the U.S. Since he had to wait for his visa from the U.S. Consulate in Shanghai, he and his parents first went to Israel where he volunteered to join the army. After seven months, his parents returned to Austria. Meisel moved back to Austria in 1951, and two years later he finally immigrated to the U.S. by himself.

Several reasons contributed to the Jewish dispersion from Shanghai. The primary reason was that Shanghai was the last resort for the European Jews, and most preferred to go to Western countries such as the U.S., Canada, Australia, and England. As the Western countries closed their gates to European Jews, Shanghai, a free port with no visa and passport control, became their only alternative. For most of the Jewish refugees, Shanghai was only a transient home as Blumenthal's sister, Stefanie Blumenthal Dreyfuss, said in an interview, "We all thought our stay in Shanghai was going to be interim and we would all go someplace else" (Chen, 2011).

Originally, the European Jews were unwilling to consider China because they thought of Shanghai in the 1930s was an undeveloped society (Gao, 2013: 128). Although Shanghai spared their lives, most of the refugees viewed their experience in Shanghai as "unpleasant" (Gao, 2013: 130). Blumenthal expressed the sentiment that was shared by many Shanghai Jew survivers: "Shanghai was a tough place for most of us. Many of us, indeed virtually all of us, were there unwillingly. We were grateful to be alive, but we wanted, above all, to get away—to get away to another place—to go somewhere where we could begin a new life and turn our backs on everything that had happened in Germany and in the course of our headlong flight" (Blumenthal, 1996: 4). Their difficult experience in Shanghai over the ten-year-period certainly impacted their decision to leave China, and the end of war brought new possibilities of immigration to their preferred countries.

While in Shanghai, most refugees were unable to create the life they desired. Asked why remaining in Shanghai was not an option, Meisel's replied simply as "there was no future for us." Few Jewish refugees learned Chinese language or the local customs. Meisel said that he picked up little Chinese while shopping in Chinese stores in Shanghai. Whereas in other countries such as European countries and the U.S., Jews learned the languages and integrated into society. Instead, the refugee parents encouraged their children to learn English, just as Meisel's father had sent him to the Jesuit School to have an education in English. This indicated that many of the European Jews had their hearts set on settling in the English-speaking countries such as the U.S., Canada, and Australia early on, and the United States was the most popular destination. Blumenthal expressed his regret that he did not learn much Chinese while in Shanghai because he had to work to support his family. He also commented that most of the Jews did not learn Chinese partially due to their arrogance which they shared with other Westerners such as the British and Americans who looked down on the Chinese (Chen, 2011).

Hochstadt and Gao also recounted some anti-foreign incidents in Shanghai after the war (Hochstadt, 2012: 180-1; Gao, 2013: 133-4). However, these incidents were not as threatening to the refugees as Mao's Communists who were approaching Shanghai. Ilse Greening said, "The Communists make it quite clear they could do without the foreigners. The poorer people were indoctrinated, they became antiforeigner, too" (Hochstadt, 2012: 198). Ilse's husband Herbert Greening stated, "We were afraid of the Communists, we didn't know what they would bring, we felt that we had to get out of there" (Hochstadt, 2012: 197). Meisel expressed a similar fear, "We did not know what to expect."

The unknown future which would come from the imminent change of regime in China was terrifying to the Jewish refugees. However, Pan Guan and Wang Jian, two leading scholars on Jewish studies in China, hold a different view. They contend that "the political climate change in China at the time was not directly responsible for the departure of the Jews from Shanghai" (Pan & Wang, 2010: 226, 337, with my translation). Their interpretation seems to contradict the fear expressed by the refugees.

Conclusion

During the Holocaust, while Jews in Europe were suffering the Nazis' persecution, most of the world, including the Western democracies, chose to look away. Due to China's unique semi-colonial status having been jointly controlled by Western powers and the Japanese occupying forces, Shanghai became the only sanctuary for the European Jews. Despite the difficult circumstances—the poverty, the threat of disease, and the ill-treatment by the Japanese—the refugees of Hongkou created an astonishingly rich cultural life which not only helped them endure the harsh conditions but also enriched the cultural life of the Shanghainese. While six million Jews in Europe perished, 17,000 Jewish refugees in Shanghai survived. Their survival reflects the tolerance and kindness demonstrated by the Chinese. It also gives a testimony of the resilience of human spirit, the magnitude of hope and courage, and the significance of community. The opportunities that emerged at the end of the war and the threat of China's Communists prompted the exodus of the Jewish refugees from China. Seventy years have been passed since World War II ended. Nevertheless, the stories of European Jewish refugees' survival and the radiant cultural life in the Hongkou Ghetto remains as an indelible tribute to their resilience in an otherwise tragic episode of human history.

Bibliography

BLUMENTHAL, M. (2005). The Shanghai experience and history. In B. Falbaum (Ed.), *Shanghai remembered...: Stories of Jews who escaped to Shanghai from Nazi Europe* (foreword, pp. 13-19). Royal Oak, MI: Momentum Books.

BLUMENTHAL, M. (1996 March). Shanghai: The persistence of interest. *Points East 4*: 2-4.

CHEN, WEIHUA (2011 November 4). With thanks to Shanghai. *China Daily.* https://usa.chinadaily.com.cn/weekly/2011-11/04/content_14035490.htm

FALBAUM, B. (Ed.) (2005). *Shanghai remembered....: Stories of Jews who escaped to Shanghai from Nazi Europe.* Royal Oak, MI: Momentum Books.

GAO, BEI (2013). *Shanghai sanctuary: Chinese and Japanese policy toward European Jewish refugees during World War II.* Oxford: Oxford University Press.

GOLDSTEIN, J., & SWARTZ, B. (1999). *The Jews of China: v. 1: Historical and Comparative Perspectives.* New York: M.E. Sharpe.

HO, MANLI (1999). *Feng Shan Ho and the rescue of Austrian Jews.* Vancouver: Vancouver Holocaust Education Centre.

HOCHSTADT, S. (2012). *Exodus to Shanghai: Stories of escape from the Third Reich.* New York: Palgrave Macmillan.

KRANZLER, D., & DUKER, A. (1976). *Japanese, Nazis & Jews: The Jewish refugee community of Shanghai, 1938-1945.* New York: Yeshiva University Press.

KREMER, R. (1999). *Diplomat rescuers and the story of Feng Shan Ho.*

Vancouver: Vancouver Holocaust Education Center.

PAN, GUANG, & JIAN WANG (2010). *Youtai ren yu Zhongguo jin dai yi lai liang ge gu lao wen ming de jiao wang he you yi* [Jews and China: contact and friendship between two old civilizations in modern times]. Beijing: Shishi Chubanshe.

ROSENSON, H. (1999). Jewish musicians in Shanghai: Bridging two cultures. In J. Goldstein (Ed.), *The Jews of China, Vol. 1* (pp. 239-250). *Historical and comparative perspectives.* New York: M.E. Sharpe.

ROSS, J. (1994 July 10). Germans didn't plot to kill Shanghai Jews. *New York Times*, Sec. 4, p. 18. https: //www.nytimes.com/1994/07/10/opinion/l-germans-didn-t-plot-to-kill-shanghai-jews-630977.html

SAKAMOTO, P. (1998). *Japanese diplomats and Jewish refugees: A World War II dilemma.* Westport, CT: Praeger.

SCHWARCZ, V. (1999). Who can see a miracle? The language of Jewish memory in Shanghai. In J. Goldstein (Ed.), *The Jews of China, Vol. 1. Historical and comparative perspectives* (pp. 277-98). New York: M.E. Sharpe.

WANG, JIAN (2004). *Shanghai youtai ren shehui shenghuo shi [The history of Shanghai Jews].* Shanghai: Shanghai cishu chuban she.

YAD VASHEM (2022). The Holocaust Martyrs' and Heroes' Remembrance Day through the years. [Film]. https://www.yadvashem.org/remembrance /archive.html.

YAN, XIAOYING (Director). (2015). *Survival in Shanghai.* [DVD, three episodes]. https://www.amazon.com/Survival-in-Shanghai/dp/B07HK R2LWT

YING, MINGYONG (Producer). (2010). *Ark Shanghai* [DVD]. Shanghai: Shanghai Jewish Refugees Museum Production.

ZHOU, XIAO (Producer), & Du Cane, P. (Director). (2004). *Shanghai Jews: Refuge from Hitler's Germany* [DVD]. https://www.films.com/ecTitleDetail.aspx?TitleID=30529.

The two Chengdu J-20s that made its first public appearance at Airshow China 2016.
Photograph by Alert5. CC BY-SA 4.0

Chapter 5

The Effects of Chinese Displays of Force
on the U.S.-Taiwan Relationship

by Ian Murphy

During his July 1, 2021, speech for the Chinese Communist Party's 100th anniversary, Chinese President Xi Jinping vowed to defeat attempts aimed at Taiwan's independence as part of Chinese Communist Party's historic mission to reunify with Taiwan (Xinhua, 2021). President Xi's comments on the question of reunification came amid growing international attention on the Taiwan Question. Often described as a "nightmare scenario," a Chinese invasion of Taiwan is viewed by political and military thinkers as a threat to both U.S. and international security. Taiwan, often with the help of the United States, has long prepared to defend itself against China. China's growing confidence and military capabilities has pulled the Taiwan Question back into public debate as many in the United States and Taiwan Question the effectiveness of the United States' ambiguous defense strategy.

The People's Republic of China (PRC) views the modern Taiwan conflict as a holdover from the Chinese Civil War. In the decades since it came to power, the Chinese Communist Party (CCP) has refused to renounce its goal of unifying Taiwan under the PRC or renounced the use of force to accomplish this goal (Bush, 2019). China has a history of being a credible threat to the security of Taiwan. After the Guomintang (KMT) government fled resurgent CCP forces on the mainland and established the Republic of China (ROC) in Taiwan in 1949, Mao's forces prepared to take the island of Taiwan by force. The outbreak of the Korean War in 1950 disrupted Mao's invasion plans by forcing the PRC to shift its military resources to aid North Korea in their fight against United States (Tudor, 2012). The CCP quickly lost the opportunity to take Taiwan by force since the prominence of the domino theory in Washington's foreign policy circles led the United States to position its Seventh Fleet in the Taiwan Strait to prevent the spread of conflict in the region (Department of State, 2009). After the United States established diplomatic relations with the PRC and derecognized the Republic of China in 1979, Taipei abandoned its ambitions to reunify with the mainland under the Republic of China, and subsequently abolished martial law, which led to gradual democratization on the island. Under the leadership of China's second premier, Deng Xiaoping, China underwent an economic transformation and began to assert itself in the realm of foreign policy (Economy, 2010). Over the last six decades, the United States has asserted itself in the Indo-Pacific during times of Cross-Strait hostilities to deter Chinese aggression towards Taiwan, even after the establishment of the One China Policy.

These instances of Chinese aggression towards Taiwan are collectively known as the Taiwan Strait Crises. Despite deterring Chinese aggression during the Taiwan Strait Crises, the United States learned that it would need to counter the capabilities of the People's Liberation Army (PLA) if it is to continue deterring Chinese aggression towards Taiwan in the Indo-Pacific. China's current military capabilities and the use of gray zone tactics—aggressive tactics used to achieve military objectives that fall short of justifying war—have been posing a significant challenge for U.S. policymakers and defense planners. China's recent months-long aggression campaign towards Taiwan began in 2020 and employs gray zone tactics such PLA Air Force incursions into Taiwan's Air Defense Identification Zone (ADIZ), confrontations with Taiwan's coast guard and private naval vessels, and the use of cyberattacks to weaken Taiwan's command and control system. While this paper will only analyze data on China's air incursions into Taiwan's ADIZ, the frequency and nature of these tactics have led scholars and policymakers in the United States and Taiwan to question the effectiveness of Washington's policy of strategic ambiguity regarding defense commitments to Taiwan.

The nature of China's current aggression campaign is fundamentally different from previous displays of aggression towards Taiwan. During the Taiwan Strait Crises, the United States was able to deter Chinese aggression through unilateral, conventional shows of military force. One such example took place during the Third Taiwan Strait Crisis from 1995-96. This crisis was sparked by PLA missile tests and troop mobilization in the province of Fujian aimed at sending a message to Taipei for undertaking pro-independence actions. The United States responded by disapproving of these hostile missile tests, dispatching two aircraft carrier battle groups to the Indo-Pacific, and sailing the Nimitz battle group through the Taiwan Strait (Elleman, 2014: 130). This unilateral action displayed China's inability to prevent the United States from coming to Taiwan's assistance in the near future. However, these unilateral responses have lost their potency and no longer deter PLA acts of aggression. U.S. aircraft carriers have increased their presence in the Taiwan Strait in recent years as part of the United States' freedom of navigation operations in the Indo-Pacific and were not envisioned as a deterrent against Chinese aggression (Feng, 2021). Although unilateral U.S. military action still serves a purpose, past methods of deterrence no longer hold the power they once had over decision makers in Beijing.

Many observers and defense planners now worry that the People's Liberation Army possesses the capabilities to defeat the United States' forces in the Indo-Pacific (Maizland, 2020). As part of expanding the PLA's role in foreign policy, China adopted the use of gray zone tactics towards Indo-Pacific nations. Gray zone tactics are used as part of a state's hybrid warfare strategy and can be defined as "an effort or series of efforts beyond steady-state deterrence and assurance that attempts to achieve one's security objectives without resort to direct and sizable use of force" (Chorn, 2019). China uses gray zone tactics to coerce governments into making political concessions, which helps China to weaken its adversaries (Zhang, 2018). In the past, the United States was able to deter Chinese aggression without making explicit defense commitments to Taiwan since its unilateral responses were effective against a less capable PLA. The United States is now questioning the conventional wisdom of strategic ambiguity in the search of a new defense strategy.

The purpose of this research study is to document how recent Chinese aggression towards Taiwan influences Washington's relationship with Taipei. This analytical study uses mixed methods to evaluate the connection between PLA gray zone tactics and the reactions of officials in the United States. Historically, Washington has been reserved in its official relations with Taipei so as to avoid violating the One China Policy, which China cites as a red line justifiable with war (Manson, 2021). The conceptual framework of this study operates on the assumption that the United States acts in response to Chinese actions. Any actions taken by Washington subsequently influences the direction of its bilateral relationship with Taipei. In this conceptual model, the dependent variables include proposed and passed U.S. legislation on Taiwan, U.S. arms sales and transfers, and diplomatic visits to Taiwan. The causative factors are China's use of air incursions into Taiwan's ADIZ as a gray zone tactic. Understanding the dynamic between the conceptual model's independent and dependent variables serve as a conceptual framework to understand the bilateral U.S.-Taiwan relationship and avoid confusion caused by misinformation and misunderstanding of the causative and reactive factors in this model.

This research study will take China's behavior into account from the Taiwan Strait Crises as well as the PLA's use of gray zone tactics. These Chinese tactics are used with the intention of putting pressure on the population, gathering information while weakening Taiwan's defense capabilities, and isolating Taiwan diplomatically. This paper hypothesizes that the United States is inherently reluctant to establish a well-defined relationship with Taiwan, but China's increasing use of gray zone tactics have led policymakers in the United States to clarify their defense commitments to

Taiwan. If Beijing continues to threaten Taiwan's security, the United States will seek closer and more explicit diplomatic and security ties with the island.

Review of the Literature

The existing literature provides a conceptual and intellectual background upon which a conceptual model can be imposed. The United States had to carefully balance its bilateral relationship with Taiwan in the context of a trilateral relationship, which included the People's Republic of China after 1979. Détente and the derecognition of Taiwan was a tricky task for U.S. diplomats given their need to establish warm relations with China during the Cold War while maintaining the security of Taiwan. The United States used ambiguity to temporarily appease both Beijing and Taipei. The two leading policies that remain in place today are the One China Policy and the unofficial policy of strategic ambiguity. In 1979, Congress passed the Taiwan Relations Act, which preserved the United States' legal rights to "make available to Taiwan such defense articles and defense services in such quantity as may be necessary to enable Taiwan to maintain a sufficient self-defense capacity" with the expectation "that the future of Taiwan will be determined by peaceful means" (H.R.2479, 1979). Scholars and policymakers continue to debate the extent that the United States should commit itself to the defense of Taiwan. To fully understand how Chinese aggression towards Taiwan influences Washington's diplomatic engagement with Taipei, it is helpful to analyze why the United States would want to defend Taiwan and its concepts for doing so.

The biggest factor affecting the direction of the bilateral U.S.-Taiwan relationship is the role of strategic ambiguity and whether it is adequate in defending Taiwan against Chinese air incursions and aggression. Strategic ambiguity is a risk aversion strategy that employs vague language and intentional ambiguity in foreign policy. Strategic clarity would make the United States' defense commitments to Taiwan clearer and more credible to potential adversaries, whereas ambiguity hedges against overcommitment and the risk of being dragged into a large-scale conflict with China. Determining whether the shift from strategic ambiguity to strategic clarity is taking place will reveal new trends in the U.S.-Taiwan relationship and introduce a new set of parameters for the bilateral relationship that did not previously exist. Establishing these parameters requires an understanding of the importance of Taiwan to U.S. national security, the factors necessary to maintain deterrence, the competing defense concepts for Taiwan, and the reasons influencing the voices in favor of strategic clarity on Taiwan's defense.

Two distinct camps can be identified throughout the literature on the U.S.-Taiwan defense relationship. Defense skeptics are advocates for limiting or eliminating U.S. defense commitments to Taiwan as a way of reducing both the costs and risks of maintaining current security commitments. Proponents of Taiwan's defense recognize the costs involved with continuing to defend Taiwan against the threat of a Chinese invasion, but they advocate for a clear, unambiguous U.S. defense commitment as a way of reestablishing deterrence in the Taiwan Strait. Each group makes a set of subjective assumptions on China's military capabilities and the ability to invade Taiwan, as well as the United States' and Taiwan's ability to deter and defend against such an invasion. This debate is occurring amid the collective realization that China is a rapidly growing military power, and that deterrence is a moving target in the Taiwan Strait. The most telling aspect of these arguments is that neither the proponents of defense nor the defense skeptics are calling for the United States to fully recommit itself to the policy of strategic ambiguity, which indicates that the United States is reevaluating and making changes to its decades-long Taiwan strategy.

U.S. Interests with Taiwan

Notable defense skeptic Charles Glaser (2021) examines the United States' defense commitments to Taiwan in the context of a shifting balance of power between a declining United States and a rising China. Glaser challenges the consensus in Washington that the United States must engage in competition with China to mitigate the security threats posed by a more capable adversary by weighing the value of protecting the status quo in the Pacific with the potential high cost of going to war with China over the defense of Taiwan. As a rising power, it is only natural that China would assert itself in the region. China has gradually acquired anti-access/area-denial capabilities to push back the operational range of U.S. forces from Chinese shores. China's new military capabilities have weakened U.S. deterrence in the region. The United States does not have the same power to deter an assertive China as it did during the Taiwan Strait Crises. A weak deterrence coupled with frequent maritime disputes raises the risk of sparking an accidental war in the Asia-Pacific. Since Charles Glaser views the United States as a declining power, he believes that the United States should cut back on its security commitments to avoid conflict with a rising China. Glaser does not view a reduction of U.S. security commitments in the Asia-Pacific as jeopardizing vital security interests because of the geographical distance between China and the United States. If China does reach a point where it can threaten the U.S. mainland, the United States can fall back on its nuclear deterrent. Additionally, Glaser believes that Japan can defend against a Chinese attack since it resides outside of China's anti-access area denial strike capabilities and has advanced military capability in which it can defend itself.

Like Charles Glaser, Lyle Goldstein (2020) is an advocate of abandoning U.S. security commitments in Asia. Goldstein further analyzes the costs of a U.S. defense commitment to Taiwan and views the cost of a potential war as too high for the preservation of Taiwan's de facto sovereignty. Referring to the Porcupine Defense Strategy, Goldstein asserts that in the event of an invasion, China could subdue Taiwan's defenses in two weeks and can defeat U.S. forces stationed in the Indo-Pacific. Additionally, the United States is unlikely to defend Taiwan to the extent that it would defend the Philippines, which it fought to defend in the Second World War and now shares a formal defense treaty. He also views the removal of U.S. forces and nuclear weapons from Taiwan after the Vietnam War as a positive step in U.S.-China relations, since Beijing views the stationing of troops in Taiwan as a redline. Goldstein's major arguments are that Taiwan is neither the "cork in the bottle" that can counter China's naval ambitions nor the lynchpin of the United States' alliance structure in Asia. Goldstein views it as unwise to treat Taiwan as an "unsinkable [U.S.] aircraft carrier" since defending the island increases the risk of "sleepwalking" into a major war with Beijing. However, Goldstein contradicts his main argument by assuming that China is not an aggressive power. Although he cites China's lack of involvement in a major war in over four decades and a lack of overseas Chinese military bases, Goldstein ignores the Chinese government's rhetoric about taking Taiwan by force, and China's use of aggressive gray zone tactics in the Indo-Pacific. Additionally, other authors note that reunification with Taiwan is a primary objective for the Chinese Communist Party and a driving force in its military modernization program, so the PLA will not be easily distracted by other military engagements.

Steven Jackson's (2016) research provides a counterweight to Goldstein's assumptions about the Chinese Communist Party by exploring China's large-scale aggressive behavior by examining evidence of a Chinese "regional exclusion doctrine," which has implications for the United States' national security and international security. Jackson examines observable behavior in the Indo-Pacific rather than explicit Chinese doctrines that declare a regional exclusion or a spheres of influence strategy. He finds that although China has not developed or articulated a formal regional exclusion strategy like the Monroe Doctrine, China has exhibited behavior conducive to gradual regional exclusion of outside powers. Knowing the power of rhetoric, Chinese politicians are also likely being careful to avoid overtly articulating a regional exclusion doctrine due to the region's historical memory of the Japanese Empire and the European powers' attempts to create spheres of influence and set up regional exclusion doctrines in Asia. An explicit doctrine would also contradict the Chinese government's claims of "peaceful development." Jackson outlines three areas where China exhibits exclusion behavior, 1) the articulation, development, and enforcement of Chinese claims in the South China Sea along the Nine-Dashed Line, 2) the unilateral establishment of an Air Defense Identification Zone in the East China Sea by the disputed Senkaku Islands, and 3) statements regarding and ambitions on the control of the First and Second Island Chains as part of China's maritime defense strategy. Although China continues to promote rhetoric such as "peaceful development," its actions are more in line with Deng Xiaoping's saying, "hide your capabilities and bide your time," while getting things done.

Jackson agrees with Charles Glaser and Lyle Goldstein that China is rising as a military power. However, Jackson was able to articulate the duality of Chinese actions: rhetoric versus observable behavior. J. Michael Cole (2021) notes that the views of Charles Glaser and Lyle Goldstein are closely aligned with the Chinese Communist Party's official narrative. Cole criticizes the two defense skeptics for providing a lack of evidence to back up their claims that fewer U.S. commitments in the Asia Pacific will reduce the security threat posed by China. According to Jackson, Chinese behavior does pose a risk for U.S. national security. China also seeks to control the narrative by rejecting outside influence in Asian affairs and has done so by rejecting the International Court of Justice's 2016 ruling on the illegality of Chinese actions in the West Philippine Sea, and by rejecting international dissent on Tibet and Taiwan, which Beijing considers to be "core issues." Generally, in situations where a single power exerts influence in a region, the regional hegemon can limit the sovereignty of states and even annex them. Another point that Glaser and Goldstein overlook is that the value of Taiwan's sovereignty amounts to more than just Taiwan's military capabilities. Jackson asserts that once China is able to successfully unify Taiwan under the People's Republic of China, the PLA will redirect its naval power beyond the First Island Chain to the Second Island Chain, bringing the Chinese military closer to the U.S. mainland. Allowing the PLA to occupy the First Island Chain not only puts the Philippines and Japan at risk, two states that the United States shares explicit defense commitments with, but it also puts the U.S. homeland at risk of Chinese aggression. The United States is also unlikely to tolerate Chinese hegemony in the Second Island Chain due to its historical memory of the Japanese sphere of influence in Asia that directly threatened the U.S. homeland.

Maintaining Deterrence

The United States has fundamental security interests in the preservation of Taiwan's de facto autonomy. Although the options of abandoning Taiwan and protecting Taiwan both come with costs, Washington is following precedent set by the Taiwan Relations Act and is unlikely to abandon its role in providing for Taiwan's defense. The larger debate is on how to defend Taiwan in the most cost-effective way without provoking war with China. The most likely cost in defending Taiwan is the misallocation of defense resources and provoking backlash from China. The offense-defense balance is a widely accepted theory of deterrence. This theory states that when defense has the advantage over offense, and it is clearly known by the attacking power, then a major war can be avoided. Glaser and Kaufmann (1998) analyzed the role of geography, military technology, size and quality of military forces, nationalism, and the cost ratio of defense and offense in deterring war. Glaser and Kaufman find that it is easier for states to defend territory than to take territory by force due to the cost ratio of defending forces to attacking forces. Military forces are either offensive or defensive by nature, which makes it difficult for offensive forces to shift strategies. Defense also holds the advantage over offense because defense can affect offensive operations by changing offensive tactical battles. In this way, asymmetric defense capabilities can complicate the overall operational offense strategy by posing challenges to tactical domains. Although Glaser and Kaufmann may be correct in that defenders hold the advantage over attackers, offensive operations planners may suffer from a lack of imagination or an abundance of confidence and underestimate the high costs of offense while underestimating defense's capabilities, which can lead to a major war.

The offense-defense balance assumes that both sides in a conflict are rational and that there is information symmetry. Leon Wieseltier (1985) disputes the assumptions made by Glaser and Kaufman by pointing out that the theory of the offense-defense balance does not necessarily match reality. Wieseltier asserts that deterrence is fragile and must be constantly defended. The fragility of deterrence stems from the gradual acceptance of once terrifying technologies and routine human error in calculating risks. Leon Wieseltier describes deterrence as "a wager upon the human heart" (Wieseltier, 1985). For deterrence to remain effective, it must maintain credibility in the eyes of hostile powers, policymakers must hold confidence that deterrence works, and the conviction to use methods of deterrence when the initial deterrence fails. Defense skeptics fail all three of Wieseltier's criteria for maintaining a strong deterrent. Abandoning Taiwan amid a rising Chinese military threat would weaken the United States' credibility internationally and thus weaken its ability to deter adversaries in other domains while weakening the confidence of allies. Deterrence is a social construct that must be upheld as military technology, capabilities, and methods change. Visibility also plays an important psychological role in maintaining deterrence since perceptions play a role in game theory. Forrest Morgan (2013) finds that the presence of bombers in a troubled region helps to maintain "crisis stability" amid a conflict since bombers are powerful and highly visible to potential adversaries. Despite also being highly powerful, submarines are much less effective at deterring adversaries because they usually operate undetected. However, submarines can be used to restore deterrence if used in the right contexts and in a visible way. In 2010, the United States Navy surfaced three Ohio-class submarines in the Asia-Pacific and Indian Ocean in response to PLA missile tests in the East China Sea (Morgan, 2013). Deterrence is a moving target since the variables of the offense-defense balance and human perception are constantly changing. Thinkers on deterrence agree that deterrence must be known to the adversary to prevent miscalculations and the outbreak of major war.

Defense Strategies

The Porcupine Strategy seeks to reconcile the threat of a modernizing PLA with Taiwan's smaller defense budget and restore balance in the Taiwan Strait. The Porcupine Strategy is defined as a purely defensive strategy that seeks to deter hostile powers with the knowledge that the defenders can inflict a large cost on the invading forces. In the context of Taiwan, a Porcupine Strategy emphasizes the development and survivability of Taiwan's army and counter-insurgency capabilities in the event of a Chinese invasion of the island. This strategy assumes that China could use its advanced missile capabilities to subdue Taiwan within two weeks by using preemptive, targeted strikes against Taiwan's Air Force and Naval installations. Under these assumptions, the strategy views Taipei's request for U.S. maritime patrol and F-16 fighters, destroyers, and submarines as a misperception of the threats posed by the PLA and a misallocation of Taiwan's limited defense budget (Murray, 2008). Instead, the strategy urges Taipei to concentrate its resources on developing a professional standing army, create survivable defense infrastructure, and arm itself with short-range and mobile defense articles. When discussing the prudence of a Porcupine Strategy, William Murray views the sale of U.S.-made and the indigenous development of Taiwan's counter strike capabilities as unnecessarily provocative towards Beijing, compared to short-range, defensive weapons systems. In 2008, Murray classified Taiwan's defense strategy as one of "offensive defense," and believed that shifting to a Porcupine Strategy would enhance Taipei's ability to deter a Chinese invasion and defend against an invasion for weeks or months, giving the United States time to react.

Although Liang-Chih Evans Chen views the Porcupine Strategy as conducive to the island's defense, he views the strategy as outdated given the alternatives better suited for Taiwan's defense. The Porcupine Strategy was devised by Washington when China held less of a military advantage over Taiwan. Chen's main argument is that a "defensive" defense policy is no longer sufficient in deterring Chinese aggression alone, and that Taiwan must establish an "active defensive" strategy (Chen, 2019). Specifically, he refutes Murray's assertion that a purely defensive defense strategy would be less provocative to Beijing since China has held onto its ambition of unification. The difference between a defensive or offensive defense strategy is irrelevant to a hostile power intent on forcible unification. Additionally, a Porcupine Strategy underestimates the advantage that Taiwan's current Air Force and Navy would have in defending against air and sea bombardments. Taiwan's Ministry of National Defense (2017) reflects Chen's views in their plan to meet non-traditional security threats by developing Taiwan's next-generation capabilities, improving force survivability during a first strike, strengthening air-defense and long-distance strike capabilities, and improving joint command and control. The Ministry of National Defense's strategy relies heavily on modern information and communications technology to improve early warning and a joint response to threats. This joint response capability significantly improves the coordination and thus the capability for Taiwan's Air Force, Navy, and Army to defend against an invasion.

The Push for Strategic Clarity

The policy of strategic ambiguity played a central role in the United States' relations between China and Taiwan after the derecognition of Taiwan in 1979. Strategic ambiguity provided the United States with a flexible foreign policy by allowing for multiple interpretations to exist simultaneously (Eisenberg, 1984). Ambiguity allowed the United States to intervene on Taiwan's behalf and restore the balance of power in the Taiwan Strait without signaling that Taipei can declare full independence. However, many observers are critical of strategic ambiguity and Washington's late reaction to Chinese aggression. Oriana Mastro (2021) notes that the United States is only now waking up to the threat that China poses to Taiwan. Mastro's analysis points to weakening deterrence and a shift in favor of offense in an invasion scenario. In addition to PLA growth and modernization, the Chinese public is also increasingly supportive of armed unification (Sun, 2021). Armed unification will only happen if Chinese leaders are confident that the PLA and security forces can control all of Taiwan. According to Mastro, such a scenario will likely be conducted in four parts, 1) PLA airstrikes to force the island into submission, 2) a naval and cyber blockade to isolate the island from the international community, 3) airstrikes against U.S. forces stationed in the region to cripple a quick U.S. response, and 4) an amphibious assault on Taiwan's main island (Mastro, 2021). While China already has the capability to execute the first three phases of this plan, an amphibious assault appears much riskier. Chinese officials are confident in their ability to consolidate power on the island after a successful landing due to China's resources and refined experiences in internal repression. Instead, the main challenge for an invasion force would be the middle stage of reaching Taiwan's shores. In this way, China will likely be deterred by Taiwan and the United States' offensive long-range capabilities, not a Porcupine Strategy that mainly focuses on the final stage of occupation.

Bonnie Glaser (2020) focuses on the workings of Taiwan's defense. As one of China's "core interests," the reunification of Taiwan is Beijing's top priority. It is also the main justification behind the PLA's military modernization programs. Bonnie Glaser takes "gray zone" tactics into account as part of China's pressure and intimidation strategy against Taiwan. These gray zone tactics include air and naval operations around Taiwan as well as cyberattacks on Taiwan's command and control infrastructure. The economic and military rise of China has reduced Taiwan's comparative military advantage. While the island has been increasing its defense budget in recent years and adopted an asymmetric warfare strategy called the Overall Defense Concept in 2017, the United States will need to reestablish deterrence against Chinese aggression. The United States has the legal precedent to provide support for Taiwan's defense through the Taiwan Relations Act, which stipulates that the United States shall provide the defense articles necessary for Taiwan to maintain its self-defense capabilities. While the United States' armed forces also engage in military training and joint exercises with Taiwan, the Taiwan Relations Act is far from a defense treaty and thus is not adequate as a deterrent. To reestablish deterrence, the United States will have to move towards strategic clarity. Strategic clarity will not only involve issuing statements against the use of force against Taiwan, but instead require the United States to build up its defensive capabilities in the region in order to maintain credibility in the eyes of Chinese policymakers. Much like the defense skeptics Charles Glaser and Lyle Goldstein, Bonnie Glaser shares the concern that defending Taiwan will come with an increased risk of military confrontation with China. Washington will need to balance the risks in the pursuit of deterrence through strategic clarity. Part of this balancing act will involve the need to avoid green lighting Taiwan to pursue policies contrary to U.S. interests, such as declaring independence, which can needlessly raise the risk of conflict with Beijing.

Reflecting on past U.S. interventions that prevented Taiwanese independence and Chinese aggression, Richard Haass and David Sacks (2020) concluded that strategic ambiguity fulfilled its dual mandate of appeasing Beijing and tempering Taipei's ambitions but will not play a role in safeguarding Taiwan or contribute to the balance of power in East Asia going forward. While they are in favor of moving towards strategic clarity, Haass and Sacks would disagree with Bonnie Glaser that strategic clarity will increase the risk of Taiwan declaring independence and provoking war with Beijing. They note that although President Tsai Ing-wen, who is part of the pro-independence Democratic Progressive Party, was elected twice, fewer than 10% of Taiwan's population supports formal independence. Taiwan understands the risks associated with declaring independence and have instead focused on implementing other policies that manage Taiwan's relations with China. Haass and Sacks also assert that failing to respond to Chinese aggression will further destabilizethe Indo-Pacific by eroding South Korea and Japan's confidence in their security partnership with the United States. Strategic clarity does not nullify the One China Policy, support Taiwan's independence, or upgrade the U.S.-Taiwan relationship. Rather, strategic clarity will prevent a Chinese miscalculation by pledging the United States' willingness to defend Taiwan against an aggressive attempt at unification.

A great number of scholars on the Taiwan conflict approach deterrence from a unilateral frame of reference. Certainly, the United States has played a key role in deterring Beijing's aggression towards Taiwan, and it will likely play a role in the future. However, Blackwill and Zelikow (2021) argue that the United States should clarify its defense strategy to prevent war and to preserve Taiwan's political and economic autonomy, but the United States should not act alone in these endeavors. They also do not approach the subject of defending Taiwan from a binary perspective— deterrence without conflict and rapid escalation to a large-scale war with China. Blackwill and Zelikow also believe that the United States would be unwilling to intervene in an invasion scenario not because of a lack of political will, but rather that the United States does not have credible options to confront the Chinese PLA and deter a crisis scenario. Building off of previous research, the authors identify key recommendations for U.S. leadership to avoid major conflict with China while reestablishing deterrence: 1) make clear that the United States will not seek to change Taiwan's status, 2) engage in defense cooperation with allies while placing the burden of war on China, 3) make defense plans visible to Chinese leadership, and 4) make it known that conflict shall not escalate to the Chinese, Japanese, or U.S. homelands. Blackwill and Zelikow's recommendations are useful for framing the roadmap towards strategic clarity. These recommendations provide clarity and predictability to the trilateral U.S.-Taiwan-China relationship and set precedent to expand areas of the bilateral U.S.-Taiwan relationship without crossing China's redlines.

The United States allowed itself to coast on the Taiwan issue for the past four decades and is now beginning to react to the changing balance of power in the Indo-Pacific. The scholars, with the exception of William Murray's Porcupine Strategy, are urging the United States to become proactive instead of reactive in its dealings with Taiwan. Staunch defense skeptics view the risk of war with China as too high for the value of maintaining security commitments in Indo-Pacific, while proponents of defense seek greater clarity to prevent a miscalculation that could lead to a major war. The defense skeptics analyze the United States' defense commitments to Taiwan through a narrow focal point, while proponents of defense view security commitments to Taiwan through the theory of deterrence. Examining the aims of defense skeptics through the theory of deterrence reveals that abandoning defense commitments to Taiwan is an irrational behavior. If defense skeptics convince the United States to reduce its presence in the Indo-Pacific amid a rising China, it will signal a lack of confidence in the U.S.'s ability to deter adversaries, a lack of conviction to use methods of deterrence against violators and reduce the United States' credibility to defend itself and its allies elsewhere in the world. On the other hand, strategic clarity will strengthen deterrence, but it will also mean clearly defining the rules of engagement for the U.S.-Taiwan relationship.

The authors note that strategic clarity on Taiwan will entail a buildup of U.S. defense capabilities in the Indo-Pacific and a willingness to use those military capabilities in addition to statements reaffirming Washington's commitments to Taiwan's defense. Pledging the United States' willingness to defend Taiwan against Chinese aggression will not entail nullifying the One China Policy, support Taiwan's formal independence, or guarantee an upgraded bilateral relationship. Although the authors agree on a set of steps that are conducive to strategic clarity, they largely view strategic clarity as a unilateral action. During the Taiwan Strait Crises, the United States deterred Chinese aggression unilaterally because it had the capability and flexibility to do so. Despite seeing past success, deterring a more capable China will take a multilateral approach and involve a closer defense relationship between Washington and Taipei. This research study builds on the literature by evaluating variables such as arms sales that reflect Taiwan's Overall Defense Concept, the shift away from the Porcupine Strategy, engagement with allies on the multilateral defense of Taiwan, and diplomatic visits to Taipei. Although the United States has not articulated a formal doctrine of strategic clarity, it has been engaging in activities conducive to a closer defense relationship with Taiwan.

Methodology and Research Strategy

This research study seeks to analyze the relationship between recent Chinese aggression towards Taiwan and its effects on the bilateral U.S.-Taiwan relationship. The research operates under the assumption that the United States is inherently reluctant to establish a well-defined relationship with Taiwan, while the Taiwan authorities seek increased support from Washington. This assumption is critical to understanding the dynamic between Washington and Taipei and the ways in which the bilateral relationship will develop in the future under certain conditions. Since the hypothesis is that China's use of gray zone tactics will lead Washington to develop a clearer relationship and clarify its defense commitments to Taipei, it is expected that the United States would avoid developing the bilateral relationship further if Chinese aggression towards Taiwan is not present. In this way, United States policy on Taiwan has historically been reactive, not proactive. The dynamic between China and the United States means that China acts independently of the United States until deterrence is reached. Since the United States was not able to deter China's aggression campaign, for the purposes of this research paper, it is assumed that Chinese aggression acted independently from U.S. responses from November 1, 2020, to July 1, 2021. Independent variables include the number, frequency, location, and threat level of PLA Air Force incursions into Taiwan's Air Defense Identification Zone.

During the Taiwan Strait Crises, the United States reacted unilaterally with military might as a way of restoring deterrence in the Strait. Strategic clarity is now the next best concept of deterring Chinese aggression once unilateral military interventions fail. If the United States is reacting to Chinese aggression by developing its bilateral relations with Taiwan, it will do so as described by the scholars that are advocating for strategic clarity. Just as strategic ambiguity defined the parameters of the U.S.-Taiwan relationship in the past, strategic clarity will likely serve as the defining concept of the bilateral relationship going forward. The importance of deterrence combined with a lack of confidence in strategic ambiguity leaves few alternatives for U.S. policymakers to pursue. Without an adequate deterrence against Chinese aggression, any gains made in the bilateral U.S.-Taiwan relationship will quickly be lost in an invasion scenario. Analyzing the qualities of the dependent variables will reveal whether the U.S.-Taiwan relationship is developing in the direction of strategic clarity or remaining ambiguous.

An ambiguous defense commitment will reflect the priorities outlined in the Porcupine Defense Strategy and will continue to involve unilateral U.S. military action and statements in response to Chinese aggression towards Taiwan. An ambiguous political response would only involve the proposal and passage of minor legislation clarifying the Taiwan Relations Act and minor consular changes, and the continuation of routine, non-disruptive diplomatic engagement with Taipei, as seen in the past. If the bilateral relationship is developing towards greater strategic clarity, then actions taken by the United States in response to Chinese aggression will reflect the recommendations outlined by Blackwill and Zelikow. If the United States is trending towards strategic clarity, then its defense commitments will reflect the priorities set by Taiwan's Overall Defense Concept, which emphasizes the development of active defense, modern communications systems for the military, and the transfer of U.S. defense articles that strengthen Taiwan's joint forces. Clarity will also involve the proposal and passage of novel legislation that expands on the Taiwan Relations Act and breaks diplomatic taboos or self-imposed restrictions. A defense policy driven by the idea of strategic clarity will also involve multilateral engagement with allies, which could include joint planning, military exercises, joint statements, and multilateral engagement with Taipei.

As noted in the literature, the United States is going through a deliberative phase regarding its relationship with Taiwan. The United States used the Taiwan Relations Act and unilateral displays of military force to deter Chinese aggression and avoid tough questions on its ambiguous relationship with Taipei. While the goal of deterring China remains the same, the United States is questioning its methods of doing so. This research study provides value to political leaders and defense planners concerned with the defense of Taiwan by providing a current account of how relatively new Chinese gray zone tactics are influencing the bilateral U.S.-Taiwan relationship. Subsequent research could expand on this research study to include more variables, apply the lessons learned to other governments facing Chinese coercion, and lead to research that helps the United States reclaim its status as the independent variable. Political science research can also be conducted on political camps within the Chinese Communist Party and the split between Party members on the Taiwan Question, as well as the future of a "One Country, Two Systems" deal for Taiwan. Wolf Warrior Diplomacy is also a relatively new development and may play a role in China's recent aggression campaign towards Taiwan. Conducting research on China's major uses of gray zone tactics and its effects on the U.S.-Taiwan relationship will open multiple avenues for further research and discoveries.

This research study takes a mixed methods approach and uses data taken from November 1, 2020, to July 1, 2021. Data on both the independent and dependent variables are taken from U.S. and Taiwanese sources that include government agencies and independent sources. The independent variable includes the number, frequency, location, and threat level of Chinese PLA Air Force incursions into Taiwan's Air Defense Identification Zone. The dependent variable includes proposed and passed U.S. legislation on Taiwan, arms sales and technology transfers to Taiwan, diplomatic engagements with Taipei, and defense planning with U.S. allies regarding the protection of Taiwan. Dependent variable data will be coded through content analysis and categorized as favorable and groundbreaking to prevent redundancy and duplicates within the dataset, while secondary sources such as media reports and public political statements will corroborate the findings. Analyzing the quantity and qualities of both variables provides a clearer picture of the threat and nature of a U.S. response. The independent and dependent variables will be graphed to reveal trends in the data through a convergent parallel design.

Limitations and Bias

This research study assumes that the Chinese government, think tanks, and the media in China are unreliable sources due to historic inconsistency and government censorship. The Chinese Communist Party holds a monopoly on the media and think tanks through the Publicity Department, which is also known as the Propaganda Department (McGregor, 2010). The close association between government and non-government sources means that it is difficult to accurately corroborate government claims with non-government sources. Another limitation for the independent variable is the ability of Taiwan and the United States to accurately report Chinese air incursions since their timing, location, and number of aircraft is often unpredictable. China makes this gray zone tactic intentionally difficult to report and predict, which creates a need for better detection and response capabilities. Data on the dependent variable is subject to biases when collected through U.S. sources. Although the United States government seeks to deter China from invading Taiwan, policymakers and academics may have alternative motives for producing materials in support of Taiwan. These biases include broader anti-CCP sentiment, the U.S.-China Trade War, leverage over other regional issues, and career enhancement or alternative political motives. Using independent sources to corroborate government reports will reduce bias in the primary dataset.

ANALYSIS AND FINDINGS

As previously stated, this paper explores both the reactive relationship of U.S. policy to Chinese aggression towards Taiwan as it impacts U.S. policy and the reactive relationship of U.S. policy as it impacts the bilateral U.S.-Taiwan relationship. Formally, this relationship can be thought of as a recursive mathematical system of two equations, where Chinese actions are independent (or exogenous) to the system while U.S. policy and changes in the U.S.-Taiwan relationship are dependent (or endogenous) within the system. The conceptual system could be mathematically defined as follows:

$$\text{U.S. Policy} = f(\text{Chinese actions})$$
$$\text{U.S.-Taiwan Relationship} = f(\text{U.S. Policy})$$

Chinese actions are independent of the system while U.S. policy and the bilateral U.S.-Taiwan relationship are dependent and are ultimately reactions to Chinese action. The United States might switch to an offensive posture in the future, but the analysis for doing so is outside the scope of the present model. This two-equation recursive system is hypothesized to explain the current political environment of strategic ambiguity. A more proactive political model, in which U.S. policy and development of the bilateral relationship is independent of Chinese action, would not be described by this model. This paper does not make any statement about whether a potential proactive model would provide a safer world environment than the current reactive model, but instead attempts to make a statement as to whether the proposed reactive model accurately explains the current environment and can be used as a framework to analyze the current environment. The bulk of the analysis presented in this paper focuses on the first equation as it relates to air incursions. Other forms of Chinese behavior such as sea and cyber activities and the relationship of U.S. policy as it impacts the bilateral U.S.-Taiwan relationship are left for future research.

Flight Incursions into Taiwan's ADIZ

Between November 1, 2020, and July 1, 2021, the PLA Air Force had a near constant presence in Taiwan's Air Defense Identification Zone, with 149 incursions over the course of 243 days. According to David Welch, an ADIZ "is a publicly defined area extending beyond national territory in which unidentified aircraft are liable to be interrogated and, if necessary, intercepted for identification before they cross into sovereign airspace" (Welch, 2013). Although not a perfect equivalent due to the complexities of the One China Policy, this ADIZ roughly defines Taiwan's airspace. China has respected Taiwan's ADIZ in the past, but has violated it in recent years to display its displeasure at Taiwanese authorities. Although the establishment of an ADIZ does not guarantee legal rights to the airspace, international customs are generally abided by as a safety precaution both for the authorities that established the ADIZ and for aircraft entering the area. PLA Air Force flight incursions into Taiwan's ADIZ pose both short-term and long-term threats to Taiwan's security. For most of these overflights (95/149), Taiwan responded by sending out airborne sorties, issuing radio warnings to the offending aircraft, and deploying missile systems to monitor aircraft activities. The ROC Air Force also responded by issuing radio warnings and deploying CAP aircraft and missile defense systems to monitor PLA air activity for 54/149 of incidents (MND, 2021). Since the ROC Air Force routinely intercepts PLA aircrafts in its ADIZ, it can be reasonably assumed that the PLA Air Force is not self-identifying to the Taiwan authorities, which demonstrates hostile intent. Beijing has used this tactic in the past as a way of voicing its political displeasure towards the island, but it has only recently conducted a prolonged campaign to violate Taiwan's ADIZ, which can be likened to a war of attrition (Chang, 2020). This recent aggression campaign prompted Taiwan's Ministry of National Defense (MND) to publish opensource reports on the PLA's flight paths starting on November 1, 2020.

When first viewing the data on a day-to-day basis, the number of PLA

Month	Number of Crossings	Number of Aircraft	Average Aircraft per Crossing
November, 2020	22	41	1.86
December, 2020	19	32	1.68
January, 2021	29	81	2.79
February, 2021	17	40	2.35
March, 2021	17	53	3.11
April, 2021	21	105	5.00
May, 2021	17	28	1.65
June, 2021	10	43	4.30

Air Force aircraft flying into Taiwan's Air Defense Identification Zone appears to be random. However, when viewed as a whole, there is a clear upward trend in the number of aircraft being sent into the ADIZ on any one given day. What is less predictable is the schedule of flights with less than ten aircraft. Although it may appear that the PLA is conducting these overflights for fewer days from May to June, the PLA Air Force is continuing to break its records on the total number of aircraft that it is able to dispatch on any given day. This is significant because it signals the PLA Air Force's ability to safely dispatch and coordinate a large number of aircraft in the Taiwan Strait at one time. In theory, China can send hundreds of aircrafts into the Taiwan Strait, but it cannot do so effectively until its pilots have adequate over-ocean training and until the PLA Air Force can effectively utilize electronic intelligence aircraft.

One aspect of Chinese air incursions reflected in this plot is the PLA Air Force's increasing ability to coordinate a large number of aircrafts in the Taiwan Strait at any one point in time. Early on, China would only send a few aircraft into flight at any one time. However, China has increasingly demonstrated an ability to move larger numbers of aircrafts into Taiwan's ADIZ at any given time. The ability to maneuver a large number of aircraft in the Taiwan Strait is a direct threat to Taiwan for several reasons. This

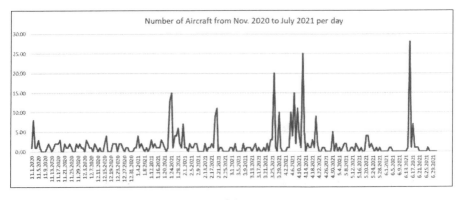

Number of Aircraft from Nov. 2020 to July 2021 per day

ability suggests that Chinese forces are receiving training directly related to a Taiwan invasion scenario. Previously, PLA Air Force pilots received little over-ocean training out of fear that they may defect to Taiwan. Taiwanese pilots receive about 120 flight hours of over-ocean training compared to just 60 flight hours for PLA Air Force pilots (Shambaugh, 2000). Over-ocean training and coordination is a dangerous activity, even in the less chaotic environment of flight training. From 2020-2021, the ROC Air Force experienced three deadly training incidents. In October and November 2020, one F-5 and one F-16 crashed, killing their pilot as a result. A higher profile crash occurred on March 22, 2021, when two Taiwanese F-5E fighters collided off Taiwan's Southeastern coast (Reuters, 2021). These incidents raised public concern over the training of ROC pilots and the maintenance of aircraft, both of which are under the stress of responding to Chinese flight incursions into Taiwan's Southwestern ADIZ.

The PLA Air Force has displayed an ability to use multiple kinds of aircraft during these flight incursions. Although any PLA Air Force accidents and crashes are likely to go underreported, the PLA Air Force has displayed an ability to contest Taiwan's ADIZ using a maximum of 28 aircraft on June 15, 2021, which included one Y-8 ASW, one Y-8 EW, two KJ-500 AEW&C, Four H-6, six, J-11, and fourteen J-16 aircraft (MND, 2021). A constant presence in the Taiwan Strait past Taiwan's ADIZ also serves Beijing's political objective of eroding the perception that Taiwan's ADIZ is exclusive to the Taiwan authorities.

Not reflected in the initial data plot is the proximity of these flights to Taiwan's main island. Initially, flight incursions were concentrated around the perimeter of Taiwan's Southwestern ADIZ, and gradually expanded to the Southeastern corner of the ADIZ over the course of several months. Southern Taiwan is home to various defense installations including two major naval bases in Makung and Zaoying, and air bases in Makung, Tainan, Kangshan, Pingtung, and Taitung (Stratfor, 2015). Strategists also identify potential amphibious invasion sites near Tainan, Linyuan, and Jialutang (Holmes, 2019). Retired ROC Air Force lieutenant general Chang Yan-ting (張延廷) asserts that the PLA Air Force is conducting these operations to 1) collect data on Taiwan's response times, 2) put stress on the ROC Air Force's human and defense resources, 3) increase the maintenance cost of newer ROC aircraft by triggering a jet sortie response, and 4) declare Chinese sovereignty in the Taiwan Strait (Chang, 2020). Although Taiwan articulated an asymmetric defense policy through the Overall Defense Concept and began producing its own submarines and jet trainers (Taipei Times, 2020), Chang Yan-ting believes that there is still a need for U.S. arms to deter and defend Taiwan against an air assault from China.

U.S. Arms Sales to Taiwan

The United States has been historically reluctant to provide Taiwan with the weapons it requests. In addition to bureaucratic scrutiny, providing arms to Taiwan is also subject to political scrutiny. The Taiwan Relations Act of 1979 allows the United States to provide Taiwan with weapons in a sufficient manner to provide for its own defense. Although the United States is presented with the general challenge of China's military rise, policymakers still express hesitancy over supplying Taiwan with its requested provisions. Hesitancy exists around arms sales due to China's political and military influence in the region (Kastner, 2017). Some policymakers view the sale of offensive long-range military provisions as more provocative towards China, while others argue that defensive provisions are equally provocative in the eyes of a potential invader. China has sought to punish United States for selling arms to Taiwan by sanctioning the defense companies that provide arms to Taiwan (Reuters, 2020). Despite its economic influence, China's efforts to deter the United States from selling Taiwan weapons only seems to work when Taiwan's security is perceived to be at minimal risk.

Aircraft Type	Y-8 RECCE	Y-8 ASW	Y-8 EW	Y-8 ELINT	KJ-500 AEW&C	Y-9 EW
Total number deployed	49	113	40	4	17	8
Number deployed at once	2	2	1	1	2	1

Aircraft Type	SU-30	J-16	J-11	J-10	J-7	JH-7	H-6K
Total number deployed	4	90	10	47	4	10	22
Number deployed at once	2	2	1	1	2	4	8

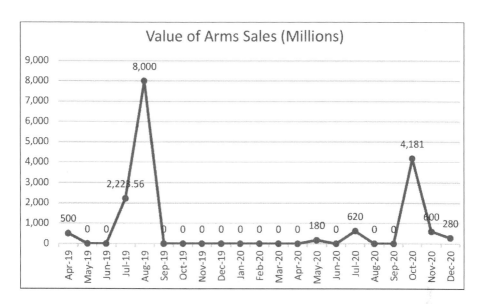

Although it is important to note the timing of arms sales, the number, and the dollar value of arms sales to Taiwan do not accurately reflect the changes in U.S. policy due to Chinese aggression. Instead, these quantitative measures may be more indicative of Taiwan's procurement budget or general bureaucratic procedures. Looking at the timing of arms sales provides little information on the political environment in which such agreements are made. It is not uncommon for the United States to approve multiple arms sales for multiple countries at the same time. On July 8, 2019, the United States approved two arms sales to Taiwan for $223.56 million and $2 billion. On October 21, 2020, the United States approved three arms sales to Taiwan for $436.1 million, $1.008 billion, and $367.2 million, with a fourth arms sale on October 26 for $2.37 billion (DSCA, 2021). Arms sales negotiations involve multiple government entities and private contractors, so they take a long time to negotiate and are often proposed months ahead of their announcement date. Since the qualities of the October 2020 arms sales vary, it can be assumed that they were proposed at different times in response to specific military needs but were finalized and approved at the same time. In March 2021, various news agencies reported that the Biden Administration was reviewing its first arms deal with Taiwan. Secrecy around arms sales leaves out important details such as the timing of the initial request, rejected requests, and specific reasons for requests. When it comes to approved arms sales, the Defense Security Cooperation Agency publishes reports that detail the quantity, value, and quality of arms being sold to U.S. counterparts, as well as the reasons for approval by the State Department and gives a sense of the specific threat being responded to. The qualities of the arms sales and the reasons for why they were issued have changed from 2019 to 2021.

TIMELINE OF U.S. ARMS SALES TO TAIWAN, 2019-2021
Descriptions from Defense Security Cooperation Agency Reports

April 15, 2019: "Continuation of a pilot training program and maintenance/logistics support for F-16 aircraft currently at Luke Air Force Base, Arizona for an estimated cost of $500 million.

- These services and equipment will support the continuing pilot training program currently at Luke Air Force Base, Arizona. This program enables the recipient to develop mission ready and experienced pilots through CONUS training. The training provides a "capstone" course that takes experienced pilots and significantly improves their tactical proficiency. Training is a key component of combat effectiveness.

July 8(a), 2019: Stinger missiles and related equipment and support for an estimated cost of $223.56 million.

- The recipient intends to use these defense articles and services to modernize its armed forces and expand its existing air defense architecture to counter threats. This will contribute to the recipient's military goal to update its capability while further enhancing greater interoperability between the recipient, the U.S., and other partners.

July 8(b), 2019: M1A2T Abrams Tanks and related equipment and support for an estimated cost of $2 billion.

- The proposed sale of M1A2T tanks will contribute to the modernization of the recipient's main battle tank fleet, enhancing its ability to meet current and future regional threats and to strengthen its homeland defense. These tanks will contribute to the recipient's goal of updating its military capability while further enhancing interoperability with the United States and other partners.

August 20, 2019: Sixty-six F-16C/D Block 70 aircraft and related equipment and support for an estimated cost of $8 billion.

- This proposed sale will contribute to the recipient's capability to provide for the defense of its airspace, regional security, and interoperability with the United States. The recipient currently operates the F-16 A/B.

May 20, 2020: Eighteen MK-48 Mod6 Advanced Technology Heavy Weight Torpedoes and related equipment at an estimated cost of $180 million.

- The proposed sale will improve the recipient's capability in current and future defensive efforts. The recipient will use the enhanced capability as a deterrent to regional threats and to strengthen homeland defense.

July 9, 2020: Recertification of Patriot Advanced Capacity-3 missiles at an estimated cost of $620 million.

- This proposed sale will help sustain the recipient's missile density and ensure readiness for air operations. The recipient will use this capability as a deterrent to regional threats and to strengthen homeland defense.

October 21, 2020: Eleven High Mobility Artillery Rocket Systems M142 Launchers and related equipment for an estimated cost of $436.1 million.

- The recipient will use this capability as a deterrent to regional threats and to strengthen homeland defense. Acquisition of HIMARS will contribute to the recipient's goal of updating its military capability while further enhancing interoperability with the United States and other allies.

October 21(2), 2020: One hundred thirty-five AGM-84H Standoff Land Attack Missile Expanded Response (SLAM-ER) Missiles and related equipment for an estimated cost of $1.008 billion.

- This proposed sale will improve the recipient's capability to meet current and future threats as it provides all-weather, day and night, precision attack capabilities against both moving and stationary targets. The recipient will be able to employ a highly reliable and effective system to increase their warfighting effectiveness as needed, which can counter or deter aggression by demonstrated precision against surface targets.

October 21(3), 2020: Six MS-110 Recce Pods and related equipment for an estimated cost of $367.2 million.

- This proposed sale will improve the recipient's capability to meet current and future threats by providing timely intelligence, surveillance, and reconnaissance capabilities for its security and defense. The enhanced capability is a deterrent to regional threats and will strengthen the recipient's self-defense.

October 26, 2020: One hundred Harpoon Coastal Defense Systems and related equipment for an estimated cost of $2.37 billion.

- This proposed sale will improve the recipient's capability to meet current and future threats by providing a flexible solution to augment existing surface and air defenses. The recipient will be able to employ a highly reliable and effective system to counter or deter maritime aggressions, coastal blockades, and amphibious assaults.

November 3, 2020: Four Weapons-Ready MQ-9B Remotely Piloted Aircraft and related equipment for an estimated cost of $600 million.

- This proposed sale will improve the recipient's capability to meet current and future threats by providing timely intelligence, surveillance, and reconnaissance, targeting acquisition, counter-land, counter-sea, and anti-submarine strike capabilities for its security and defense. The capability is a deterrent to regional threats and will strengthen the recipient's self-defense.

December 7, 2020: Field Information Communications System and related equipment for an estimated cost of $280 million.

- The proposed sale is designed to provide mobile and secure communications. It will contribute to the recipient's goal to modernize its military communication's capability in support of their mission and operational needs." (DSCA, 2021)

Although Taiwan's Ministry of National Defense did not start publicly publishing PLA Air Force flight data until November 1, 2020, both news reports and Defense Security Cooperation Agency arms sales reports point to violations of Taiwanese airspace starting in March 2019. This was the first time that Chinese PLA Air Force aircraft intentionally flew into Taiwan's ADIZ since 1999 (Xie, 2021). The above timeline details the arms sales approved by the U.S. State Department from 2019-2021 along with the reasoning for approving such provisions, as provided by the Defense Security Cooperation Agency (DSCA, 2021). These descriptions show a shift in mindset regarding the types of provisions the United States is willing to sell to Taiwan as well as a shift in how the U.S. views Taiwan's security. Initial arms sales revolve around modernizing and maintaining Taiwan's existing forces, with little change in overall operational direction. The reports first start using language that supports deterrence on May 20, 2020, when it linked "defensive efforts" to the use of enhanced capabilities as a "deterrent to regional threats" (DSCA, 2021). The language of deterrence against regional threats continued in subsequent arms sales reports. In the second October 21, 2020, report, the language linked "precision attack capabilities" with the ability to "counter or deter aggression," before the sale of tactically significant intelligence, surveillance, and reconnaissance capabilities.

Early arms sales reports focused on countering threats by selling Taiwan provisions that expanded its current defense infrastructure rather than changing Taiwan's overall operational advantage. The emphasis on ground operations and short-range defenses such as M1A2T Abrams Tanks displays the United States' early adherence to the Porcupine Defense Strategy, which prioritizes the development of Taiwan's army over an active defense strategy. The United States shifted its mindset in the direction of active defense as described by Taiwan's Overall Defense Concept with the sale of precision attack capabilities on October 21, 2020. The Overall Defense Concept also prioritizes the development of Taiwan's joint response with the help of modern communications equipment. Communications equipment is viewed as provocative to Beijing because such equipment extends the range and improves coordination between missile systems and jet fighters. Only after this language was established, did the United States begin selling Taiwan provisions supporting its intelligence, surveillance, and reconnaissance capabilities and modernizing its military communication's capability.

The language used by the Defense Security Cooperation Agency continues to support Taiwan's self-defense through deterrence capabilities and will likely reflect aspects of the Porcupine Defense Strategy going forward. It is unlikely that the State Department would approve of arms sales that solely serve offensive purposes or could be used to attack the Chinese mainland. Instead, future arms sales will likely involve dual-use technology such as communications systems as well as porcupine-like defense systems to deter an invasion of the island. The Biden Administration appears to be continuing this trend with an anticipated arms sale of Patriot Advanced Capability 3 Missile Segment Enhancement missiles from Lockheed Martin (Lee, 2021). These advanced surface-to-air missiles will directly support Taiwan's defense against an aerial assault from the PLA Air Force and raise the cost of an invasion for China. Also, critical to deterring Chinese aggression towards Taiwan is U.S. legislation. In recent months, the United States has proposed and passed legislation regarding the defense of Taiwan and its overall relationship with the island.

U.S. Legislation

The United States has actively responded to threats from China through legislative activity. In this research study, legislative activity includes bills, amendments, and resolutions being introduced into the House and Senate. Since switching diplomatic recognition to the People's Republic of China, the United States has mainly used the Taiwan Relations Act of 1979 as a guide for navigating its bilateral relationship with the Republic of China. Even though the Taiwan Relations Act set legal precedent for providing Taiwan with defensive articles, it left other aspects of the bilateral relationship intentionally vague. Vague guidance coupled with Chinese political disapproval stalled aspects of the bilateral U.S.-Taiwan relationship such as trade, diplomatic engagement, and defense. There has been a notable uptick from 2019 to 2021 in U.S. legislative activity regarding Chinese threats to U.S. national security, treatment of the people of Hong Kong, and the U.S.-Taiwan bilateral relationship.

Taiwan has received a lot of attention from lawmakers due to Chinese threats in other domains. When reviewing legislative actions, there is an urgent push to maintain Taiwan's status as a democratic enclave in the Indo-Pacific, especially after China imposed limits on democratic institutions in Hong Kong. U.S. legislators have consistently issued new bills and resolutions on Taiwan from 2020-2021 that support elevating U.S. engagement with Taiwan through increased economic trade, diplomatic engagement, and plans to defend the island in an invasion scenario. Even though legislation takes anywhere from several months to several years to

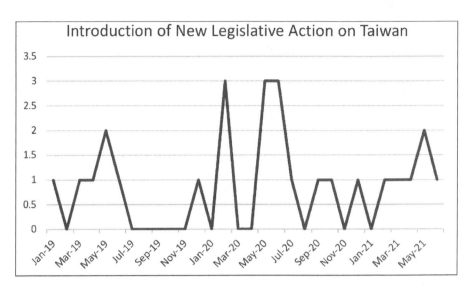

be passed, the introduction of new legislation displays a renewed interest in the U.S.-Taiwan bilateral relationship. However, U.S. legislation regarding Taiwan is still a function of Chinese actions. The wording of introduced legislative action suggests that Chinese actions in all domains affect U.S. legislation on Taiwan, which makes it more difficult to pinpoint legislative actions that are in response specifically to Chinese air incursions into Taiwan's ADIZ. While the above chart reflects new legislative actions specific to Taiwan, the reasoning for introducing such legislation is varied.

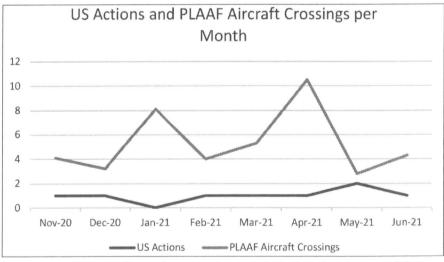

- U.S. Actions = Sum of arms sales combined with House and Senate legislation introduced for a given month.
- PLAAF Aircraft Crossings = The total number of aircraft that crossed into Taiwan's ADIZ for a given month, divided by ten to allow for easy visual comparison.

This paper has attempted to present information, which either supports or rejects the hypothesis that U.S. policy is influenced and reactive to Chinese actions and that the status of the U.S.-Taiwan relationship is dependent upon U.S. policy. The data collection has focused on air incursions into Taiwan's Air Defense Identification Zone and the impact this has had on U.S. policy as reflected by arms sales and legislative activities. The nature of air incursions provide data that is very specific as to the date of the incursion and specifics concerning the number and types of aircraft used by the PLA Air Force and their flight path. United States legislative activity spans a wider time period and is less specific as to the dates of initial legislative activity and lacks clear statements of what the official policy on Taiwan is. The dates of the introduction of various House and Senate proposed legislation is well documented while the specific reasoning is more ambiguous and up for interpretation. Additionally, the dates when Congress ultimately created public laws is well documented. What is less clear is how to interpret legislative activity that does not culminate in public law. As to public law created by Congress, there have only been three significant laws relating to Taiwan:

1) Taiwan Relations Act of 1979,
2) Taiwan Assurance Act of 2019,
3) Taiwan Allies International Protection and
   Enhancement Initiative (TAIPEI) Act of 2019.

The first was passed during the Carter Administration and seeks to create a stalemate situation where the United States does not identify Taiwan as an independent country while also ensuring that China does not use military force to invade Taiwan and preserving the United States' obligation to provide for Taiwan's defense (H.R.2479, 1979). The second and third pieces of legislation both passed in 2019 during Trump Administration. The Taiwan Assurance Act calls for the U.S. State Department to review previous guidance governing the U.S.-Taiwan bilateral relationship and reissue guidance to account for changes as well as to encourage engagements between U.S. and Taiwanese government officials (H.R.2002, 2019). The TAIPEI Act builds on the Taiwan Assurance Act by requiring the U.S. State Department to annually report to Congress on steps the State Department has taken to strengthen Taiwan's international diplomatic relationships (S.1678, 2019). Given the long-time interval over which a House or Senate resolution becomes a public law, it is very difficult to assign a specific point in time to the creation of public law. Arms sales have greater specificity as to time, type, and quantity. My reading and analysis of U.S. legislative efforts and arms sales suggests that they are reactions to a broad set of Chinese activities. Nothing that I have researched provides any evidence to suggest that this paper's hypothesis that U.S. policy is a reaction to Chinese aggression towards Taiwan should be rejected.

Implications for the Future

The relationship between China, Taiwan, and the United States is complex and involves many more dimensions than the ones presented in this paper, with many aspects of the U.S.-Taiwan relationship still in development. While the Trump Administration consistently broke long-standing taboos regarding the U.S. relationship with Taiwan, observers were less certain of the incoming Biden Administration's Taiwan strategy (Bader, 2016). The Biden Administration has continued the trend of reducing the United States' self-imposed restrictions on its engagement with Taiwan in a more systematic way by allowing for more official contact between the two and by swiftly responded to Chinese economic and diplomatic pressure on Taiwan (Culpan, 2021). Despite bipartisan conflict around domestic affairs, Taiwan also enjoyed bipartisan support for stronger defense and economic ties in the U.S. House and Senate, most notably with Senators and Congress members issuing a formal letter encouraging U.S. Trade Representative Lighthizer to begin negotiating a trade agreement with their Taiwanese counterparts (SCFR, 2020). As support for Taiwan continues to grow in Washington, observers note that Taiwan often faces the brunt of Chinese retaliation for developments in Cross-Strait tensions (Hass, 2021). Although it may seem like U.S. support for Taiwan can yield infinite political gains for Taipei, there are limitations to how far both the U.S. and Taiwan are willing to develop their relationship.

The United States has long made its objections to formal Taiwanese independence clear. What is not clear is the extent that the United States is willing to defend Taiwan against an invasion, which this research paper sought to explore. Another factor limiting the scope of this paper is that it only explores three international actors, China, Taiwan, and the United States, and does so in a limited manner by solely focusing on the theory of deterrence and not including the declaratory theory of recognition. In international law, the declaratory theory of recognition equates international practice to the act of recognition by stating that "recognition signifies no more than the acceptance of an already-existing factual situation" (Britannica, 2021). Future research could combine these two theories to produce a clearer prognosis on the propensity of specific countries to protect or engage with Taiwan. One contemporary example of this theory in action is the precedent set by a Czech business delegation's visit to Taiwan. Headed by the Czech Senate President and Mayor of Prague, this delegation spoke with Taiwanese political and business leaders to form stronger bilateral economic ties. Under scrutiny from China, Senate President Vystrcil asserted, "I do not feel like I crossed the 'red line' whatsoever, because I think we didn't do anything that infringed the 'One China' Policy" (Aspinwall, 2020). After Vystrcil decoupled economic relations from the purview of the One China Policy, several countries, including the United States, sent delegations to Taiwan for the purpose of bolstering bilateral economic relations (VOA News, 2020). Relations between Taiwan and the United States might be influenced by the declaratory theory of recognition, but only concrete research can tell.

Future research could also utilize a recursive model to explain the relationship between Chinese actions, the responses of other countries to those actions, and its effect on their relationship with Taipei. In late 2020 and early 2021, several countries took actions similar to the United States, such as increasing their diplomatic engagement with Taiwan, increasing their naval presence in the Indo-Pacific, and advocating international bodies to admit Taiwan as a member (Van Der Made, 2021). As one of the members of the Quadrilateral Security Dialogue and one of the countries most concerned by a Chinese-occupied First Island Chain, Japan has been particularly involved in laying the groundwork for deterrence in the Indo-Pacific. Japan is quickly becoming a credible security partner of Taiwan. On August 4, 2021, *Taiwan News* reported that Japan's Ministry of Defense plans to deploy missile unites on the Japanese island of Ishigaki, only 300km from Taiwan's Taoyuan International Airport, and will be manned with up to 600 troops (Everington, 2021). The missile units include ground-to-air and surface-to-ship missiles, which serve as a deterrent to both an attack on Japan and Taiwan from the PLA Navy and Air Force. Japan further appears to fit Blackwill and Zelikow's criteria for effectively balancing deterrence and the risk of escalating into a major conflict with China. Japan is not seeking to change Taiwan's status. However it does engage in defense cooperation with allies, makes visible defense plans in the region, and seeks to place the burden of war on China. Japanese Defense Minister Yasuhide Nakayama warned that it is necessary for Japan to protect Taiwan as a fellow democracy and as an integral part of Japan's own defense (Brunnstrom, 2021). Using the recursive model [Japan Policy = f(Chinese Action), Japan-Taiwan Relations = f(Japanese Policy)] could clarify the relationship between Chinese actions and a Japanese response.

Ultimately, all nations hold competing defense priorities, and their actions can serve multiple purposes. While it may be difficult to establish a causal relationship between specific Chinese actions and a U.S. response regarding Taiwan, the United States, Europe, and Asian nations are taking a wholistic approach to their relationship with Taiwan. Long gone are the days when world leaders paid little attention to Taiwan. Even if the actions of certain countries do not directly contribute to a military deterrent against a Chinese attack, an ongoing discussion over Taiwan as well as robust diplomatic, military, and economic relations could potentially avert a major crisis over Taiwan.

Bibliography

ASPINWALL, N. (2020 September 5). Czech delegation pledges support for Taiwan, vows not to bow to Chinese threats. *The Diplomat.* https://thediplomat.com/2020/09/czech-delegation-pledges-support-for-taiwan-vows-not-to-bow-to-chinese-threats/.

BADER, J. (2016 December 3). Trump, Taiwan, and a break in a long tradition. *Brookings.* https://www.brookings.edu/blog/order-from-chaos/2016/12/03/trump-taiwan-and-a-break-in-a-long-tradition/.

BLACKWILL, R., & Zelikow, P. (2021 February 17). The United States, China, and Taiwan: A strategy to prevent war. *Council on Foreign Relations.* https://www.cfr.org/report/united-states-china-and-taiwan-strategy-prevent-war.

BRITANNICA (2021). Declaratory theory of recognition. *Britannica.* https://www.britannica.com/topic/declaratory-theory-of-recognition.

BRUNNSTROM, D. (2021 July 1). Japan minister says necessary to 'wake up' to protect Taiwan. *Reuters.* https://www.reuters.com/world/asia-pacific/japan-minister-says-necessary-wake-up-protect-taiwan-2021-06-28/.

BUSH, R. (2019 November). From persuasion to coercion: Beijing's approach to Taiwan and Taiwan's response. *Global China.* https://www.brookings.edu/research/from-persuasion-to-coercion-beijings-approach-to-taiwan-and-taiwans-response/

CHANG, YAN-TING (2020 September 9). Outfoxing China's war of attrition. *Taipei Times.* https://www.taipeitimes.com/News/editorials/archives/2020/09/09/2003743059.

CHANG, E. (2021 January 8). Chinese early warning aircraft intrudes into Taiwan's ADIZ. *Taiwan News.* https://www.taiwannews.com.tw/en/news/4097024.

CHEN, LIANG-CHIH EVANS (2019). Revisiting Taiwan's defense strategy. Institute for National Defense and Security Research, *Defense Security Brief 8*(1), pp. 28-41.

CHORN, A. & SATO, M. (2019 October 1). Maritime gray zone tactics: The argument for reviewing the 1951 U.S.-Philippines Mutual Defense Treaty. *Center for Strategic & International Studies.* https://www.csis.org/maritime-gray-zone-tactics-argument-reviewing-1951-us-philippines-mutual-defense-treaty.

COLE, J. M. (2021 May 20). Abandoning Taiwan would create a far more dangerous world. *Inside Policy.* https://macdonaldlaurier.ca/abandoning-taiwan-create-far-dangerous-world-j-michael-cole-inside-policy/

CULPAN, T. (2021 January 25). China gets a message that Taiwan is a bipartisan U.S. issue. *Bloomberg.* https://www.bloomberg.com/opinion/articles/2021-01-25/china-gets-a-u-s-message-that-taiwan-is-a-bipartisan-issue-for-biden.

Department of State (2009). The Taiwan Strait crises: 1954-55 and 1958. *U.S. Department of State Archive.* https://history.state.gov/milestones/ 1953-1960/taiwan-strait-crises.

DSCA (2021). Major arms sales. *Defense Security Cooperation Agency.* https://www.dsca.mil/press-media /major-arms-sales.

Economy, E. (2010). The game changer: Coping with China's foreign policy revolution. *Foreign Affairs, The World Ahead 89*(6): 142-152.

Eisenberg, E. (1984). Ambiguity as strategy in organizational communication. *Communication Monographs 51,* 227-242.

Elleman, B. (2014). *Taiwan Straits: Crisis in Asia and the role of the U.S. Navy.* Lanham, MD: Rowman & Littlefield.

Everington, K. (2021 August 4). Japan to deploy missiles 300km off coast of Taiwan in 2022 to deter China. *Taiwan News.* https:// www.taiwan-news.com.tw/en/news/4263918.

Feng, J. (2021 April 7). U.S. warship, carrier ramp up maneuvers in Taiwan Strait and South China Sea. *Newsweek.* https://www. newsweek.com/ us-warship-carrier-ramp-maneuvers-taiwan-strait-south-china-sea-1581617.

Glaser, B., Bush, R., & Green, M. (2020 October). Toward a stronger U.S.-Taiwan relationship. *A report of the CSIS task force on U.S. policy toward Taiwan.* https://csis-website-prod.s3.amazonaws.com/s3fs-public/publication/201021_Glaser_TaskForce_Toward_A_Stronger _USTaiwan_Relationship_0.pdf

Glaser, C. (2021 April 28). Washington is avoiding the tough questions on Taiwan and China. *Foreign Affairs.* https://www.foreignaffairs.com/articles/asia/2021-04-28/washington-avoiding-tough-questions-taiwan-and-china

Glaser, C., & Kaufmann, C. (1998). What is the offense-defense balance and can we measure it? *International Security 22*(4): 44-82.

Goldstein, L. (2020 December 2). No American lives should be lost to defend Taiwan. *The American Conservative.* https://www. theamericanconservative.com/articles/no-american-lives-should-be-lost-to-defend-taiwan/.

H.R.2002 (2019). H.R.2002 – Taiwan Assurance Act of 2019. *Congress.gov.* https://www.congress.gov/bill/116th-congress/house-bill/2002

H.R.2479 (1979). H.R.2479 – 96th Congress (1979-1980): Taiwan Relations Act. *Congress.gov.* https://www.congress. gov/bill/96th-congress /house-bill/2479

H.R.2479 (1979). H.R.2479 – Taiwan Relations Act. *Congress.gov.* https:// www.congress.gov/bill/96th-congress/house-bill/2479

Haass, R., & Sacks, D. (2020 September 2). American support for Taiwan must be unambiguous: To keep the peace, make clear to China that force won't stand. *Foreign Affairs.* https://www.foreignaffairs.com/articles/united-states /american-support-taiwan-must-be-unambiguous

HASS, R. (2020 January 25). The path to protecting bipartisan US support for Taiwan. *Brookings*. https://www.brookings.edu/blog /order-from-chaos/2021/01/25/the-path-to-protecting-bipartisan-us-support-for-taiwan/.

HOLMES, J. (2019 October 17). Taiwan needs a Maoist military. *Foreign Policy*. https://foreignpolicy.com/2019/10/17/taiwan-maoist-military-china-navy-south-china-sea/.

JACKSON, S. (2016). Does China have a Monroe Doctrine? Evidence for regional exclusion. *Strategic Studies Quarterly 1*(4): 64-89.

KASTNER, S., CHEN PING-KUEI, & REED, W. (2017). A farewell to arms? US security relations with Taiwan and the prospects for stability in the Taiwan Strait, 221-238. In D. Lowell (Ed.), *Taiwan and China: Fitful embrace*. Berkely, CA: University of California Press.

LEE, YIMOU (2021 March 31). Taiwan to buy new U.S. air defense missiles to guard against China. *Reuters*. https://www.reuters.com/article/taiwan-defence-idINKBN2BN1EA.

MAIZLAND, L. (2020 February 5). China's modernizing military, backgrounder. *Council on Foreign Relations*. https://www.cfr.org/backgrounder/chinas-modernizing-military.

MANSON, K. (2021 January 9). US risks enraging China by easing limits on Taiwan. *Financial Times*. https://www.ft.com/content/debd 932f-48f7-4933-a596-a4663b442002.

MASTRO, O. (2021 June 3). The Taiwan temptation: Why Beijing might resort to force. *Foreign Affairs*. https://www.foreignaffairs.com/articles / china/2021-06-03/china-taiwan-war-temptation

MCGREGOR, R. (2010). *The party: The secret world of China's communist rulers*. New York, NY: HarperCollins.

MINISTRY OF NATIONAL DEFENSE (2017). Chapter 3: Force buildup. *Quadrennial Defense Review*, Ministry of National Defense ROC, pp. 44-47.

MND (2021 August 19). Military news update: Air activities in the southwestern ADIZ of ROC. *Ministry of National Defense ROC*. https://www. mnd.gov.tw/English/PublishTable.aspx?types=Military%20News% 20Update& Title=News%20Channel.

MORGAN, F. (2013). Crisis stability and long-range strike: A comparative analysis of fighters, bombers, and missiles. *Project Air Force*. https:// www.rand.org/pubs/monographs/MG1258.html

MURRAY, W. (2008). Revisiting Taiwan's defense strategy. *Naval War College Review 61*(3) Article 3. Available at: https://digital-commons.usnwc .edu/nwc-review/vol61/iss3/3

REUTERS (2020 October 26). China to impose sanctions on U.S. firms over Taiwan arms sales. *Reuters*. https://www.reuters.com/article/usa-china-taiwan/china-to-impose-sanctions-on-u-s-firms-over-taiwan-arms-sales-idUSKBN27B0P0.

REUTERS (2021 March 22). Taiwan loses two fighter jets in apparent collision, third such crash in six months. *Reuters.* https://www.reuters.com/world/china/taiwan-loses-two-fighter-jets-apparent-collision-third-such-crash-six-months-2021-03-22/.

S.1678 (2019). S.1678 – Taiwan Allies International Protection and Enhancement Initiative (TAIPEI) Act of 2019. *Congress.gov.* https://www.congress.gov/bill/116th-congress/senate-bill/1678/text.

SCFR (2020 October 1). Risch, Inhofe, Menendez, Colleagues Urge Lighthizer to Begin Talks for a Trade Agreement with Taiwan. *United States Senate Committee on Foreign Relations.* https://www.foreign.senate.gov/press/chair/release/risch-inhofe-menendez-colleagues-urge-lighthizer-to-begin-talks-for-a-trade-agreement-with-taiwan.

SHAMBAUGH, D. (2000 Spring). A matter of time: Taiwan's eroding military advantage. Center for Strategic and International Studies and the Massachusetts Institute of Technology. *The Washington Quarterly 23* (2): 119-133.

STRATFOR (2015 May 5). Taiwan's new military strategy. *Risk Assistance Network.* https://worldview.stratfor.com/article/taiwans-new-military-strategy

SUN, YUN (2021 January 22). Top conflicts to watch in 2021: The danger of *U.S.-China confrontation over Taiwan.* Council on Foreign Relations. https://www.cfr.org/blog/top-conflicts-watch-2021-danger-us-china-confrontation-over-taiwan.

TAIPEI TIMES (2020 November 25). Taiwan starts submarine production. *Taipei Times.* https://www.taipeitimes.com/News/front/archives/2020/11/25/2003747541.

TUDOR, D. (2012). *Korea: The impossible country: South Korea's rise from the ashes.* Rutland, VT: Tuttle Publishing.

VAN DER MADE, J. (2021 July 5). French Senate's Taiwan vote triggers Beijing's anger again. *Radio France Internationale.* https://www.rfi.fr/en/international/20210507-french-senate-s-taiwan-vote-triggers-beijing-s-anger-again.

VOA NEWS. (2020 November 21). US, Taiwan boost economic cooperation. *Voice of America.* https://www.voanews.com/east-asia-pacific/us-taiwan-boost-economic-cooperation.

WELCH, D. (2013 December 9). What's an ADIZ?: Why the United States, Japan, and China get it wrong. *Foreign Affairs.* https://www.foreignaffairs.com/articles/east-asia/2013-12-09/whats-adiz.

WIESELTIER, L. (1985 Spring). When deterrence fails. *Foreign Affairs.* https://www.foreignaffairs.com/articles/russian-federation/1985-03-01/when-deterrence-fails

XIE, J. (2021 January 6). China is increasing Taiwan airspace incursions.

Voice of America. https://www.voanews.com/east-asia-pacific/voa-news-china/china-increasing-taiwan-airspace-incursions.

Xɪɴʜᴜᴀ (2021 July 1). Resolving Taiwan Question a historic mission of CPC: Xi. *Xinhua.* http://www.china.org.cn/china/2021-07/01/content_7759 9535.htm

Zʜᴀɴɢ, K. (2018). *Calculating bully – Explaining Chinese coercion.* Unpublished doctoral dissertation, Massachusetts Institute of Technology, Cambridge.

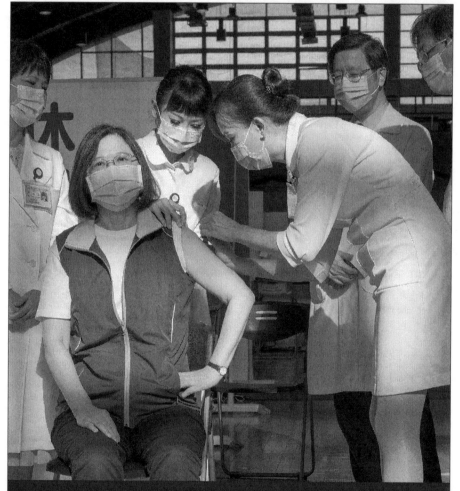

President Tsai Ing-wen receiving her first dose of COVID-19 vaccine.

Official Photo by Makoto Lin / Office of the President. Courtesy of the Presidential Palace.
Top page credit: Photo 175496947 / Covid Virus © Mykhailo Polenok | Dreamstime.com

Chapter 6

Taiwan's COVID Response

by Jiayi Zhang

As COVID-19 became a deadly pandemic, Taiwan represented a useful example on how a nation can battle coronavirus. This paper aims to answer the following questions: was Taiwan's COVID response effective? What factors contributed to Taiwan's COVID success if that is the case? What did Taiwan's leadership do to combat the virus? What lessons can other countries take away from Taiwan's COVID response? The research for this paper includes a phone interview, an email interview, a WeChat exchange with a senior Taiwanese government official, a U.S. foreign exchange student who studied in Taiwan, and a local Taiwanese couple. This paper concludes that Taiwan implemented an appropriate COVID response based on what it learned from previous pandemic experiences and established policies and enhancements to Taiwan's online health system. In addition, Taiwanese leaders played an essential role in mobilizing private and public sectors and its citizens to combat the virus. Taiwan not only contained the virus it also cooperated with the United States and European countries to develop effective vaccines and donated masks to countries that experienced mask shortages.

Learning from previous pandemic experiences

In an interview hosted by Johns Hopkins University, the Dean of Johns Hopkins' Public Health School, Ellen McKenzie, invited Taiwan's former Vice President Chen Chien-Jen to discuss Taiwan's actions during the pandemic and how it served as a model for the world. Vice President Chen stated that the rapid COVID-19 pandemic response was based on Taiwan's "containment of SARS in 2003 and H1N1 Flu in 2009" (McKenzie & Christenson, 2020). Based on its experiences with past pandemic responses, Taiwan implemented a border quarantine and required a fourteen-day self-management period for travelers entering the country. Taiwan also mobilized its health care system to expand the supplies of personal protective equipment (PPE) and other medical supplies and adjusted its protocol for announcing travel alerts and warnings.

Using lessons from SARS and H1N1, Taiwan developed effective strategies and policies to combat the novel coronavirus. Taiwan's health care system was well-prepared to provide early warnings of new outbreaks. In addition, Taiwan's Central Epidemic Command Center (CECC), managed several disease outbreaks, including the 2009 H1N1 pandemic as well as the current COVID-19 pandemic, including conducting daily conferences to provide transparent health guidelines and administering risk management protocols. Taiwan's CECC issued regular updates on COVID development to keep its citizens informed; it also addressed inquiries from the media. At the same time, the CECC also advised people to avoid large gatherings and to keep a distance from one another.

Taiwan's CECC sought to develop the solutions to contain the fast-spreading pandemic. Taiwan's former Vice President Chen Chien-Jen said that Taiwan learned from the SARS outbreak and devised the following strategies:

1. Continue monitoring infectious diseases outside Taiwan, especially in populous areas like mainland China;
2. Optimize border quarantine;
3. Strengthen the health care reporting of contagious diseases;
4. Implement a combination of responses to emerging infectious diseases and contact drills;
5. Upgrade labs to allow for early detection and diagnosis;
6. Provide public health education to school children and the public;
7. Convey overt and transparent COVID-19 information; and
8. Enhance international cooperation and COVID research development.

To summarize, when the COVID-19 pandemic began in January 2020, the CECC acted quickly to establish border control and community containment (Hsieh et al., 2021). The SARS outbreak in 2003 was the first time Taiwan experienced the threat of an epidemic. It started in Guangdong province and was soon transmitted to Taiwan. Taiwan was initially unprepared and lacked any type of crisis management mechanism that allowed the central government to communicate with local governments and hospitals (Hsieh et al., 2021). The 2003 SARS outbreak caused panic in Taiwanese society and created shortages that left medical workers without masks. At that time, 346 people were infected by the epidemic in Taiwan, resulting in thirty-seven deaths; over 131,000 people were quarantined in hospitals or homes due to close contact with SARS patients. The government realized it needed to set up a holistic and integrated approach to any future public health-related crisis. One year after the outbreak, the Taiwanese government established the National Health

Command Center (NHCC), designed to manage diseases, and address emergent public health issues. The NHCC also serves as a central point of direct communication among governments at all levels and provides relevant information to the central government. Furthermore, the NHCC gathers and integrates epidemic information in real-time and makes it available to citizens via mobile devices and daily news briefings. This public health emergency management system has proven to be effective in dealing with the COVID-19 situation.

Taiwan was unprepared during the 2003 SARS epidemic which led to its rapid spread among its population. This prompted Taiwan's CECC to become vigilant and prepared for subsequent pandemics. "As of October 2021, [Taiwan] ranked lowest in a total number of COVID-19 cases and second-lowest in deaths per 100,000 population among comparable [Organisation for Economic Co-operation and Development] OECD countries" (Cheng, 2021). Even though mainland China was experiencing an increasing number of confirmed cases, Taiwan was not overly concerned as the senior official at Taipei's Economic and Cultural Representative Office in D.C. stated, "[after] SARS, we established new regulations that gave our health officials greater authority in a health crisis like this" (Chang, 2020). He said that Taiwan learned how to prepare early for a health crisis and be hypersensitive to enigmatic reports of illnesses and always lean to the side of caution. Taiwan has learned from its past failures and established a robust system for confronting future public health issues. Its success in managing the COVID-19 pandemic can be attributed to its past experiences with epidemic diseases and its emergency management system. When mainland China reported its first case in Wuhan, the Taiwanese government requested a health screening for all travelers arriving from Wuhan on December 19, 2019. It also adopted two approaches: the first was to keep the virus out, and the second was to prevent and control community spread (Cheng 2021). On February 6, 2020, Taiwan banned all travelers coming from mainland China. It also required Taiwanese citizens returning from mainland China, Hong Kong, or Macau (Hsieh et al., 2021) to quarantine for fourteen days. Five days later, the Taiwanese government restated the ban of mainland Chinese citizens to include those from Hong Kong and Macau. On March 19, 2020, Taiwan banned all foreigners. Taiwanese officials knew they had to act quickly and decisively thus they adopted strict border control and quarantine policies that were essential at the beginning of the COVID-19 outbreak.

In addition, Taiwan learned from the harsh lessons of SARS about the need to be well prepared for a crisis such as COVID-19. The CECC enacted preventive measures that required their citizens to cultivate personal hygiene habits such as washing hands frequently and wearing masks when leaving their homes. The Taiwanese government and citizens understood the need to wear masks to reduce infections from the 2003 SARS outbreak so the COVID-10 masking policy was swiftly implemented. On January 22, 2020, Taiwan's Center for Disease Control (CDC) started distributing surgical masks to local convenience stores. On January 31, 2020, the government required that all surgical masks be produced by domestic manufacturers forcing Taiwan to become self-reliant in this area. Soon, on February 6, Taiwan established a name-based system associated with people's insurance cards, and the Taiwanese people could use their National Health Insurance cards to purchase two masks per week. Soon after, the number of masks that people could purchase was increased to nine per person in a 14-day period (Su & Han, 2020).

Taiwan began assembling a massive database combining its national health insurance database and its immigration and customs database. This system generates real-time alerts based on clinical visits, online reports of travel history, and health symptoms to classify travelers' infectious risks based on flight origin and travel history over the last 14 days (Wang et al., 2020). Besides the CECC and the CDC's role in the fight against COVID-19, Taiwan's central and local governments, private sectors, and individual Taiwanese all played essential roles in the pandemic and came together to fight this disease. For instance, an engineer collected the number of masks in convenience stores and put the information on Google Maps so that people were able to see how many face masks were left in each store without having to wait in long lines.

President Tsai Ing-wen said, "Taiwan also had an advantage because of our extensive experience in disease prevention from fighting SARS, H1N1, H7N9, and dengue fever" (Koski et al., 2020). She believed that this body of qualified Taiwan's professionals could capably lead the COVID-19 response. Taiwan mobilized the whole island to join the collective effort to manage the disease. The central government set up a public health emergency management system, and the NHCC effectively dealt with the coronavirus outbreak. The communication between Taiwan's central and local governments was also quick and effective. Taiwanese citizens not only cautiously followed the government's advice but also developed the technology that served the effort to control the outbreak.

First to Inform WHO

When the officials from Taiwan's Centers for Disease Control identified some references on the internet to a SARS-like disease, they were concerned about the possibility that it might be transmissible to humans. On December 31, 2020, Taiwan was among the first governments to send an alert to the World Health Organization (WHO) "on the potential human-to-human transmission of a novel coronavirus in Wuhan, China" and requested that the WHO provide information (Lee et al., 2020). At the same time, Taiwan had set up its own mechanism to prevent the disease from entering Taiwan and it carefully monitored passengers returning from Wuhan and tightened its border controls.

In 2009, WHO created means within the International Health Regulations for the Taiwanese government to report public health information to WHO even though Taiwan is not recognized as a member state by the UN. The International Health Regulations require nations to share information on significant public health issues. However, unlike WHO member states, the information Taiwan provided to the World Health Organization through the International Health Regulation did not reach WHO member states because of Taiwan's status. Taiwan was also prevented from attending WHO regular meetings and activities (Bardi & Bollyky, 2020). Taiwan's Minister of Foreign Affairs Joseph Wu said in an interview, "If you look at the way we want Taiwan to be covered by the WHO, it's very clear, and we don't try to hide anything." He continued, "the first is we want to receive information so that Taiwan can be protected by the international community when there is a disease going on, and the second is that we want to be able to help the international community if there is a need for Taiwan to provide assistance" (Bardi & Bollyky, 2020). Taiwan's message was clear; it wanted to be transparent about the pandemic and to offer help to the international community. However, it was becoming increasingly difficult for Taiwan to achieve representation at the World Health Organization. Despite the rejection from an international organization, Taiwan continues to seek participation in WHO which has the support of the United States and some European countries.

Leadership Matters

Taiwan's President Tsai Ing-wen endeavored to unify the Taiwanese people in the fight against COVID-19. President Tsai stated, "leadership means inspiring unity, which was the real key to our success in combating COVID-19" (Koski et al., 2020). President Tsai knew that to control COVID-19, the leaders had to devise effective policies, gain public confidence, and work closely with Taiwan's government institutions. In a survey conducted by the Taiwan Public Opinion Foundation on February 17-18, 2020, more than 70 percent of 1,079 randomly chosen Taiwanese respondents approved of how Tsai and her cabinet handled the health crisis (Wang 2020). President Tsai was selected by *Time* magazine as one of the top 100 most influential people of 2020 due to her government's policies to curb the coronavirus. Tsai's decisive actions helped avoid lockdowns of entire cities, closures of schools, and an economic shutdown.

Vice President Chen also assumed a visible role in this global health crisis, emphasizing the need for each Taiwanese to follow the guidelines, including providing accurate information about their travel history. He reminded the people of the fines and penalties for not complying with quarantine rules and how the names of people who violated the rules would appear on national television, as public shaming is a tactic of government enforcement in Asian societies.

Taiwan, with a population of 24 million, had only 34,507 confirmed cases and 854 deaths as of April 18, 2022 (Our World, n.d.).

Home Quarantine with Care Services

Taiwan has implemented many quarantine and isolation measures, including health and symptom checks, quarantine hotel reservations, and mobile phone announcements regarding home quarantine. Local health officers check in with quarantined people once or twice daily by phone and arrange for the delivery of daily meals and supplies for quarantined individuals. In addition, those Taiwanese citizens who are in quarantine received 30 dollars in compensation per day (Su & Han, 2020). Besides tracking travel histories, occupations, and contact histories, the government also used innovative software to track clusters of people. Each Taiwanese citizen has a health care record that can be accessed online by doctors and nurses. People who are under home quarantine and isolation by Taiwan's local governments receive a range of supportive services, including a 24/7 hotline for consultations, family visits, daily meal deliveries, settlement assistance, and health care support. Therefore, Taiwan not only organizes quarantine protocols, it also provides direct care for effected citizens.

Cooperation with Other Nations

President Tsai said that "We cannot stop the spread of COVID-19 simply by preventing an outbreak within Taiwan. All members of the international community must pool their capabilities and work together to overcome this challenge" (Chen, 2020) thereby indicating her willingness to cooperate with the international community to fight the spread of the disease. The United States and Taiwan signed a joint statement a few months after the outbreak to enhance their collaboration in preventing the spread of the coronavirus. Moreover, Taiwan joined the world effort, collaborating with the U.S. and other European nations, to develop antivirals and vaccines for methods of rapid diagnosis. In March 2020, Taiwan's most prestigious research institution, Academia Sinica, organized a video conference with the United States, the Czech Republic, and Canada to discuss test kits, vaccines, and the development of reagents for COVID-19 (Chen, 2020). Taiwan also collaborated with Australia by providing fabric masks in exchange for alcohol for making hand sanitizer. Despite being a small power, Taiwan found its own way to survive and has worked hard to build relations using skillful diplomacy during the pandemic. By working with various nations, Taiwan not only demonstrates its ability to join the collective efforts against COVID-19, but also increases Taiwan's chance of expanding economic ties since many countries in recognition for Taiwan's contributions to the rapid development of antivirals and vaccines.

Donating Masks to Other Countries

Taiwan worked with its domestic manufacturers to progress from being an importer of face masks to becoming the world's second-largest producer of face masks. Besides producing masks for its own citizens, Taiwan also donated masks to countries in need. President Tsai said on Twitter, "In times of crisis, countries around the world must come together. Taiwan is indispensable to global efforts to stop the spread of COVID-19, but no country can stop this virus alone. That is why we are willing to offer medical supplies to countries most in need." To do so, Taiwan launched a global campaign called "Taiwan Can Help." Taiwan wanted to show the world that not only "Taiwan can help" but "Taiwan is actually helping other nations" (Chen, 2020). As of April 2020, Taiwan has donated 17 million masks to the United States, Japan, European Union, and its allies (McKenzie & Christenson, 2020). President Tsai recognized how medical workers throughout the world had demonstrated "countless acts of bravery and sacrifice" during the early months when COVID was at its worst (Chen, 2020). President Tsai indicated that Taiwan would continue to donate masks to the front-line's medical workers around the world and appreciated their bravery in saving lives. Even though Taiwan was excluded from entering the international medical community of the WHO, this did not inhibit Taiwan from helping other countries, especially those in need.

Former Vice President Chen stated that "our president of Taiwan once said that Taiwan cannot stand by while other countries are in need of help, and Taiwan is actively fostering cooperation with all countries and is willing to provide assistance to the international community in the areas of face masks, pharmaceuticals, and technologies" (McKenzie & Christenson, 2020).

Interviews

Interviews were conducted to gauge public opinion on Taiwan's COVID response including a senior official from the Taipei Economic and Cultural Representative Office (TECRO), and three individuals living in Taiwan.

The senior officials at TECRO addressed five issues relating to: the current COVID situation in Taiwan, the public's reaction to COVID, the government's measures and policies to stop the spread of the virus, Taiwan's donations of masks to other nations, and the data that the government has released on the incidents of COVID in Taiwan.

According to the senior official at TECRO, Taiwan recently experienced a surge in the number of cases. As of April 20, 2022, Taiwan had an increase of more than 3,000 cases. He said that "this is very different from most of the time during the last two years where we have either single digit or zero cases; however, the severity of these cases, most of them are either asymptomatic or have light symptoms." He also mentioned that even though the number of confirmed cases has risen, Taiwan's health system was able to meet the needs of most people. He indicated that Taiwan is more prepared than two years ago given the fact that now 80 percent of its population has been fully vaccinated. The senior official said that the vaccines have been effective in keeping people out of the hospital and preventing serious symptoms. He believes that Taiwan is prepared to deal with the high number of cases.

When asked about people's reaction toward COVID, he mentioned that in the beginning, people did not know much about COVID, so there was a lot of anxiety among the public about how to deal with the virus. He emphasized that the CECC focused on educating and communicating with the public on what the virus is about, which is reflected in the CECC's communication with the public on various levels. Taiwan has a robust border control policy; people who are not Taiwanese citizens or residents are unable to enter Taiwan freely. However, Taiwan has not instituted lockdowns, the schools have been open, and businesses and restaurants are running as normal. He said that most people have adjusted to this new normal.

When asked about the measures that Taiwan implemented, the senior official replied that at the beginning of the pandemic, Taiwan had been using contact tracing measures to curb the spread of the virus; however, due to the surge of confirmed cases, contact tracing is no longer effective. Therefore, the government focused on urging the public to wear masks, obtaining the vaccine, and maintaining social distancing. He said, "we have conducted contact tracing for a long time. As we have progressed, the problems have evolved, therefore the method to address the problem needed to change as well." In this case, Taiwan has demonstrated its ability to adapt to the changing environment. It should be noted that an app for tracking contacts called "Taiwan Social Distancing App" (臺灣社交距離 App) was designed by both Taiwan's Centers for Disease Control and a private research organization. The app uses wireless technology such as Bluetooth and WIFI to inform people when they've been in close contact with someone with COVID without collecting people's private information. While downloading this app is not mandatory for Taiwanese citizens, having such an easy-to-use app has the potential to benefit the overall population. In this case, Taiwan has mobilized the private sector to create a voluntary app that tracks people's contact history anonymously.

The senior official was also interviewed about Taiwan's cooperation with other countries. He indicated that "in terms of active cooperation, there are many of them, the most memorable cooperation is the exchange of [protective materials] supporting one another in the time of the COVID." He then explained that during the first two years, Taiwan had few cases, and the government mobilized the private sector to ramp up the production of face masks. Once Taiwan had a surplus of masks, it began to provide and donate masks and other PPE to countries all over the world. For instance, it donated millions of masks to the U.S., including medical masks and N95 masks. He added that Taiwan also donated masks to critical sectors within Taiwan, to the health workers, firefighters, government officials, specific businesses, nurseries, and the places that care for the elderly. He said that "we are donating masks because we have the ability to do so, we are doing it with goodwill. It shows friendships." As a result of these relationships, when Taiwan needed vaccines, countries like the United States and other European countries that received assistance from Taiwan donated a significant number of doses of vaccines to Taiwan. The senior official commented on this "I think it is truly heartwarming. It was not planned, but we had the ability to help others and we did it, and when we needed their help, they came to our aid."

The senior official mentioned that Taiwan's Central Epidemic Command Center has daily briefings and handles communication with its citizens. Taiwan's governmental response to the pandemic has emphasized transparency and openness.

In another interview intended to gain a perspective on public opinion to Taiwan's COVID response, a U.S. student who is currently studying business at National Taiwan Normal University said that few people expected to see tightened restrictions despite the rise in cases because most Taiwanese people received the vaccines. The vaccines, which were produced by AstraZeneca, Pfizer, or Moderna, were donated from other countries. It was the student's belief that the vaccines gave people the confidence to trust their government and not to fear COVID. Then, he added that "opening the economy helps Taiwan to be part of the global system in a meaningful way." Taiwan did not shut down any cities or businesses during the pandemic time, which helped it to maintain a steady economy.

In email interviews with the research assistant in Taiwan and two Taiwanese people, they all confirmed what the official said about how the number of newly confirmed cases in Taiwan being on the rise. The CDC requires asymptomatic and mild patients to be isolated at home and not tax Taiwan's medical resources. When I asked about the government measures and policies, they said that Taiwan's success is attributed to the government's strict border control, and the Taiwanese people voluntarily wearing masks to cooperate with the government's pandemic prevention measures. They felt Taiwan's pandemic guidelines, such as washing their hands frequently, wearing masks, and avoiding gatherings as well as the cooperative nature of the Taiwanese people were important factors in the virus' containment.

Conclusion

Taiwan's success in managing the pandemic not only demonstrated its ability to adapt to changing circumstances. It has worked with various sectors to keep the people safe while also maintaining steady economic growth during a global pandemic (Koski et al., 2020). Since the beginning of the pandemic, Taiwan has initiated specific approaches for identifying cases, containing the outbreak, and allocating resources to protect the public health of its citizens. Unlike mainland China, Taiwan minimized the impact on its society; Taiwanese citizens have generally maintained their normal routine. Taiwanese cities have not faced strict lockdowns like those in mainland China. Taiwan's success in combating COVID is inseparable from the efforts of the public and private sectors, President Tsai's leadership, and most importantly, the cooperation of the Taiwanese people. Prompt action, freely sharing information, innovative technology, robust communications between various levels, and the cooperative nature of the Taiwanese people have all contributed to Taiwan's successful COVID response.

Bibliography

BARDI, J., & BOLLYKY, T. (2020 May 15).Taiwan's response to COVID-19 and the WHO: Think global health. *Council on Foreign Relations.* https://www.thinkglobalhealth.org/article/taiwans-response-COVID-19-andwho.

BCF/MOFA (2022 February 24). Bureau of Consular Affairs, Ministry of Foreign Affairs, Republic of China (Taiwan). Entry restrictions for foreigners to Taiwan in response to COVID-19 outbreak [on-line]. https://nspp.mofa.gov.tw/nsppe/news.php?post=171182& unit=377.

CHANG, I-WEI JENNIFER. (2020 November 10). Taiwan's model for combating COVID-19: A small island with big data. *Middle East Journal* [on-line]. https:// www.mei.edu/publications/taiwans-model-combating-covid-19-small-island-big-data

CHEN, SHIH-CHUNG (2021 March 26). Taiwan's experience in fighting COVID-19. *Nature Immunology* [on-line]. https://www.nature.com/articles/s41590-021-00908-2.

CHENG, TSUNG-MEI (2021 December 1). How has Taiwan navigated the pandemic? *Economics Observatory* [on-line]. https://www.economicsobservatory. com/how-has-taiwan-navigated-the-pandemic.

CHEN, S. (2020 April 1). Taiwan to donate 10 million masks to countries hit

hardest by coronavirus. *ABC News.* https://abcnews.go.com/Health/tai
wan-donate-10-millionmasks-countries-hit-hardest/story?id=699
18187.

HSIEH, C., WANG, M., WONG, N., & HO, L. (2021 June 10). A whole-of-nation
approach to COVID-19: Taiwan's national epidemic prevention
team. *Sage Journals* [on-line]. https://journals.sagepub.com/doi/full/
10.1177/01925 121211012291.

KOSKI, J., BROUWER, C., & SINKOW, S. (2020 January 6). As Taiwan's resident,
alumna leads fight against COVID-19. *Cornell Chronicle* [on-line]. https:
//news.cornell.edu/stories/2020/01/taiwans-president-alumna-
leads-fight-against-COVID-19.

LEE, PO-CHANG, ET AL. (2020 July 21). What we can learn from Taiwan's
response to the COVID-19 epidemic. *British Medical Journal* [on-line].
https://blogs.bmj.com/bmj/2020/07/21/what-we-can-learn-from-
taiwans-response-to-the-COVID-19-epidemic/.

MCKENZIE, E. & CHRISTENSON, B. (2020 April 25). Taiwan model: Response to
COVID-19. *Johns Hopkins Bloomberg School of Public Health.* https://
www.jhsph.edu/covid-19/news-and-events/events/_documents/
2020-04-24-inside-taiwanas-response-to-covid-19-transcript.pdf

MOHW (2021 November 8). 「臺灣社交距離app」已上架 鼓勵全民下使
用掌握疫情擴散相關資訊. (Taiwan Social Distance App has been
launched, and everyone is encouraged to download and use it to grasp
information about the spread of the epidemic). *Ministry of Health and
Welfare* [on-line]. https://www.mohw.gov.tw/cp-5016-60680-1.html.

NHCC (2022). NHCC-Taiwan Centers for Disease Control [on-line]. https://
www.cdc.gov.tw/En/Category/MPage/gL7-bARtHy NdrDq8 82pJ9Q.

OUR WORLD (n.d.). Daily and total confirmed COVID-19 deaths, Taiwan. *Our
World in Data* [on-line]. https://ourworldindata.org/grapher/total-
daily-covid-deaths?tab=chart&country=~TWN

SU, SHENG-FANG, & HAN, YUEH-YING (2020 June). How Taiwan, a non-who
member, takes actions in response to COVID-19. *Journal of Global
Health* [on-line]. https://www.ncbi.nlm.nih.gov/pmc/articles/PMC
7307800/.

WANG, J., NG, C., & BROOK, R. (2020 March 3). Response to COVID-19 in
Taiwan: Big data analytics, new technology, and proactive testing. *Journal of the American Medical Association* [on-line]. https://jamanet-
work.com/journals/jama/fullarticle /2762 689/.

WU, YUANXI 吳元熙 (2022 April 13). 「台灣社交距離App」優化，通知比
實聯制還快！怎麼下載、怎麼用一次看懂 (Taiwan's social distance
app replaces the real-time SMS system! How to download, how to use
once to understand). *Business Next* [on-line]. https://www.bnext.com.
tw/article/62626/taiwan-social-distance-app.

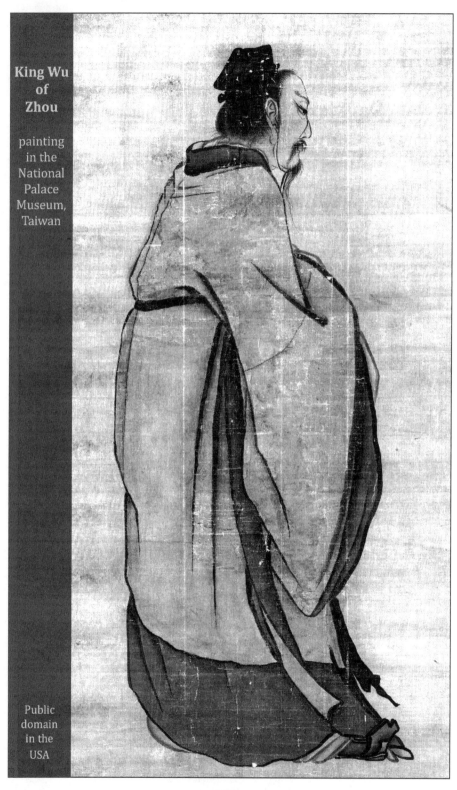

Chapter 7

Dispelling the Myth of the Mandate of Heaven as a Rationalization for Regime Change — A Rebuttal

by Gloria Shen

One important notion of ancient Chinese history was the idea of the "Mandate of Heaven" (*tianming* 天命), which has been dismissed in the West over the second half of the last century. Professor Herrlee Creel, a most revered authority on Western Zhou civilization, was one of the first to put forward the view that the doctrine of the *tianming* was invented by the Zhou rulers to justify their take-over, and that it did not previously exist in the mind-set of the Shang dynasty (1770-1045 BCE) (Creel, 1936; 1937).[1] Professor Wing-tsit Chan in his *A Source Book in Chinese Philosophy* (1963) also claimed that "having overthrown the Shang, founders of the Zhou had to justify their right to rule. Consequently, they developed the doctrine of the Mandate of Heaven. . ."[2] As a consequence, many other contemporary historians[3] in the West have followed suit and held that the notion was "innovated" and "developed," "fabricated" and "created" by the rulers of the Western Zhou (1045-771 BCE) to justify their overthrow of the Shang.

Prof. Creel's reasoning that the "Mandate of Heaven" was a Zhou rationalization reflected the views and methodology of the contemporary modernist scholars of the school of "Skepticism towards Ancient History" (疑古派), which started in China in 1920s headed by Gu Jiegang's (顧頡剛) and others. According to the contemporary modernist scholars, who have skeptically re-evaluated early Chinese history, many traditional, time-honored views of ancient history should be treated as mythology which has no basis in historical fact. The modernist interpretation of ancient Chinese history began to gain strength in China in the 1930s with Gu Jiegang's Gushibian 古史辨 school of context criticism and spread to the West in the 1980s via the PhD dissertations of Edward Shaughnessy and Richard Kunst. *Gushibian*, 'Debates over Ancient History', is the title of the

---

[1] Creel, 1970, pp. 84-85.
[2] Chan, 1963, p. 3.
[3] See, for instance, Hansen's discussion on the notion of the "Mandate of Heaven", 2000, pp. 40-41.

journal (1923-35) in which many modernist studies were published. A key figure who spread the views and methodology into the West, Prof. Creel, in the wake of the campaign initiated by the journal *Gushibian*, published in two consecutive years two books on early Chinese history: *The Birth of China* (1936) and *Studies in Early Chinese Culture* (1937), both addressing, in a similar vein, the "Decree of Heaven" (his earlier rendition of the later established term of the "Mandate of Heaven" that appears in his *The Origins of Statecraft in China* (1970), where he initiated and advanced his beliefs that the traditional association of the Zhou rulers, King Wen, King Wu and the Duke of Zhou as sage rulers is simply a myth and that the time-honored notion of the Mandate of Heaven was a "doctrine" full blown during the very first years of the Zhou rule (Creel, 1936: 368, 371), and that it was "innovated" and "developed" as a "propaganda" ploy at the beginning of the dynasty to justify their legitimacy to overthrow the previous dynasty of the Shang (Creel, 1970: 84). [As a young budding scholar of early Chinese history, Prof. Creel might have been so greatly inspired by the studies of these contemporary modernist scholars that he adopted the journal's founder's last name as his last name in his trans-literated Chinese name of 顧立雅]. Though there are still a great many traditional scholars of ancient history in China, they do not appear to have felt any necessity to defend their beliefs against the modern research that has undermined the tradition. Consequently, in the academic world the modernist view of the Mandate of Heaven is now pre-eminent. Tradition has effectively become moribund, and a new consensus has taken hold.

1. The traditional views have held that the sage ruler Yao (ca. 2500 BCE) abdicated his throne to the sage ruler Shun and Shun to the sage ruler Yu, and that sage ruler Tang of the Shang (ca. 1750 BCE) and King Wen and King Wu of the Zhou (ca. 1100 and 1045 BCE) answered to the higher authority of *Di* or *Shangdi* (the "Lord" or "Lord on High" for the Shang) or *Tian* ("Heaven" for the Zhou). Commenting on what he deems as a "rather remarkable occurrence", Prof. Creel dismisses the rulers Yao, Shun, Yu of the Xia, Tang of the Shang, King Wen and King Wu of the Zhou as sage rulers, and claims that the "Mandate of Heaven" was merely legendary and its "rationalization" was "developed" by the rulers of the Zhou for their political purpose to control a large territory and divers groups of conquered peoples, since, he maintains, no written records or documents of the Xia and the Shang were available for evidence around the time when the Zhou started their rule. Prof. Creel cited Gu Jiegang to support his view but slightly modified the latter's assertion by stating that some of the forged books of the *Documents* were written as early as the Western Zhou (Creel, 1937: 63). However, the "official version of Chinese history" is still accepted by the vast majority of Chinese

scholars, and until very recently accepted by virtually all of them. It has also been accepted, until very recently, by a large number of foreign scholars..." (Creel, 1937: 368-371).

2. The notion of *Tian-ming* (the Decree of Heaven), as Prof. Creel believes, is derived from the Zhou's idea of *Tian* (Heaven) being a personal God of the Zhou people, the script of which, as he maintains, was not found among the Shang oracle-bones inscriptions. Instead, the *Di* (Lord) or *Shangdi* (Lord on High) appeared frequently in Shang oracle-bones inscriptions to refer to the personal God of the Shang kings (Creel, 1937: 51). Derived from a "context criticism" based solely on the handwork of the graphs of the Shang inscriptions, Prof. Creel concluded that the doctrine of the Mandate of Heaven was a political "propaganda" ploy "developed" by the rulers of the Zhou that "helped to create a psychological and cultural vacuum among the Shang people" (Creel, 1970: 84, 87) for the sake of controlling a large territory and converting the conquered Shang people to the Zhou rule. This conception, Prof. Creel deems, involves what might be called an "embryonic philosophy of history" that lasted for three thousand yeas till the end of the last dynasty in China (Creel, 1970: 83).

3. Prof. Creel readdresses the issue in an appendix to *The Origins of the Statecraft in China* (1970), where he adopted a textual approach and thus modified his assertions. He first points out that in the twelve Western Zhou sections of the *Documents*, especially in the two speeches of the Duke of Zhou, both the deities *Di* or *Shangdi* (Lord or Lord on High) of the Shang people and the deity *Tian* (Heaven) are mentioned. As Prof. Creel states, the Duke of Zhou "repeatedly uses the two names as synonyms, and once uses a combined name, *Huang Tian Shangdi* 皇天上帝, 'August Heaven *Shangdi*.' He repeatedly tells the Shang people that *Tian* gave the Mandate to the founder of their own Shang dynasty... the Duke makes it very clear that it is useless for the Shang to hope for help, in regaining their independence from the Zhou, from their deity, *Di*. For he says repeatedly that not merely *Tian*, but *Di*, rejected the last Shang King and commanded the Zhou to overthrow him and take over the Mandate to rule (Creel, 1970: 500-501). The juxtaposition of the names in the same speech to the officials of the conquered Shang, which were originally claimed by Prof. Creel to be associated with different deities of two different peoples, in my opinion, proves that there was no need to "invent" the doctrine of the "Mandate of Heaven" on the part of the Zhou rulers in the first place, since the audience of the two speeches could have already identified the two names as names of the same deity. In addition, as Prof. Creel points out that, by the Western

Zhou times the character *tian* had already denoted the very definite deity, *Tian*, who could decree the transfer of the Mandate and to whom the King could be understood to stand in relationship as "Son of Heaven," that the Zhou must be diligent and careful, and that they must look upon the terrible fate that overtook Yin and draw a lesson from it (Creel, 1970: 504).

Given the innate connection between the different branches of humanities, I intend to adopt an inter-textual and interdisciplinary approach and conduct a dialogue between history, literature and thought to re-examine the key notion of the "Mandate of Heaven" and clusters of related ideas scattered in ancient texts of Western Zhou and the Spring and Autumn period (770-481 BCE), such as the *Book of History*, the *Book of Songs*, the *Analects*, and other early texts of the pre-Qin period (221-207 BCE). It is my hope that, through the inter-textual and interdisciplinary analysis, the notion of the "Mandate of Heaven" and its related ideas scattered in books of different disciplines can, in fact, sustain one another and coalesce into a meaningful tapestry to bring about/restore the time-honored understanding of the "Mandate of Heaven" and dispel the myth that the Mandate of Heaven was simply a "doctrine" created by the founders of the Western Zhou dynasty (1045-771 BCE) to "justify their right to rule." It is my hope that my interpretation developed in this study will go some way to redress the balance.

I would like to start my discussion on the notion of the Mandate of Heaven with some segments of two poems from the *Odes* and three entries from Confucius' *Analects*. First, the two poems, one from the collection grouped under the poems of the Shang:[4]

天命降監, 下民有嚴。 不僭不濫, 不敢怠遑。 命于下國, 封建厥福。
<詩經-商頌-殷武>

The Mandate of Heaven descended to (the king) to inspect;
The people below were reverent.
There were no disorders, no excesses;

---

[4] On the validity of the oral tradition, both literary scholars and historians have invariably commented on the validity and reliability of the orally transmitted corpus of literature as a stable tradition passed on from master to disciple in ancient times. Martin Kern states that materials written and preserved in books were done so because they were considered ritual or sacred, which left little room to forgeries or distortions for the individuals' interests. Orally-transmitted texts found in the library collections of Mawangdui, Guodian, Shanghai Museum all prove that this stable tradition and a mastery of cannon by those who had access to books was responsible for the collectively—and communally-shared knowledge that existed in ancient China. See Kern, 2005: 149-193, "The Odes in Excavated Manuscripts"; see also Hansen, 2000: 123.

He dared not be lazy or indolent.
It charged him in the states below
Grandly to establish his blessings.[5]
<*Book of Odes* - "Shang song-yinwu">

明明在下，赫赫在上，天難忱斯，
不易為王，天位殷適，使不挾四方。

有命自天，命此文王，于周于京。
篤生武王，保右命爾，燮伐大商。
<詩經-大雅-大明>

Shining brightness below,
Majestic on high,
Heaven is difficult to rely on;
It is not easy to be king.
The lawful heir of the Yin on the throne of Heaven
Was not permitted to embrace the four quarters.

The Mandate came from Heaven;
It charged this King Wen,
In Zhou, in the capital…
Staunchly was borne King Wu.
(Heaven said: "I shall protect and help you and appoint you,
To march and attack the great Shang."[6]
<*Book of Odes* - "Daya-daming">

Next, the two entries concerning the notion found in the *Analects*:

孔子曰:"君子有三畏: 畏天命，
畏大人，畏聖人之言。"
<論語 · 季氏>

Confucius said, "The superior man stands in awe of three things. He
stands in awe of the Mandate of Heaven; he stands in awe of great men;
and he stands in awe of the words of the sages."[7]

堯曰： 「咨！ 爾舜！ 天之曆數在爾躬， 允執其中！
四海困窮， 天祿永終。」舜亦以命禹。<論語-堯曰>

---

[5] Karlgren, 1950a, p. 266. The English translation is slightly modified from Karlgren's
rendition (K#305).
[6] Ibid. The English translation is slightly modified from Karlgren's rendition (K#236).
[7] Chan, 1963, p. 45.

Yao said:

"Oh, Shun,
The execution of rulers' duties in accord with
accurate calendar calculations has now fallen upon you.
Hold thou firmly to the middle way.
If the Empire should be reduced to dire straits,
The emolument bestowed on thee by Heaven
will be terminated forever."
It was with these same words that Shun commanded Yu.[8]

The "Mandate of Heaven 天命," sometime simply the "Mandate 命" (not the "charge 命" received by a vassal from his Lord), is a key word that appears frequently in the Western Zhou texts of the *Book of Odes*, the *Book of Documents* and the *Analects* among others. The term was used to refer to the divine approval which had been purportedly given to the sage-kings of the Three Dynasties of Xia 夏, Shang 商, and Zhou 周. It was claimed that the divine right and subsequent bestowment of the political power to reign was given to an individual or a ruling house to replace the old one which had fallen out of favor with Heaven through the ruler's inappropriate deeds or evil conduct, foul practice in polity and negligence of his sacrificial duties to both Heaven above and his ancestors. The warnings of the divine disapproval would manifest in unusual celestial phenomena, natural disasters, or war. The Mandate of Heaven was believed to be given by Heaven Above to King Wen (fl. 1111 BCE) to replace the last king of the Shang dynasty and found a new dynasty. King Wen started but did not complete the plans before he passed away. The Mandate was then given to his son King Wu, who founded the Western Zhou dynasty.

The notion of the Mandate of Heaven emerged as early as the time of the Zhou Conquest launched by King Wu over the last king of the Shang, Zhou Xin 紂辛. It had been commonly accepted by traditional historians as being legitimate, and ancient Chinese books of dynastic history could have been considered as a compendium of disaster records and downfalls of dynasties. The notion of the Mandate of Heaven has a concurrent appearance throughout major ancient texts.

A more elaborated instruction was given in chapter "Daoyu Mo 大禹

---

[8] *Lunyü*, Chapter XX, "Yaoyue". While Wing-tsit Chan in his translation of the *Lunyü* skips the whole chapter, D.C. Lau in his translation of the *Lunyü* renders the expressions figuratively as "The succession, ordained by Heaven, has fallen on thy person. Hold thou truly to the middle way." My translation is modified from his. See Lau, 1979, pp. 200-201.

謨" of the *Shangshu* 尚書,[9] where Shun is recorded in saying to Yu when he passes on his throne:

帝曰: "來! 禹! …天之歷數在汝躬, 汝終陟元后。
人心惟危, 道心惟微, 惟精惟一, 允執厥中…
慎乃有位, 敬修其可願, 四海困窮, 天祿永終。"[10]

The Sovereign said:
Come! Yu! . . .
The execution of rulers' duties in accord with
accurate calendar calculations has now fallen upon you.
You have finally become the ruler.
The hearts of humans are too precarious to rely on,
The mind of Dao is too flimsy to maintain;
Only by absolute earnest and single-mindedness
Can you hold truly to that middle way...
Prudence will guarantee the throne to you,
Respectfully cultivate your vows.
If the Empire should be reduced to dire straits,
The emolument bestowed on thee [dynasties] by Heaven
will be terminated forever.

The recognition of the will of a higher authority, whether it was God on High 上帝 at earlier times or simply Heaven at later times, became the reason why sovereigns in the past were all in awe of overstepping the scope of their authority. They took upon themselves to exercise their heavenly-mandated authority with great caution when they implemented their responsibilities as rulers on behalf of this Supreme Power, the higher authority to whom they had to answer. They seemed to be fully aware or, otherwise, constantly reminded that they could only maintain their status when they continued to perform their allotted obligations to care for and

---

[9] Of the "New Text" chapters included in my presentation, the various chapters concerning the Three Dynasties in the work certainly do not date from the time of the legendary emperors of Yao, Shun, and Yu, but were rather composed in the last centuries of the Zhou dynasty; some could be written down as late as the Qin dynasty in the third century BCE. The *Tang shih* of the *Shangshu* (Book of Documents), as many scholars argued, could have been created by the Zhou founders to justify their own conquest of the Shang. The three chapters of the *Zhoushu*, the *Mu shi, Hong fan*, and *Jin teng*, all attributed to the time of King Wu (r. 1045-1043 BCE), are also generally regarded as later creations. The chapters of *Kang gao, Shao gao, Jun shi* and *Gu ming*, generally attributed to the reign of King Cheng (r. 1042/35-1006 BCE), and especially the first seven years of the reign during which time the Duke of Zhou acted as regent, were said to be the heart of the authentic *Book of Documents*. See Loewe, 1993, pp. 377-379.

[10] *Shangshu zhengyi*, 1972, p. 26.

provide for the people. In the meantime, they admonished their successor against committing acts that would slight or deviate from the will of Heaven or God on High. In the same section of Chapter "Yao yue 堯曰 of the *Analects* 論語, Tang 湯 (r. 1766 BCE) of the Shang was recorded in conveying a tremendous amount of caution and fear when addressing the Supreme Being Di:

曰:"予[小子履，敢用玄牡，] 敢昭告于皇皇后帝:
有罪不敢赦，帝臣不蔽，簡在帝心!
[朕躬有罪，無以萬方；萬方有罪，罪在朕躬。]" 11

[Tang] said, "I . . . dare to . . . make this declaration before you, the great Lord. I dare not pardon those who have transgressed. I shall present thy servants as they are so that the choice rests with Thee alone."12

In Chapter *Tang shi* 湯誓 of the *Shangshu* 尚書, we find a passage where the same King Tang made a vow to God on High and announced his intention when fighting with the troops of the last evil ruler Jie 桀 of the Xia 夏 (2200?-1766 BCE). This passage conveys the same kind of fear as in the preceding lines:

"非台小子，敢行稱亂；有夏多罪，天命殛之。…
予惟聞汝眾言；夏氏有罪，予畏上帝，不敢不正。…
爾尚輔予一人，致天之罰…"13

The king said: "It is not that I, the small child, dare act so as to start rebellion. The lord of Hsia has much guilt, Heaven has charged me to kill him . . . I have heard the words of you all; the lord of [Xia] has guilt, I fear God on High, I dare not but punish him . . . May you support me, the One Man [sc. the sovereign], to apply Heaven's punishment. . . .14

The anthropomorphic Supreme Being, who was recognized and addressed both as Heaven and God on High, and whom the sovereigns admonished against each other was revered with the same kind of fear that Shang rulers felt towards him. It was indeed so genuine and profound

---

11 Legge, 1991, p. 350.
12 Lau, 1979, p. 201.
13 *Shangshu zhengyi*, 1972, p. 49.
14 Karlgren, 1950b, p. 20. The English translation is slightly modified from Karlgren's rendition.

that it was passed on to the rulers of the succeeding Zhou. The rulers of Zhou had been subjects to the Shang for generations and stood in awe as well. When King Wu 武 (r. 1045 BCE) of the Zhou was ready to launch an attack against the last ruthless sovereign of the Shang, he made a declaration at *Muye* 牧野 (the Mu fields) which is in the same spirit as the one made by Tang of the previous Shang dynasty. Both rulers were purported sage rulers, whose responsibilities it was to fulfill their ordained destiny, i.e., the Mandate of Heaven. They both were to right the wrongs of the evil rulers and to carry out the "punishment" on behalf of the Supreme Being. In Chapter *Mushi* 牧誓 of the *Shangshu* 尚書, King Wu of the Zhou enumerates the reasons for his righteous act. King Zhou 紂 (d. 1045 BCE) of the Shang 商 was said to have neglected his duties and done all the evil-doings and King Wu was to "execute Heaven's punishment[15] (惟恭行天之罰)."[16]

The termination of the "emolument bestowed by Heaven (*tianlu* 天祿)" means none other than the termination of the Mandate of Heaven, as its accompanying consequence. In the *Book of Odes*, King Wen of the Zhou was celebrated as the one to replace the Shang as the new receiver of the Mandate of Heaven because of his great "virtue":

> The Mandate of Heaven, how beautiful and unceasing!
> Oh, how glorious, was the purity of King Wen's virtue![17]
> (Ode no. 267, "The Mandate of Heaven")

> 維此王季，帝度其心。貊其德音，其德克明。
> 克明克类，克长克君。⋯ 既受帝祉，
> 施于孙子。⋯
> Now this King Wen, God probed his heart:
> Settled was his reputation of virtue ⋯
> He received God's blessings;
> It reached to his grandsons and sons . . ."[18]
> (*Book of Odes*, ode no. 241, "August")

The chapter of *Kang Gao* 康誥 in the *Shangshu* 尚書 attests to the occasion: "The king [King Cheng 成 (ca. 1020 BCE), son of King Wu] said, 'Oh, then, you youngster Feng! The mandate is not constant. You should

---

[15] *Shangshu zhengyi,* 1972, p. 72.
[16] *Shangshu zhengyi,* 1972, p. 72.
[17] Karlgren 1950a, pp. 239-240. The English translation is slightly modified from Karlgren's rendition.
[18] Karlgren, 1950a, pp. 194-196. The English translation is slightly modified from Karlgren's rendition.

keep it in mind. 嗚呼！肆汝小子封。惟命不於常；汝念哉'".[19]

The *Book of Odes* 詩 also records songs that illustrate how unreliable the Mandate of Heaven could be and how constantly it could change hands. The following is one which typically exemplifies the keen awareness that only "virtue" of the ruler can help secure the source of lasting blessings from Heaven Above:

文王，於緝熙敬止。假哉天命，有商孫子。
商之孫子，其麗不億。上帝既命，侯於周服。
侯服於周，天命靡常。⋯王之藎臣，無念爾祖。⋯
聿脩厥德。永言配命，自求多福。
殷之未喪師，克配上帝。宜鑒於殷，駿命不易。⋯

August was King Wen, continuously bright and reverent;
Great, indeed, was the Mandate of Heaven;
There were Shang's grandsons and sons . . .
Was their number not a hundred thousand!
Now God on High has given his Mandate,
And so they became subject to Zhou.
Heaven's Mandate is not for ever . . .
Do not think of your ancestors, but cultivate your virtues.
Forever be worthy of (Heaven's) Mandate,
And seek for yourself much felicity;
When Yin had not lost the multitudes,
It was able to be a counterpart to God on High.
You ought to mirror yourself in (the fate of) Yin;
The great Mandate is not easy (to keep) . . .[20]
(*Book of Odes*, ode no. 235, "King Wen")

The recognition of the shifting of the Mandate of Heaven and of the possibility of losing it at any time was equally shared by members and members other than those of the royal family.

To the rulers of Zhou, Heaven or God on High was a supreme being who was ruthless, ready to strike, take away the Mandate of Heaven and send down disasters or destruction. Warnings to each other among rulers or between ruler and subject against offending Heaven or God on High are found throughout the documents (of both Shang and Zhou dynasties) in the *Shangshu*. The only effective means that could appease God on High and reverse Heaven's will to send destruction to a ruling house and prevent

---

[19] Karlgren, 1950b, pp. 41-43. The English translation is slightly modified from Karlgren's rendition.

[20] Karlgren, 1950a, p. 186. The English translation is slightly modified from Karlgren's rendition.

more impending disasters was through the demonstration of virtue in the rulers (皇天無親，惟德是輔).[21] The ruler served to link God on High with his subjects. If he governed well, God on High would continue to support him, but if he violated Heaven's intent, Heaven could send various portents to warn him of his misconduct in the form of eclipses, floods, droughts, or any other calamity. All Chinese history could be understood as the manifestation of a larger pattern of disaster records and downfalls of dynasties. The conduct of the ruler had direct, almost immediate, effects upon both the natural and the human worlds.

II. Proper Conduct of the Ruler Stipulated According to the Seasons

In the "Grand Norm" of the *Documents*, we are given a list of "Nine Categories 九疇," where both human conduct and the natural phenomena corresponding to the human realm are enumerated. Under the second category, we read,

二、五事：
一曰貌，二曰言，三曰視，四曰聽，五曰思。
貌曰恭，言曰從，視曰明，聽曰聰，思曰睿。
恭作肅，從作乂，明作哲，聰作謀，睿作聖。

Second: the Five Conducts.
The first is called appearance; the second, speech; the third, seeing; the fourth, hearing; the fifth, thinking. The virtue of appearance is respectfulness; that of speech is accordance [with reason]; that of seeing is clearness; that of hearing is distinctness; that of thinking is penetration and profundity. Respectfulness leads to solemnity; accordance with reason, to orderliness; clearness, to wisdom; distinctness, to deliberation; and penetration and profundity, to sageness.

This passage reminds us of the concerns of Confucius about the morally "superior man" expected of his disciples who would become rulers or assistants to rulers of the states eventually. To quote for comparison:

孔子曰：＂君子有九思：視思明，聽思聰，色思溫，
貌思恭，言思忠，事思敬，疑思問，忿思難，見得思義。＂
＜論語·季氏＞

Confucius said, "The superior man has nine wishes. In seeing, he wishes to see clearly. In hearing, he wishes to hear distinctly. In

---

[21] "Cai Zhong zhi ming" in *Shangshu zhengyi*, 1972, p. 114.

his expression, he wishes to be warm. In his appearance, he wishes to be respectful. In his speech, he wishes to be sincere. In handling affairs, he wishes to be serious. When in doubt, he wishes to ask. When he is angry, he wishes to think of the resultant difficulties. And when he sees an opportunity for a gain, he wishes to think of righteousness."[22]

The Confucian concept of *junzi* 君子, originally meaning and referring to the "son of the ruler," has been rendered commonly by modern scholars as the "superior man." As it appeared in the *Analects*, it had been radically modified by Confucius, who believed in the perfectibility of all men and used it to denote a morally superior man since to him nobility was no longer a matter of blood, but of character.[23] Nevertheless, the quality and character of the Confucian "superior man" had been in ancient times those expected of a sage ruler. In the eighth of the Nine Categories, we come to what is called the Various Verifications, namely, ways to check governmental measures against natural phenomena. It reads,

八、庶徵：曰雨，曰暘，曰燠，曰
寒，曰風，曰時。五者來備，各

Eighth: the various verifications. They are called rain, sunshine, heat, cold, wind, and their seasonableness [timeliness]. When the five come in a complete way, and each in its proper order, all the plants are rich and luxuriant. If anyone is complete to the extreme, it is baleful; if anyone is lacking to the extreme, it is baleful. Some are called the lucky verifications: the solemnity [of the sovereign] – seasonable rain responds to it; his orderliness – seasonable sunshine responds to it; his wisdom – seasonable heat responds to it; his deliberation – seasonable cold responds to it; his sageness – seasonable wind responds to it. Some are called unlucky verifications: the wildness [of the sovereign] – lasting rain responds to it; his arrogance – lasting sunshine responds to it; his indolence – lasting heat responds to it; his rashness– lasting cold responds to it; his stupidity – lasting wind responds to it.[24]

---

[22] Chan, 1963.

[23] The traditional concept of *junzi* 君子, or superior man, originally "son of the ruler," was radically modified by Confucius, who believed in the perfectibility of all men and used it to denote a morally superior man since to him nobility was no longer a matter of blood, but of character. See Chan, 1963, p. 15.

[24] Wing-tsit Chan and Yu-Lan Fung both cited this entry in their discussion of the *Book of Documents*. My translation is primarily modified from Karlgren, 1950b, pp. 30-33. See also Chan, 1963, p. 9 and Fung, 1963, p. 132.

138

What is immediately noticeable in these passages is the close one-on-one correspondence between the human and natural worlds. The human and natural worlds are interlinked; bad conduct on the part of the human results in the appearance of abnormal phenomena in the world of nature. This correspondence, which was greatly developed in later times, is known as that of "the interaction between Heaven and man" 天人感應. The natural phenomena, almost like mirror images, reflect/respond to the causative corresponding virtuous conducts in the human world. Fung Yu-Lan and Wing-Tsit Chan both claim that the "sovereign" was the one for whom the five types of virtuous conduct are designed and by whom they should be cultivated.[25] The Second Category seems to suggest that there is the need for an appropriate educational and moral program, designed not for the commoner 小人 in general, but primarily for the "sovereign," by which he could cultivate himself to become a sage-ruler 聖王. Suffice it to say for now that this program was later adopted and cultivated by the Confucian superior men 君子[26] as their goal for character training. In the three passages, the king and minor rulers of the states are, indeed, the intended audience to follow the ordinances outlined in the "Grand Norm" because they play a crucial role in the interconnecting worlds of the humans and nature. In the Shang and Early Western Zhou beliefs, wrong conduct on the part of the sovereign causes Heaven to become angry, resulting in abnormal natural phenomena, taken to be warnings of disapproval given by Heaven to the sovereign, and his "Mandate of Heaven" was at stake. In later times after the Eastern Zhou period, the sovereign's bad conduct was believed to automatically result in a disturbance of nature and thus produces abnormal phenomena. The whole universe, like an "organism," goes out of harmony. When one part of it becomes out of order, the other part must be affected.

A very important early document to prove the interconnection of the two realms of the natural and the human can be found in the passage taken from the *Guanzi* by Guan Zhong (? -645 BCE), the prime minister of the state of Qi during the Spring and Autumn period. Master Guan 管子, who predated Confucius and was not a precursor of Confucianism was recorded explaining the extreme importance of the "Four Seasons," by

---

[25] In his translation of the Eighth of the "Nine Categories," Yu-Lan Fung takes the liberty of adding the word "sovereign" to "solemnity"—"the solemnity of the sovereign"; and in Wing-Tsit Chan's translation, when speaking of the Conducts listed as the Second Categories, he places the qualifying expression in brackets—[all of which should be cultivated by the ruler]. See Fung, 1963, p. 132, and Chan, 1963, p. 9.

[26] Literally "son of the ruler," it came to acquire the meaning of morally "superior man" in the teaching of Confucius, on his idea that nobility was no longer a quality determined by status, associated with a hereditary position, but of character. See Chan, 1963, p. 15.

which sage rulers in ancient times managed to rule their states successfully:[27]

令有時，無時，則必視順天之所以來⋯ 唯聖人知四時。
不知四時，乃失國之基。不知五穀之故，國家乃路⋯
刑德者，四時之合也。刑德合於時，則生福；詭則生禍。
然則春夏秋冬將何行？

The ordinances, whether timely or untimely, have to be carried out in accordance with Heaven . . . Only sages know [the importance of] the four seasons. He [the ruler] who does not know [the importance] of the four seasons will lose the foundation on which the nation is built. He [the ruler] who does not know about the five grains will put his nation and state in danger . . . The infliction or remission of a penalty has to accord with the four seasons. When they are done according to the time, blessings will be produced; when they are not done timely, disasters will be produced. In that case, for the four seasons of spring, summer, autumn and winter, how does [the ruler] know what he should and should not do?

The "timely act" was to be understood as an act performed appropriate to its corresponding climatic season. The time-honored expression of the Chinese since ancient times is "To plant 春生, to grow 夏長, to harvest 秋收, and to put away for storage 冬藏". What is "appropriate," then, depends on the climatic characteristics and tendency of the individual seasons; when tasks corresponding to the climatic tendency of the individual deeds are performed, it is called "in accordance with Heaven 順天". And it will result in abundance in vegetation and happiness in humans:

柔風甘雨乃至。百姓乃壽，百蟲乃蕃⋯

The gentle breeze and beneficial rain will arrive.
All objects will live long lives and all insects will thrive.

However, when tasks of different seasons are performed, the result will be undesirable:

是故春行冬政則雕，行秋政則霜，行夏政則欲⋯

---

[27] My translation of the segments cited is entirely based on the annotations of the book by Li, 1988, pp. 689-699.

140

Therefore, when the administrative programs for the winter are carried out in spring, they will wilt the crops; when the administrative programs for autumn are carried out [in spring], they will bring frost to descend; when the administrative programs for the summer are carried out, it will arouse desires.

The appropriate tasks for spring needed to be initiated right at the beginning of the first month of spring as five programs mostly in the nature of political and social services. "If the five programs are conducted timely, the spring rain will arrive as a result . . . The king's tasks must be executed appropriately in order for his state to last for long 五政苟時，春雨乃來⋯ 王事必理，以為久長。"[28]

The concise instruction of Master Quan was enumerated in greater details in another document, "Monthly Ordinances" (*Yueling* 月令), which also predates Confucius by half a century first found in the *Lüshi Chunqiu* 呂氏春秋 (comp. in 239 BCE) and later included in the *Liji* 禮記, a collection of treatises written by Confucian scholars in the third and second centuries BCE. The cosmological world-view in the "Monthly Ordinances" reflects the same but fully developed system of correlations. Being a text of "almanacs," it tells the ruler in particular what he ought to do month by month in order to retain harmony with the forces of nature and maintain a balance between the two interconnected worlds of the natural and the human. All the ordinances in concordance with the right timing and seasonal appropriateness should be strictly observed in order to avoid interrupting the natural order of the seasons and causing untimely undesirable effects:

月令: 孟春行夏令，則雨水不時，草木蚤落，國時有恐。
行秋令則其民大疫，猋風暴雨總至，藜莠蓬蒿并興。
行冬令則水潦為敗，雪霜大摯，首種不入。

The Monthly Ordinance: If in the first month of spring, the governmental proceedings proper to summer are carried out, the rain will fall unseasonably, plants and trees will decay prematurely, and the states will be kept in constant fear. In the first month of summer, if the proceedings proper to autumn are carried out, there will be great pestilence among the people, violent winds and torrential rain will frequently descend; fescue, darnel, tumbleweeds, and wormwood will grow up together. In the first month of fall, if the proceedings proper to winter are carried out, floods of water will produce destructive effects, and

---

[28] Li, 1988, p. 699.

snow and frost will do such great damage so that the first sown seeds will not take root in the ground.

The crucial idea underlying and purporting both the "Grand Norm" and the "Monthly Ordinances" is the notion of "appropriate timing" (時) of natural phenomena which are in a reciprocal relationship with the conduct of the sovereign. When his conduct is good and appropriate, the sovereign will bring about "lucky verifications" (休徵), manifesting in the "seasonableness" or "timeliness" of natural phenomena; when the conduct of the sovereign is not proper, he will bring about "unlucky verification" (咎徵), manifesting disasters in nature. If, in each month, the sovereign fails to act in the manner befitting that month, but, instead, follows the conduct appropriate to another month, abnormal natural phenomena will result. The delineation of the dos and don'ts proper to each month for the sovereign to perform dutifully in the "Monthly Ordinances" mark one-on-one corresponding and reciprocal correlations between nature and proper human efforts or misconduct.

III. The Enigmatic Interlocution Between Sage Rulers Yao and Shun, and Shun and Yu:

"天之曆數在爾躬，…允執其中 The execution of rulers' duties in accord with accurate calendar calculations has now fallen upon you.... Hold thou firmly to the middle way."

The ancients tried to explain natural phenomena in terms of timing and maintained that these phenomena were closely interrelated with human conduct. A sovereign of sagacity, a sage-ruler, had the ability to discern the seasonal patterns of the ceaseless motion in nature and to act upon them correctly to avert the calamities that occurred due to any inappropriate conduct in the human realm, manifest primarily in the sovereign himself. If a ruler could not govern or perform his expected tasks properly, Heaven would show that it had withdrawn support for the dynasty by sending natural disasters in the form of excessive winds or rain, drought, earthquakes, unusual celestial events, or man-made disasters in the form of foreign invasions or domestic rebellions. While later thinkers interpreted the Mandate of Heaven as a check on evil rulers, the early Zhou rulers were noted for being in perpetual dread of losing it, earnestly reminding each other that "Heaven's Mandate is not constant"[29] (天命不于常—the *Shijing*) and that "the Mandate of Heaven is not easily preserved

[29] *Shijing*, ode #235, "Wen Wang". See ode #235: "King Wen" in Karlgren, 1950a, p. 186.

and Heaven is hard to trust (天命不易，天難諶—the *Shangshu*)".[30] It was seen not only as a check on the evil government, but as a reminder of the possibly excessive conduct of the rulers or the negligence of his duties. Prudent rulers, then, were obliged to monitor the skies and their subjects for any early signs of Heaven's disapproval. While flow and changes of seasons were believed to be the essential features of nature, the constant patterns in these changes were to be observed and recognized so that the sovereign of sagacity might direct his correct/correcting actions according to them. Being one with Heaven and living in harmony with nature, the sovereign would succeed in everything he undertook. Following the course of nature and performing his seasonal duties in accordance with the natural processes of Heaven and Earth, the sovereign would find it easy to manage the whole world, and Heaven would continue to come to support his claim to be the king. Hence, the above-mentioned enigmatic warning uttered by sage rulers, when they abdicated their thrones to one another, namely, "天之曆數在爾躬，…允執其中 The execution of rulers' duties in accord with accurate calendar calculations has now fallen upon you./... Hold thou firmly to the middle way", was an equally earnest request made not to be overlooked because the Mandate of Heaven was a genuinely lived experience to the rulers in ancient times.

In the context of all the passages cited above from seven ancient texts at different historical times, but all during the first millennium BCE, the repeated enigmatic interlocution between the sage rulers literally means that "The Calendar Calculations (the correct execution of kingly duties according to the timing specified in the calendar) has bestowed on thy person by Heaven. Hold thou properly to the middle way (without committing inappropriate acts or acts of the excesses)."

The exact meaning, now oblivious to us moderns, of the interlocution between the sage rulers, Yao and Shun, and Shun and Yu, was remembered, well recognized and recorded in the *Shiji* 史記 by Sima Qian 司馬遷 (145 - ca. 90 BCE) of the Western Han dynasty (207 BCE-CE 9). He was a direct descendent of a long lineage of uninterrupted hereditary profession of court historians/"astrologers" 太史公, whose main responsibilities had primarily been astrology for centuries.[31] To conclude my essay, I would refer to a passage, biographical or even auto-biographical in nature, from the chapter of "The Monograph of Calendar 曆書" of the *Shiji*, composed at a time when the oral tradition was still going strong. Here, the passage

---

[30] *Shujing*, "Prince Shi". My translation is modified from Karlgren, 1950b, pp. 59-62.

[31] In the "Chuyu" section of the *Guoyü*, it was confirmed by the reputable and learned Guan Yefu, whose account of Chong and Li being the ancestors of the Sima clan of the Western Zhou dynasty disclosed the long linage of the hereditary profession of Sima clan as court historians throughout the centuries. See *Guoyü weishijie*, 1968, pp. 403-404.

involves ancestors of the Sima Qian, Chong and Li, who were appointed by the sage ruler Yao to recalculate the calendar so that the correct execution of kingly duties might be timely performed and the harmony between heaven and earth might be restored again. The *Grand Historian* records the same line verbatim and emphatically states, the "correct execution of kingly duties bestowed upon rulers by Heaven was indeed what rulers in ancient times all held in high regard. It was remembered by the Grand Historian for it was the genuine reality the ancient rulers all experienced and had to observe with great care in their lives.

> 堯復遂重黎之後，不忘舊者，使復典之，而立羲和之官。
> 明時正度，則陰陽調，風雨節，茂氣至，民無夭疫。
> 年耆禪舜，申戒文祖，云「天之曆數在爾躬」。
> 舜亦以命禹。由是觀之，王者所重也。

As a result, Yao resumed once again the descendants of Chong and Li who had not forgotten their old duties and made them take charge again. He, thus, established official positions of Xi and He, who announced the seasons and regulated the time. As a result, yin and yang were in harmonious balance, winds and rains in check; the vital energy arrived and people were free from dying untimely deaths and plaques. In his old age, he abdicated and handed over the throne to Shun. He gave him earnest exhortations . . . saying, "The execution of rulers' duties in accord with accurate calendar calculations has now fallen upon you." When he abdicated and handed over the throne, Shun also used it to exhort Yu. In view of these [instances], this is indeed what rulers held in high regard.[32]

Note: An earlier version of this article was published in Ching-I Tu, et al. (Eds), (2015), An Integrated vision of Chinese scholarship: Literature, history, and philosophy. Confucius Institute of Rutgers University, pp. 43-58.

---

[32] *Shiji*, juan 26, pp. 1256-1258.

Bibliography

CHAN,WING-TSIT (1963). *A source book in Chinese philosophy.* Princeton: Princeton University.

CREEL, H. (1970). *The origins of statecraft in China, Vol. I: The Western Chou Empire.* Chicago: The University of Chicago Press.

CREEL, H. (1937). *Studies in early Chinese culture.* Baltimore: Waverly Press.

CREEL, H. (1936). *The birth of China – A study of the formative period of Chinese civilization.* New York: Reynal & Hitchcock.

FUNG, YU-LAN (1963). *A short history of Chinese philosophy.* Princeton: Princeton University Press.

Guoyü weishijie (1968). Taipei: Shijie Book Bureau.

HANSEN, V. (2000). *The open empire. A history of China to 1600.* New York: W.W. Norton & Company.

KARLGREN, B. (Trans.) (1950a). *The book of odes. Chinese text, transcription and translation.* Stockholm: Museum of Far Eastern Antiquities.

KARLGREN, B. (Trans.) (1950b). *The book of documents.* Stockholm: Museum of Far Eastern Antiquities.

KERN, M. (Ed.) (2005). *Text and ritual in early China.* Seattle, WA: University of Washington Press.

LAU, D.C. (1979). *Confucius – The analects.* Hong Kong: The Chinese University Press.

LEGGE, J. (1991). *The Chinese classics* Vols. I & II. Taipei: SMC Publishing.

LI, MIAN (Ed.). (1988). *Guanzi jinzhu jinyi* (Guanzi's annotation and translation). Taipei: Shangwu yinshuguan.

LOEWE, M. (1993). *Early Chinese texts: A bibliographical guide.* Berkeley: The Society for the Study of Early China and the Institute of East Asian Studies University of California.

SHANGSHU ZHENGYI (Book of Documents) (1972). Taipei: Guangwen shuju.

SHIJI (Historical Records), juan 26, pp. 1256-1258.

Above: Tiantai temple on Jiuhua Mountain, China. Photo 64441498 © Xin Hua | Dreamstime.com

Inset: Stained glass image of Pope Gregory the Great. Photography by Nheyob. CC BY-SA 3.0

Sin in Tiantai Buddhism and Christianity: A Comparison Between Zhiyi and Pope Gregory I

by Wangyu Tang

Introduction

What is religion? Why do people study religion? Austrian psycho-analyst Sigmund Freud thought that religion was an illusion.[1] Herbert Spencer (1820-1903), an English philosopher, biologist, and sociologist argued that ancestor worship is the root of every religion.[2] Another answer given by English anthropologist Edward Burnett Tyler (1832-1917) is that religion is a belief in spiritual beings.[3]

Tiantai Buddhism and Christianity have endured the test of time and have profoundly influenced East Asia and the West. This paper compares the subject of sin as treated by medieval Tiantai Buddhism and medieval Christianity. This paper seeks insight into the differences and similarities between the religions to achieve a better understanding of how these two faiths have evolved.

Tiantai affected the development of many of the Buddhist schools of East Asia as noted in *Sources of Chinese Tradition*: "From the philosophical standpoint, and in terms of its influence on other schools in China, Korea, and Japan, the Lotus or Tiantai teaching is of major importance."[4] Even though the basic scripture of Tiantai Buddhism, *The Lotus of the Wonderful Law* is from North India or Central Asia, it has distinctive Chinese features because it was founded based on the writings of the great Chinese monk Zhiyi (智顗, 538–597). The name Tiantai Buddhism indicates its geographical origin—*Tiantai* ("Heavenly Terrace"), which is in China's Zhejiang province where Zhiyi taught.[5]

Pope Gregory I ("the Great") (540-604) figures prominently in this analysis. He was the Pope of the Catholic Church from 590 to 604 and shaped the liturgy and mass during the medieval period and he outlined

---

[1] As quoted by Crawford, 2002, p. 2.
[2] Ibid.
[3] Ibid., p. 1.
[4] Chan, 1999, p. 444.
[5] Chan, 1999, p. 444.

the principles of monastic life. Gregory entered public life after receiving a liberal education. He became Prefect of Rome in 573. In 574, he decided to abandon his political career in the secular world and became a monk. He composed the famous and lengthy patristic work, *Morals on Job*, in Constantinople. It was based on his addresses to the community of monks who had accompanied him from Rome.[6] His other notable works are *The Book of Pastoral Rule, Dialogues*, and his *Homilies on the Gospel*.

To understand the quest to achieve salvation, it is necessary to explore how religions approach the origin of human problems—sin. In Ingram and Streng's book, *Buddhist-Christian Dialogue: Mutual Renewal and Transformation*, they noted that "in spite of the historical differences in their origins, Buddhism and Christianity present a structurally similar, two-fold problematic based on the understanding of salvation as the solution to the problem of the meaning of human existence in the world."[7]

This paper begins its comparison of medieval Tiantai Buddhism and Christianity with the contributions of Zhiyi and Gregory the Great and begin with the introduction of the lives of these great religious philosophers. This will be followed by the concept of sin in Zhiyi's teachings and the religious practice in Tiantai Buddhism. It then presents a brief introduction to Christian moral philosophy based on Pope Gregory's teachings on sin and the religious practice of contemplation in Catholicism. The paper will then analyze how the two religions share a similar concept of sin and examine the differences of how sins originate, and the meaning of cardinal sins. The analysis will explore the similarities and differences in the practice of religious contemplation in these two faiths.

Ultimately, this paper aims to help people from different religious backgrounds to understand each other in identifying the common features and differences between the religions from an academic perspective.

BACKGROUND

A. The Life of Zhiyi

According to Chappell (1940-2004), one of the major challenges in researching the development of Chinese Buddhism was the reconciliation and integration of numerous doctrines and practices from Indian Buddhism.[8]

Chinese historian and philosopher Jiyu Ren (1916-2009) noted that once Buddhism came into China, it went through four phases until it evolved into "Chinese Buddhism":

---

[6] Butler, 1922, p. 65.
[7] Ingram & Streng, 1986, p. 15.
[8] Chappell, 1983, p. 21.

1. introduction   – Han to Eastern Jin dynasty (206 BCE-420 CE)
2. reconciliation   – Northern and Southern dynasty (420-589)
3. creation   – Sui and Tang dynasty (581-907), and
4. Confucianization – Song to Qing dynasty (960-1912).[9]

Due to the language barrier, translators were needed to translate the sutras during the first phase. Inevitably, local languages and ideas were used to convey the complex concepts in the sutras. As the founder of Tiantai Buddhism, Zhiyi based his philosophy on the Lotus Sutra (法华经). Tiantai Buddhism was a milestone in the development of Chinese Buddhism.[10]

Contemporary Chinese scholar Guiming Pan says that Zhiyi was born in the late Northern and Southern dynasties and experienced the fall of the Liang (502-557) and Chen dynasties (557-589). As a descendant of officials of the Southern dynasties, Zhiyi was tormented by the political turbulence and social unrest.[11]

Another significant factor that influenced Zhiyi was the repression of Buddhism by Emperor Wu (543-578) of the Northern Zhou. The monks who crossed the river from the region controlled by the Northern Zhou into Chen territory helped shaped the later development of southern Buddhism and promoted the interaction between northern and southern Buddhism.[12]

The Northern and Southern dynasties witnessed a surge in Chinese Buddhism, especially in the Northern Wei (386-534). Despite setbacks of the first Buddhist Repression, Buddhism thrived under the encouragement of the fourth emperor of the Northern Wei, Wencheng (440-465). The reason behind this rapid recovery is that Prince Huang (428-451), the eldest son of Emperor Wu, postponed the campaign of persecution planned by the court. This gave the monks sufficient notice to hide deep in the mountains taking their Buddhist sutras and statues with them.[13]

The unprecedented development of Buddhism during the Northern dynasty brought countless societal problems and led to the second repression of Buddhism. This gives us a clue about Zhiyi's struggle to fight for Buddhism. Unlike the past, the rulers of the Southern dynasty promoted Buddhism as a method to help rule the country.[14] Zhiyi lectured for years on the text of *The Lotus*—one of the most popular of the Mahayana sutras. It was not so much a philosophical text than a guide to salvation through practice. His pupil, Guanding (561-632), recorded Zhiyi's deliberations which later became known as the "Three Great Works" of the Tiantai

---

[9] Pan, 1996, p. 2.
[10] Ibid., p. 3.
[11] Pan, 1996, pp. 3-4.
[12] Ibid., p. 5.
[13] Ibid., p. 7.
[14] Ibid., pp. 8-9.

school: *The Words and Phrases of the Lotus* (*Fahua Wenju* 法华文句), *The Profound Meaning of the Lotus* (*Fahua Xuanyi* 法华玄义), and *The Great Calming and Contemplation* (*Mohe zhiguan* 摩诃止观). As a member of the southern gentry, Zhiyi had the distinct philosophical orientation of the southern Buddhists, while his teacher Huisi (514-577) came from the north. The northern Buddhists focused on faith and discipline. Therefore, Zhiyi concluded that "the contemplative and philosophical approach to religion were like two wings of a bird." As a result, the Tiantai school assumed a strong philosophical content as well as an even stronger emphasis on the meditative practice.[15]

B. The Life of Pope Gregory I (540-604)

There is an ancient Chinese saying that heroes emerge in turbulent days (乱世出英雄). Pope Gregory I experienced the political turmoil of wars after the fall of the Roman Empire. Similarly, Zhiyi lived through the wars after the collapse of Han dynasty in China. Witnessing of human suffering strengthened the determination of both men to bring a message of salvation to the people.

Pope Gregory I was born to an aristocratic family in Rome with a strong connection to the Roman Church. As a young aristocratic he lived in a palatial estate and had the best education available. During his child-hood, between 546 to 547, control of the city of Rome shifted three times between Gothic and imperial hands. Fortunately, Gregory's family survived the political crisis. The Gothic Wars hastened the fall of the once mighty capital of the Roman Empire. The city of Rome, with its many monuments, was largely abandoned by the time Gregory reached adolescence. The experience of living in a nearly deserted city accounts for the occasional apocalyptic character of his writing.[16]

The Lombards had been ravaging Rome's cities and countryside since 568.[17] In 586, Gregory was recalled to Rome, and he returned to St. Andrew's monastery where he became its abbot. Gregory was elected Pope in 590 despite having asked Emperor Maurice (590-602) not to confirm the election.[18]

Gregory had a profound influence on Rome. He banished all the lay attendants and pages to restore monastic simplicity. Rome was in such dire circumstances that even the control of military powers fell to the Pope Gregory who also cared for the people's spiritual needs by giving countless sermons attended by immense crowds. His sermons were straight-forward

---

[15] Chan, 1999, p. 444.

[16] Demacopoulos, 2015, p. 1-2.

[17] Mcclain, 1956, p. 1.

[18] Hudleston, & Herbermann, 1909, p. 782.

and practical expositions of scripture. He regularly used anecdotes which became the model for other preachers of the Middle Ages.[19]

Remarkably, Gregory achieved many accomplishments despite being in constant ill-health. "His mind, naturally serious, was filled with despondent forebodings, and his continual bodily pains were increased and intensified."[20] His *Commentary on Job*, also known as *Moralia on Job*, and his *The Rule for Pastors* have been called "the most thorough pastoral treatises of the patristic era."[21]

SIN IN TWO RELIGIONS

I. SIN AND RELIGIOUS PRACTICE IN TIANTAI BUDDHISM

1. Zhiyi's teaching on sin

The Essentials for Practicing Calming-and-Insight and Dhyana Meditation (*Xiao Zhiguan* 小止观) is another important work of Zhiyi. Although much shorter than the *Great Calming and Contemplation* (*Moho Chih-kuan* 摩诃止观), it provides a guide to the preliminary stage for contemplation. It includes Zhiyi's teachings about how people should avoid the sins of five desires: self-hindrances, avarice, anger, foolishness, and arrogance.

a. Sins of the Five Desires

According to Zhiyi, there are five stimulations from the outside world which can lead people to sin.

- "Desire of forms such as the stately and decorous shapes and features of men and women, including alluring eyes, long eyebrows, red lips, and white teeth, as well as things regarded in the world as precious."[22]
- "Desire for sounds refers to musical sounds such as [those] from harps, zithers, or flutes, and the voices of men and women singing, chanting, hymning, or reciting."[23]
- "Desire for fragrances refers to the physical scents of men and women, food, drink, and perfumes, as well as all manner of incenses and aromas."[24]

---

[19] Ibid.
[20] Ibid., p. 786.
[21] Demacopoulos, 2007, p. 13.
[22] Dharmamitra, 2007, p. 29.
[23] Ibid.
[24] Ibid.

- "Desire for flavors refers to bitterness, sourness, sweetness, pungency, saltiness, mildness, and other such fine flavors characteristic of fine beverages and cuisine."[25]
- "Desire for touchables refers to the softness and delicate slickness of the bodies of men and women, to the sensations of their physical warmth when it is cold, their physical coolness when it is hot, as well as to all other pleasant tactile contacts."[26]

The purpose of ceasing and contemplation is to achieve detachment from secular life to reach the pure land and become Buddha. One cannot achieve this if he or she gives in to any of the five senses listed above.

b. Sins of Self-hindrances

- 弃「贪欲盖」者：前说外五尘中生五欲，今约内意根生欲。
所谓行者，端坐修禅，心生欲觉，念念相续，覆盖善心，
令不生长，觉已应弃。
The hindrance of desire: the five desires mentioned above are desires that arise from a secular life, but hindrances refer to the desires which rise from inside. That means meditators cannot practice virtuous deeds if they continue to have deluded thoughts or defilements.[27]

- 弃「瞋恚盖」者：瞋是失诸佛法之根本，堕诸恶道之因缘，
法乐之怨家，善心之大贼，种种恶口之府藏。
The hindrance of anger: anger is the root of losing pure dharma. The main cause of falling into the three realms of hell: the enemy of dharma joy, theft of good will, and source of foul mouths.[28]

- 弃「睡眠盖」者：内心惛暗，名为睡；五情暗蔽，
放恣肢节，委卧睡熟，名为眠。以是因缘，名为睡眠盖。
The hindrance of slumber: the state of when the inner conscious falls into darkness can be called lethargy. Sleep is the failing of the five senses and the loss of control of the limbs. This is called the hindrance of slumber because meditators cannot practice contemplation when they are in state of unconsciousness.[29]

- 弃「掉悔盖」者：掉有三种，一身掉、二口掉、三心掉。
身掉者：身好游走，诸杂戏谑，坐不暂安。

---

[25] Ibid., p. 31.
[26] Ibid.
[27] Zhiyi, 《天台小止观修订版》，慧辨记录，慧岳注释，1976. p. 18.
[28] Ibid., p. 19.
[29] Ibid., p. 20.

口掉者：好喜吟咏，诤竞是非，无益戏论，世俗言语等。
心掉者：心情放荡，纵意攀缘，思惟文艺，世间才技，
诸恶觉观等，名为心掉。

The hindrance of restlessness: there are three kinds of restlessness. These include a restless body, a restless mouth, and a restless mind. A restless body likes to wander around and cannot find comfort while sitting or standing. A restless mouth likes to show off, argue, make useless comments, and use worthless secular words. A restless heart lets thoughts wander, sometimes thinking about literature, art, or other distractions; and can potentially develop into bad thoughts.[30]

- 弃「疑盖」者：以疑覆5) 心故，于诸法中，
  不得信心，信心无故，于佛法中，空无所获。
  The hindrance of paranoia: paranoia will hinder the faith in dharma, so even among the dharma the person cannot find faith.[31]

c. Sins of Avarice, Anger, Foolishness, and Arrogance

Zhiyi explained in the *Great Contemplation* that one obsessed with the conventional existence of the world falls into the categories of sin designated as: avarice, anger, foolishness, and arrogance (思假者。谓贪嗔痴慢。).[32]

In the *Tripitaka Methods* (三藏法数) we find compiled interpretations of various terms of the Mahayana Buddhism. It was completed during the Ming dynasty (1368-1644) and gave further explanations about these sins:

一贪使引取之心名为贪。谓于一切物及顺情之境。引取无厌。
是为贪使。二嗔使忿怒之心名为嗔。谓于一切违情之境。
即起忿怒。是为嗔使。三痴使迷惑之心名为痴。
谓于一切事理。无所明了。妄生邪见。起诸邪行。
是为痴使。四慢使自恃轻他之心名为慢。谓由恃己
种姓富贵才能。轻蔑于他。是为慢使。[33]

First, avarice is the desire of wanting more. The person who wants everything to follow his or her will and who take things without temperance commit the sin of avarice. Second, anger is the desire that expresses itself in wrath. One gets angry every time he or she is upset. Third, foolishness involves not

---

[30] Ibid., p. 21
[31] Ibid., p. 22
[32] 智顗,《摩诃止观》第六卷上.
[33] 明沙门释一如等集注，2013，《新编三藏法数》，p. 1257

knowing the truth which generates distorted views and actions. Fourth, arrogance is thinking one is superior to others because of one's own position, wealth, or talents.

2. Religious Practice and Activity of Tiantai Buddhism

The Great Calming and Contemplation (*Mohe zhiguan*) derives from a series of summer lectures by Zhiyi in 594 CE. It was Guanding, a disciple of Zhiyi, who took notes on those lectures and later edited them into the text available today.[34] The text includes seven chapters. The following extract outlines the preparatory conditions (二十五方便) and ten modes of contemplation (十境), which serve as the instructions for meditation.

Preparations[35]

- The five conditions:
    - keeping the disciplinary code
    - having sufficient clothing and food
    - situating oneself in a quiet place
    - ending one's involvement with worldly affairs
    - acquiring worthy friends
- Suppressing the desires for the five objectives of five senses
- Discarding the five hindrances of craving, anger, sleepiness, restlessness, and doubt
- Regulating diet, sleep, body, breath, and mind
- The practice of aspiration, exertion, mindfulness, discrimination, and concentration of the mind.

Ten modes of contemplation:[36]
- contemplating objects as inconceivable
- arousing compassionate thoughts (*bodhicitta*)
- skillful means for easing one's mind
- the thorough deconstruction of dharmas (freeing oneself of all attachments)
- knowing what penetrates and what obstructs the path
- cultivating the steps to the path
- regulating through auxiliary methods
- knowing the stages
- peace through patient recognition
- avoiding passionate attachment to dharmas

---

[34] Donner, 1976.
[35] Ibid.
[36] Fa Qing, 2010, p. 6.

According to Chinese Buddhism scholar Charles Luk (1898-1978), "The right contemplation which consists of looking into all things that have no reality of their own but are creations due to direct and circumstantial causes."[37] The "things" mentioned here can be our ideas, e.g., our likes and dislikes. Such ideas can lead to prejudice which potentially could blind one's mind or even sow the seed of sin in our minds.

The passage "all things that have no reality of their own are but creations" is part of Tiantai philosophy as well as part of the threefold truth: "all things or dharmas are empty because they are produced through causes and conditions and therefore have no self-nature, but they do have tentative or provisional existence."[38]

II. SIN AND RELIGIOUS PRACTICE IN MEDIEVAL CHRISTIANITY/CATHOLICISM

1. Brief Introduction of Christian Moral Philosophy/Theology

Christian theology is an expansive topic beyond the scope of this paper; however, the following provides a brief discussion of concepts of "original sin" and the sins of pride, greed, and lust which are among the cardinal sins of Roman Catholic theology.

a. Original Sin

The doctrine of original sin (ancestral sin) is derived from the story of Adam and Eve's rebellion in the Garden of Eden—eating the forbidden fruit after being seduced by the serpent as presented in the *Book of Genesis*, chapter 3. It is worth noting that neither the word "sin" nor the concept of "original sin" appears in the story in *Genesis* or anywhere in the Jewish Bible. The narrative form of crime and punishment is told in two parts: the transgression and the punishment.[39]

As quoted by John Toews, Old Testament scholar Mark Biddle believes the transgression occurred when Adam and Eve chose to mistrust and disobey God. Power, they thought, that would make them wise. They defied God's words.[40] For the first time in Christian thought, Augustine of Hippo uses the phrase "original sin" (*Originale peccatum*), which is found in his book *First Question: Romans*.[41]

The Catechism of the Catholic Church states that everyone has original sin, but this is not a personal fault but as the results of being Adam's descendant. "It is a deprivation of original holiness and justice, but human nature has not been totally corrupted: it is wounded in the natural powers

---

[37] Luk, 1964, p. 131.
[38] Chan, 1999, p. 444.

[39] Toews, 2013, p. 4.
[40] Ibid., p. 6

[41] Ibid.

proper to it, subject to ignorance, suffering and the dominion of death, and inclined to sin—an inclination to evil that is called 'concupiscence.'"[42]

Original sin is not an evil crime committed before the birth of a human being but the separation from holiness, like the rebellion of children disobeying their parents and instead following their own rules. A similar context of discussion of original sin is that Adam's sin in the Garden of Eden was the violation of the law.[43]

St. Augustine in mid-390s and early 400s asserted that "God imputes the sin of Adam immediately to all his posterity, in virtue of that organic unity of mankind by which the whole race at the time of Adam's transgression existed, not individually, but seminally, in him as its head. The total life of humanity was then in Adam: the race yet had its being only in him. In Adam's free act, the will of the race revolted from God and the nature of the race was wounded."[44]

b. Cardinal vices

In Christian tradition, the idea of vice was of monastic origin before it was applied to the faithful life of the lay community. The names and number of vices are varied according to different authors. However, the constants outnumber the differences.[45] According to the scholar Scott Sullender, Christian writers have attempted to classify the vices since the 2nd and 3rd centuries CE. The list grew out of the experience of the Christian community, and it was used as a spiritual guide for priests to understand God's will and human nature and to help the faithful. Regardless of the variety and gravity of sins, Christian authors came to believe that seven were the worst and the root of others: pride, greed, envy, wrath, sloth, gluttony, and lust, which are now referred to as the Seven Deadly Sins.[46]

The following will focus on the vices of pride, greed, and lust which will facilitate a comparison of the two religions.

• VICE OF PRIDE

Some say that the sin of pride is the root of all evils, which is plausible in the context of the Bible, according to the book of *Ecclesiastes* 10:12: "The beginning of pride is when one departeth from God, and his heart is turned away from his Maker." This has led theologians to deliberate on the first sin as recounted in the *Book of Genesis* whereby Adam and Eve felt ashamed and hid from God in the Garden of Eden after they ate the forbidden fruit.[47]

---

[42] Catechism, Pt. I, 1994, p. 405.

[43] Strong, 1907, p. 533f.

[44] Ibid., p. 619.

[45] Solignac, 1983, vol. 12/1 column, pp. 853-63.

[46] Sullender, 2014, 2015, 64: 217-227.

[47] Bible, Ecclesiastes 10:12, Genesis 3:8, KJV version.

St. Augustine of Hippo (354-430) thinks that pride is the commencement of all sin: "because it was this which overthrew the devil, from whom arose the origin of sin; and afterwards, when his malice and envy pursued man, who was yet standing in his uprightness, it subverted him in the same way in which he himself fell. The serpent, in fact, utilized the door of pride whereby to tempt Adam and Eve, saying 'Ye shall be as gods.'"[48]

Bishop Fulton Sheen stated that "pride is an inordinate love of one's own excellence, either of body or mind or the unlawful pleasure we derive from thinking we have no superiors."[49] Then he further explains that pride comes in many forms: atheism—denial of dependence on God; intellectual vanity—people thinking they already know everything that one needs to know; superficiality—judging others by their external conditions; snobbery—sneering at inferiors to show superiority; presumptuousness—seeking honors and position beyond one's capacity; exaggerated sensitiveness—incapable of moral improvement because of not being willing to hear one's own faults and vain-glory.[50]

• VICE OF GREED

Saint Augustine gave a detailed explanation of the vice of greed. "Greed is not a defect in the gold that is desired but in the man who loves it perversely by falling from justice which he ought to esteem as incomparably superior to gold; nor is lust a defect in bodies which are beautiful and pleasing: it is a sin in the soul of the one who loves corporal pleasures perversely, that is, by abandoning that temperance which joins us in spiritual and unblemishable union with realities far more beautiful and pleasing; nor is boastfulness a blemish in words of praise: it is a failing in the soul of one who is so perversely in love with other peoples' applause that he despises the voice of his own conscience; nor is pride a vice in the one who delegates power, still less a flaw in the power itself: it is a passion in the soul of the one who loves his own power so perversely as to condemn the authority of one who is still more powerful. In a word, anyone who loves perversely the good of any nature whatsoever and even, perhaps acquires this good makes himself bad by gaining something good and sad by losing something better."[51]

This indicates that the sin of greed is a vice that lures people into losing themselves in their own desires which results in losing their virtue.

Lawrence Cunningham points out that the first three of the Ten Commandments deal with humans' relation with God. The other seven dealt with human relations with each other. Of those, the last two forbid coveting another person's wife or goods. These two commandments are

[48] Warfield, Wallis, & Holmes, 2017, p. 188.   [50] Ibid., p. 38.
[49] Sheen, 1939/2001, p. 37.   [51] Bourke, 1958, p. 235.

the only ones that prohibit an inclination rather than an act. Although "coveting" seems like an innocent envy, it is a rehearsal of action.[52] American philosopher James Ogilvy thinks that "greed is first among the seven deadliest." because "greed turns love into lust, leisure into sloth, hunger into gluttony, honor into pride, righteous indignation into anger, and admiration into envy."[53]

The category of greed not only applies to the action of taking more than one needs, like overeating or excessive drinking, it also addresses people's psychological desire to want more than they deserve.[54]

- VICE OF LUST

Cunningham points out that St. Thomas Aquinas (1225-1274) discussed lust in nineteen places in the *Summa Theologiae*. He summarizes Aquinas's idea that lust begins with "looking," next mulling over, then enjoyment, internal consent, and, finally, the action. Cunningham, on the other hand, believes lust is internal and erupts into lustful activity when occasion affords.[55] Cunningham thinks that Christian moralists tend to think of lust as reflecting animal instincts. He argues that this sin is viewed as the least sinful among the cardinal vices. For "Jesus is less condemnatory relative to public sinners, such as prostitutes, than he is with religious hypocrites." Besides, it is "a twisting of a base instinct, and typically free of the cold intellectual calculation of other sins."[56]

Fr. Joseph Francis Delany (1866-1943) thought that lust is a capital sin because it leads men to commit other evils in pursuit of it. Theologians distinguish different forms of lust, such as adultery and abduction.[57] Sullender gives a vivid example to understand the cardinal vices. The capital sins are seven trees. "The trunk of one tree is lust, and the branches that spring forth on the trunk are the various sinful manifestations of lust, i.e., adultery, fornication. . . ."[58]

To recognize these cardinal vices is a major step in the process knowing oneself and in realizing the need for redemption. In many cases, people must be tormented by their own vices and want to change before they seek help from outside. Understanding their own vices could be the first step in the process of reforming their lives.

2. Pope Gregory I's Teachings on Sin

Recent scholars have reexamined Pope Gregory I's teaching about sin in his *Morals on Job* and other works. This paper will next focus on the

---

[52] Cunningham, 2012, p. 33-34.
[53] Solomon, p. 87.
[54] Sheen, 1939/2001 p. 82.
[55] Cunningham, 2012, p. 26.

[56] Ibid., p. 25.
[57] Delany, 1913, Vol. 9.
[58] Sullender, 2014/2015.

following three topics: evil in disguise, ignorance, and a new classification of vice.

- EVIL IN DISGUISE

As G.R. Evans explains, Gregory sums up the essence of Augustine's thought that good men love the truth. Thus, they want their thoughts and actions to synchronize with God's truth. However, good men do not present themselves as they really are for their goodness is God's gift, and they do not want to take the credit falsely.[59]

In contrast with that, evil is full of twists and deceptions, just like how vices can pretend to be virtues. Thus, wicked men present a deceiving appearance. In addition, they become defensive when their carefully constructed disguise is threatened by a deep search within. Gregory sees these men as an example to people who are striving to be good and to help them identify what they must avoid. Good men are made happy by the good they do for their fellow creatures rather than for themselves.[60]

Therefore, when good men are in authoritative positions, they do not take pleasure in overpowering their fellow creatures but to see themselves as shepherds tending flocks. This is how Gregory conceived how good men will govern. Good men can remain close to the sacred and retain their goodness despite living among wicked men.[61]

- IGNORANCE

Gregory considered ignorance as one of the factors that distinguishes people in the secular life and in the afterlife in heaven. "Our peace begins in longing for the Creator, but it is perfected by the clear vision [of him]. Indeed, it will then be perfect when the mind is not blinded by ignorance."[62] Gregory also said that the saints "are not ignorant, either of God's will, or of those things which shall be." However, Gregory did not expand on his idea that people's ignorance will vanish when they reach heaven.[63] In this context, ignorance includes two parts: not knowing God's will and not seeing things as they should be. The theologian Reinhold Niebuhr (1915-1966) responded to this situation with the serenity prayer, "God grant me the serenity to accept the things I cannot change / the courage to change the things I can / and the wisdom to know the difference ... Trusting that You will make all things right if I surrender to Your will; so that I may be reasonably happy in this life and supremely happy with You forever in the next."[64]

---

[59] Evans, 1986/1988, p. 71-72.
[60] Ibid., p. 72.
[61] Ibid., p. 72-73

[62] Mcclain, 1956, p. 56.
[63] Ibid.
[64] Cunningham, 2012, p. 31.

- A NEW CLASSIFICATION OF VICE

The French theologian Aimé Solignac thinks that, under Augustine's influence, Gregory introduced a new classification of vice. "He set pride apart as the root of all evil and made the seven main vices as its offspring." Gregory modified John Cassian's (360-435) order of the eight general "thoughts": gluttony, fornication, avarice, *tristitia* (sadness), anger, acedia (sloth), vain glory, and pride. He began with such subtle moral vices because he was addressing common people rather than the monastic community.[65]

3. Christian Religious Practice and Activity

- BAPTISM

Baptism is the fundamental experience in Christianity. "The rite of admission into the Christian church, practiced by all denominations. Its origin is probably to be sought in (i) the Jewish practice of baptizing proselytes; and (ii) the baptism administered by John the Baptist of the forgiveness of sins."[66] In the Gospel (Mark, 1:2-8), John is the messenger from God who baptized people with water to help people prepare to let God into their lives, so that later God can baptize them in the Holy Spirit.[67]

According to *The Oxford Dictionary of World Religions*, the doctrine of baptism in the early church varied. For example, it might symbolize washing away of sins, dying with Christ, rebirth, or the gift of the Holy Spirit. Baptism theology became more settled in the 3rd and 4th century, especially in St. Augustine's writings. Infant baptism became the norm together with the theology of original sin. The earlier common practice of baptism on one's deathbed was replaced by infant baptism.[68]

The *Catholic Encyclopedia* defines baptism as the sacrament of regeneration by water. St. Thomas Aquinas (1225-1274) thought that "baptism is the external ablution of the body, performed with the prescribed form of words." The term of "regeneration" distinguishes baptism from every other sacrament because although penance revivifies men spiritually this is rather a resuscitation—a bringing back from the dead, rather than a rebirth. Penance does not make people Christians; on the contrary, it presumes that people have already been born of water and the Holy Spirit to a life of grace. However, baptism was instituted to confer upon men the beginning of the spiritual life, to transform people from being enemies of God to the state of adoption, as children of God.[69]

---

[65] Solignac, vol. 12/1 column, pp. 853-863.
[66] Bowker, 1999, p. 125.
[67] *Bible*, Book of Mark, 1:2-8 KJV version
[68] Bowker, 1999, p. 125.
[69] Hudleston, & Herbermann, 1909, p. 250.

• CONTEMPLATION

The Benedictine medieval scholar Jean Leclercq (1911-1993) suggests that the novelty Gregory brought to contemplative prayer in medieval western Christianity was based on his religious experiences and reflects his character and life circumstances. Gregory carefully analyzed his own state of mind. He understood human misery from his own infirmities which he thought not only resulted from original sin but also from weakness and temptation in the context of spiritual progress.[70] This leads to questions like: what is contemplative prayer and how does it relate to contemplation? Dom Cuthbert Butler (1858-1934), a Benedictine monk from England, clarified that by quoting John Cassian's teaching: contemplative prayer is "the kind of prayer in which or by which contemplation is exercised. Vocal prayer may be contemplative, and this is whether it be private vocal prayer or the public prayer of the Divine Office."[71] He further explained it by quoting from French scholar Père Ludovic de Besse (1831-1910):

Meditation carefully practiced leads on to affective prayer. This in its turn leads just as surely to the 'prayer of faith.' The grace of prayer generally terminates here, for it has reached the degree of ordinary perfection. Beyond that point prayer becomes extraordinary. When a soul is drawn to the prayer of faith, the Holy Spirit inspires no special idea in the intellect and excites no emotion in the senses. He goes directly to the will and attracts it, revealing His presence to the soul by the light of faith directed towards the highest point of the intelligence, without stirring up the imagination or the lower faculties. Feeling itself thus near to God, the will keenly perceives the need of loving Him, and of entire self-abandonment into His hands.[72]

Butler explains how Gregory believed that an active and contemplative life is appropriate for training to be preachers. Good preachers should not wholly leave one life for the other. All pastors must fulfill both lives. "The ruler (he who has the cure of souls) should be close to all by compassion but hung above all by contemplation."[73]

Furthermore, Gregory introduced different concepts of the meaning of self-observation. He divided the proximate preparation stage for contemplation into two parts: recollection and introversion. Recollection, he said, occurs when the mind recollects itself; "gathers itself to itself (se ad se colligit)." He describes introversion, the second step: "it should see itself as it is when recollected." This means that one should "turn its eyes inwards

---

[70] Leclercq, 1953, 2/2 column, p. 1933.
[71] Butler, 1922, p. 217.
[72] Butler, 1922, p. xvi.
[73] Ibid, p. 68.

upon itself and consider itself thus stripped of sense perceptions and free from bodily images. In this way the soul 'makes of itself a ladder for itself' (*sibi de seipsa gradus ascensionis facit*)."[74] Butler's summarizes Gregory's vision saying it was a "striking passage of the kind have been adduced from St Augustine, wherein is described under the act of introversion the soul's search to find God within itself, a search which for St. Augustine appears to have been a process predominantly intellectual but culminating in a fully religious experience."[75]

Additionally, Butler extracts Gregory's idea that there are two lives in which God instructs people with His holy word: the active life—such as giving bread to the hungry, teaching the ignorant the word of wisdom and tending the sick, and the contemplative life—such as retaining the love of God and neighbor while refraining from exterior action and cleaving only to the desire for the Maker.[76]

Analysis and Comparison

A. EVIL, VICE, AND SIN

To begin, it is necessary to clarify the terms in the two religions. When talking about sin, the words for vice and evil are often used interchangeably. In Christianity, the French priest Aimé Solignac (1917-2007) explains that capital sins are not sins as this word implies, meaning a conscious and voluntary action, but are tendencies that lead to evil. It was first called "thoughts in the pejorative meaning of *logismos* (thought), equivalent of *yeṣer hara'* (the evil inclination) of Judaism, 'spirits' of demonic origin, or simply 'vices.'"[77] The term 'sins' prevailed by the 13th century because these tendencies are often habits associated with conscious guilt and because they lead to truly sinful acts. Then he further points out that it was "Evagrius Ponticus (346-399) who suggested this point and Hugh of St. Victor (died 1142) who made the decisive precisions."[78]

Is there the actual concept of sin in Chinese Buddhism? Barbara O'Brien says, "Buddhism has no concept of sin; therefore, redemption and forgiveness in the Christian sense are meaningless in Buddhism."[79] Then, she uses the standard definition for sin such as "estrangement from God, an act that is regarded by theologians as a transgression of God's will and violates a law of God or a moral law."[80] She continues to argue that "the precepts are not approached as laws but as disciplines for training."[81]

Buddhism also has a doctrine of heaven and hell. However, the terms are different. Heaven is called "Pure Land (极乐世界)," where people can be with Buddha forever. As for hell, in Ksitigarbha Bodhisattva Fundamen-

---

[74] Ibid, p. 69.
[75] Ibid.
[76] Butler, 1922, pp. 171-172.
[77] Solignac, 1983, vol. 12/1 column, pp. 853-63.

[78] Ibid.
[79] O'Brien, 2014.
[80] Ibid.
[81] Ibid.

tal Vow Sutra (地藏菩萨本愿经), the ghost king named No Poison (Vandana无毒) replied to a holy woman that "since people did not perform many virtuous deeds while alive, their negative karma is guiding them into the various hells."[82] This sutra vividly describes the numerous hells and provides great detail on how people suffer there. People are sent to various hells depending on the nature of their evil deeds. The account continues with a description of the power of evil deeds.

业力甚大, 能敌须弥, 能深巨海, 能障圣道。[83]

The power of the sentient beings' negative karma is truly enormous. It rivals the size of Mount Sumeru. It can encompass the great ocean. It can even obstruct the paths to liberation.[84]

In this case, negative karma results from wrongdoings. In other words, wicked deeds block the path to salvation. The example would be an imprisoned thief. The thief is not just in prison because there is a law prohibiting people from stealing, more importantly, it is that person's actual action that leads to his or her imprisonment. Thus, the answer is that the concept of sin in Chinese Buddhism does exist, however, it is less direct when compared to Catholicism.

Neal A. Donner from the University of British Columbia defines evil "as the opposite of the Six Perfections: avarice, immorality, anger, laziness, mental distraction, and stupidity [foolishness]." The Six Perfections include generosity, morality, forbearance, exertion, meditation, and wisdom. Then he further points out that "stupidity [foolishness] from the Buddhist perspective, and pride and envy on the Christian side" do not correspond.[85] In order to reach an interreligious dialogue, this paper will recount the sins that impede humans' path to salvation.

B. Sin from Outside and Inside

Tiantai Buddhism stipulates that sins prevent people from reaching Pure Land and the sources of these sins come within and without. The five desires (eyes, ears, tongue, smell, and body touch) come from the five senses. The five hindrances (desire, anger, slumber, restlessness, and paranoia) come from within. Arrogance and foolishness are also considered to be sins. The purpose of making these distinctions is to recognize these sins when the mind or body becomes inclined towards one of them or a person has committed a given sin. The wisdom of contemplation helps free people from sins and so they may reach salvation.

For Zhiyi, understanding the five senses and five hinderances is necessary to prepare for contemplation. Pope Gregory also believed that

---

[82] Yu, 2005.

[83] 《地藏菩萨本愿经》, 实叉难陀译, 第13卷

[84] Yu, 2005.

[85] Donner, 1987.

the five senses were important. As Butler quotes in Homilies on Ezechiel (II. V.), Gregory believed that maintaining control of the five senses is crucial in the process of spiritual training: "It [Preparation] must first have learned to shut out from its eyes all the phantasmata of earthly and heavenly images, and to spurn and tread underfoot whatever presents itself to its thought from sight, from hearing, from smell, from bodily touch or taste, so that it may seek itself interiorly as it is without these sensations."[86] This correlates with Zhiyi's teaching about sins that originates from the outside world—the five desires.

C. Differences in Cardinal Sins

Apart from the sins coming from outside, vices like pride and greed come from within. A significant difference between the sin of pride in Buddhism and Christianity is that, according to Augustine, pride is the source of all evil. Pride refers not only to a feeling of superiority to others (which is hinted at in Tiantai Buddhism), but it also shows the folly of a human being trying to be like God instead of humbling oneself before a higher Power.

The concept of the sin of greed is different in the two religions. Tiantai Buddhism treats the five desires as a dangerous path towards hell; thus, people should shun these detrimental influences. Avarice is the desire of wanting more without the limits set by temperance. It is not restricted to the material world; it also could be the desire of a person forcing the world around him or her to submit his or her will. The sin of greed in Christianity is that people lose themselves in selfish desires and neglect the spiritual realm. Tiantai Buddhism's view the sin of lust—as a desire for sounds, forms, fragrances and touchables—as sins that originate from outside, and it preaches that people must reject such sins in their early stages before one gets seduced by evil thoughts.

On the contrary, Catholicism outlines the sin of lust in greater detail. It sees the actual action of committing the sin of lust as an external sin. However, lustful thoughts are treated as internal sins. This distinction is made to teach people that one should not only mind their actions, but more importantly, to be cautious about controlling their thoughts.

Furthermore, in Catholicism, "sloth is a malady of the will which cause us to neglect our duties."[87] It can be physical and spiritual. It is physical when it shows itself in laziness, procrastination, idleness, softness, and indifference. It is spiritual, when it is manifested as indifference to personal improvement, a distaste for the spiritual, and a reluctance or failure to cultivate new virtues.[88]

---

[86] Butler, 1922/1926, p. 69.
[87] Sheen, 1939/2001, p. 37.   [88] Ibid., p. 37-38.

Tiantai Buddhism categorizes the sin of sloth among the physical form. There are two sins that might lead to sloth. The sin of foolishness (the holding of distorted views due to not knowing the truth) can make people think that they are correct and do not require further effort or understanding. The other is the sin of arrogance (thinking one is superior to others) which can also lead to the sin of sloth.

D. Contemplation

Butler explains how Gregory believed that an active and contemplative life is appropriate for training to be preachers. Good preachers should neither wholly leave one life for the other. All pastors must fulfill both lives. "The ruler (he who has the cure of souls) should be close to all by compassion but hung above all by contemplation."[89] Therefore, he can accept the weakness of others by exercising the kindness inside of himself. He may also transcend himself in seeking things that are imperceptible by the loftiness of speculation. In this case, he will neither despise the weakness of his neighbors nor give up climbing the heights by adapting himself to their infirmities.[90] The teaching of contemplation in medieval Catholicism provided a sophisticated guide for the priest or pastor including instructions on how to balance an active life.

Contemplation, in both religions, is conducted in private seclusion. They both also emphasize compassion, caring for others. Tiantai Buddhism targets its message to everyone who wants to practice contemplation. Emphasizing it as a way of self-cultivation. It encourages people to practice contemplation throughout their daily lives.

Surprisingly, Gregory's prescription of how preachers should conduct themselves coincides with the theory of Threefold Truth in Tiantai Buddhism. Gregory's model of active life and contemplative life corresponds with the worldly truth and sacred truth of Buddhism. But it is not enough to answer all the questions. Therefore, there is a "Middle Path" that includes God's truth and secular truth.

In Catholicism, contemplative prayer is the process of being with God when one is alone and in a quiet place. The idea of finding God within oneself shares characteristics with the concept of the nature of Buddha in the Northern and Southern dynasties. Modern Chinese scholar Wang Zhimei noted that after the popularity of the Nirvana Sutra (涅槃经) in China many practitioners reflected on the nature of Buddha. It was believed that every sentient being could reach the ultimate truth (*nirvana*).[91]

In Christianity, only a human being can reach the truth; this is accomplished through contemplation and finding God within oneself. In Tiantai

---

[89] Butler, 1922/1926, p. 177.
[90] Ibid.
[91] 王志楣, 2012.

Buddhism all sentient beings have the potential to reach salvation. Zhiyi also pointed out that the nature of Buddha also contains evil, which adds to the uniqueness of Tiantai Buddhism. He believed that distress leads to enlightenment, and reaching nirvana is to surpass life and death (烦恼即菩提，生死即涅槃).[92] To observe and overcome greed is to reach *bodhi* (贪欲即是道).[93]

Such an idea is subtly supported by the following questions posed by Gregory. "If a man is not grieved there (in heaven) by any memory of his past sins, how does he rejoice in himself at having been freed therefrom? . . . And if he does not remember the past miseries, whence does he bestow praise for the mercies showed upon him?"[94] Gregory answered that people often recall sad things when they are happy such as when they were in good health without pain, they remember past pains. Thus, there will be memories of past sins, but that brings us closer to joy. Like a patient remembering past physical pain learns to cherish health more and knows that he or she has escaped evil.[95]

Conclusion

This paper first introduced the life of Great Master Zhiyi of Tiantai Buddhism and Pope Gregory the Great of Rome of Medieval Catholicism. After the brief overview of Tiantai philosophy on Threefold Truth, it presented the teachings of Zhiyi on sin: the sins of the five senses and five hindrances as presented in the text of *The Essentials for Practicing Calming-and-Insight and Dhyana Meditation* (*Xiao Zhiguan*). This study serves as a manual for the practice of contemplation in Tiantai Buddhism, the core of which is based on the *zhiguan* method to eliminate discrimination through the practice of contemplation.

The above sections were followed by an introduction to Christian moral theology of the medieval era with the focus on pride, greed, and lust, among the seven cardinal sins. This paper further demonstrated the theological scholarship of Gregory the Great who wrote on the topic of sin. His principal points include evil in disguise, ignorance, and a new classification of sin. Next, this paper discussed the religious practices of baptism and contemplation in medieval Catholicism. The practice of baptism was given the new meaning of regeneration during 3rd and 4th centuries. Pope Gregory stipulated that a contemplative life is crucial for pastors and should not be separated from the active life.

This paper concluded that Buddhism also has the concept of sin, and it emphasizes that everyone is responsible for his or her actions. However, there is a difference regarding the cardinal sins in two religions. The sin of

---

[92] 智顗，《妙法莲华经玄义》卷33.
[93] 智顗，《摩诃止观》卷二，大正藏46卷，第18页.

[94] Mcclain, 1956, p. 62.
[95] Ibid., pp. 62-63.

pride not only means arrogance, but in medieval Catholicism it also means not humbling oneself before God. In Buddhism and Christianity, the sin of greed indicates the avarice for money or other material things, yet in Tiantai Buddhism it also includes forcing people to follow one's will as a sin. Lust is considered a sin in both religions. The difference is that Tiantai Buddhism counts lust in the category of sins of the five senses, and thus people should immediately disassociate oneself from the source. In medieval Catholicism, the sin of lust has two forms: internal and external—lust in one's mind and in action.

Zhiyi and Gregory the Great both agree that the sins of the five senses (sight, hearing, taste, smell, and touch) are sins from outside which people should avoid at the preliminary stage of contemplation. He also taught that compassion is crucial for contemplation. Contemplation in Tiantai Buddhism encourages everyone to practice the contemplative life. Christianity directs its pastors to balance the contemplative life and active life and to search for God within themselves and serve the community with kindness.

Doubtlessly, there are differences between the two religions, yet there are more resemblances than might initially appear. As an example, Scott Sullender discussed one female patient who was suffering from depression. Her therapist revealed that she spends a lot of time in sessions of self-evaluation, constantly scanning her peers and measuring herself in many ways. Sullender thinks sin of envy accounts for her action of constantly competing with others.[96] If this patient had recognized this as her problem and followed the preaching of Tiantai Buddhism, she would have understood that material things are empty because they only have tentative existence. Therefore, there is no need to compare herself with her peers.

Finally, this paper hopes to help people from different religious backgrounds to understand each other by comparison. It calls for readers to set aside prejudice and preconceptions and see the possibility of people from different religious backgrounds cooperating to help humankind reach salvation.

Bibliography – Primary Sources

BIBLE, Book of Ecclesiastes 10:12, KJV version [on-line]. https://www.kingjamesbibleonline.org/Ecclesiastes-Chapter-10/

BIBLE, Book of Genesis 3:8, KJV version [on-line]. https://www.king james-bibleonline.org/Genesis-Chapter-3/

---

[96] Sullender, 2014/2015, p. 226.

BIBLE, *Gospel of Mark* 1:2-8 KJV version [on-line]. https://www.kingjames-bibleonline.org/Mark-Chapter-1/

CHEGWAN. *T'ien-T'ai Buddhism: An outline of the fourfold teachings.* (D. Chappell, Trans.). Honolulu, HI: University of Hawaii Press, 1983.

FA, QING (2010). *Tiantai meditation system in Mohe Zhiguan: The ten modes of contemplation.* 6th Bi-Annual International Conference, Buddhist Meditation: Texts, Tradition and Practice. Somaiya Vidyavihar University, Mumbai, India, from 3rd to 5th September 2010.

GREGORY THE GREAT. *The book of pastoral rule.* (G. Demacopoulos, Trans.). New York: St. Vladimir's Seminary Press, 2007.

ST. AUGUSTINE OF HIPPO. *City of God.* (V. Bourke, Ed.). New York: Doubleday Religion, 1958.

ST. AUGUSTINE OF HIPPO. *The anti-Pelagian writings.* (P. Schaff, Ed.; B. Warfield, R. Wallis, & P. Holmes, Trans.). Augsburg, Germany: Jazzybee Publishing, 2017.

YU, J. (Trans.) (2005). *Ksitigarbha Bodhisattva fundamental vow sutra* [on-line]. http://www.buddhism.org/Sutras/2/ksitigarbha_sutra.htm

ZHIYI. *The essentials for practicing calming-and-insight & dhyana meditation.* (B. Dharmamitra, Trans.). Seattle, WA: Kalavinka Press, 2008.

《地藏菩萨本愿经》，实叉难陀译，第13卷

龙树,《中论》,姚秦鸠摩罗什译，青目释"观四谛品"，《大正藏》卷30

智顗，《观心论》大正藏46卷

智顗，《妙法莲华经玄义》卷33

智顗，《摩诃止观》卷二，大正藏46卷

智顗,《摩诃止观》第6卷上

智顗,《天台小止观修订版》，慧辨记录，慧岳注释，(1976).

Bibliography – Secondary Sources

BOWKER, J. (1999). *The Oxford dictionary of world religions.* Oxford: Oxford University Press.

BUTLER, D. (1922). *Western mysticism.* New York: Harper & Row Press.

CATHOLIC CHURCH (1994). *Catechism of the Catholic Church.* Washington, DC: United States Catholic Conference Press.

CHAN, WING-TSIT (1999). *Sources of Chinese tradition: Volume 1: From earliest times to 1600.* New York: Columbia University Press.

CRAWFORD, R. (2002). *What is religion?* New York: Routledge Press.

CUNNINGHAM, L. (2012). *The seven deadly sins: A visitor's guide.* Indiana: Ave Maria Press.

DELANY, J. (1913). Lust, *Catholic Encyclopedia, Vol. 9.* New York: The Encyclopedia Press [on-line]. https://en.wiki source.org/wiki/Catholic_Encyclopedia_(1913)/Lust.

DEMACOPOULOS, G. (2015). *Gregory the Great: Ascetic, pastor, and first man of*

Rome. Indiana: University of Notre Dame Press.

DONNER, N. (1987). Zhiyi's meditation on evil. In D. Chappell (Ed.), *Buddhist and Taoist Practice in Medieval Chinese Society, Buddhist and Taoist Studies 2*. Honolulu: University of Hawaii Press.

EVANS, G. (1986/1988). *The thought of Gregory the Great*. New York: Cambridge University Press.

HUDLESTON, G. & HERBERMANN, C. (Eds.) (1909). *The Catholic Encyclopedia, Vol. VI*. New York: Robert Appleton Company.

INGRAM, P., & STRENG, F. (Eds.) (1986). *Buddhist-Christian dialogue: Mutual renewal and rransformation*. Honolulu, HI: University of Hawaii Press.

LECLERCQ, J. (1953). Contemplation occidentale, *Dictionnaire de Spiritualité*, 2/2 column, p. 1933. (L.E. Frizzell, Trans.). Paris: Beauchesne.

LI, SILONG 李四龙 (2001). Zhiyi's academic analysis of "The harmony of the three noble truths" [《智顗"三谛圆融"的学术分析》]. In *Religious Studies*, Issue 2: 74.

MCCLAIN, J. (1956). *The doctrine of heaven in the writings of Saint Gregory the Great*. Washington, DC: The Catholic University of America Press.

MING, SHAMEN 明沙门, SHI, YIRU 释一如 ET AL. (2013). Newly compiled Tripitaka 《新编三藏法数》, p. 1257.

O'BRIEN, B. (2014 October 29). Sins and Buddhism. ThoughtCo.com. thoughtco.com/sins-and-buddhism-3976932.

PAN, GUIMING (1996). *A critical biography of Zhiyi*. Nanjing, China: Nanjing University Press.

SHEEN, F. (1939/2001). *The seven capital sins*. New York: Alba House Press.

SOLIGNAC, A. (1983). Péchés capitaux. *Dictionnaire de Spiritualité, 12*(1), column p. 853-63. (L.E. Frizzell, Trans.). Paris: Beauchesne.

SOLOMON, R. (Ed.) (1999). *Wicked pleasure: Meditations on the seven deadly sins*. Lanham, MD: Rowman & Littlefield.

STRONG, A. (1907). *Systematic theology*. Philadelphia: Judson.

SULLENDER, S. (2014 April). The seven deadly sins as a pastoral diagnostic system. *Pastoral Psychol 64*(2): 217-227.

SWANSON, P. (1989). *Foundations of T'ien-t'ai philosophy: The flowering of the two truths theory in Chinese Buddhism*. Berkely, CA: Asian Humanities Press.

TOEWS, J. (2013). *The story of original sin*. Eugene, OR: Pickwick Publications.

WANG, ZHIMEI 王志楣 (2012). 《智顗与吉藏佛性论之思维方式比较》 [Comparison of thinking modes between Zhiyi and Jizang's theory of Buddha Nature], *Philosophical Analysis, 3*(4).

宋大文學家洪邁著

The Record of the Listener by Hong Mai

1911 lithograph Shanghai Liguang Society

夷堅志

上海黎光社藏版

Chapter 9

Curing Disease and Praying for Rain:
Two Neglected Social Functions
of Song Dynasty Shamans

by Xiang Wei

Introduction

In Chinese, the term for a shaman is *wu* 巫, which means "priest." There are records of this ancient priesthood dating back to the Neolithic era. Shamanism continued in China until the fall of the Qing empire in the early twentieth century. During the Song dynasty (960-1279), Emperor Taizu (927-976) attempted to eliminate shamanism in China. The Song court dismantled the governmental agencies that handled divination and terminated state-employed shamans. Even though shamanism was reduced to an informal religion at the start of the Song dynasty, shamanism survived, especially in Song folk communities. Shamans continued to perform societal functions like exorcisms and divination. Two of these tasks, in particular, were especially important and are frequently overlooked by modern scholars: healing and praying for rain. What methods did the shamans use to heal people and what rituals did they perform to pray for rain? Why did shamans continue to practice medicine despite the fact that relatively advanced medical care was available during the Song dynasty?

This paper will use *The Record of the Listener* 夷坚志, a collection of folktales written by Hong Mai 洪迈 (1123-1202) during the Song dynasty, as a primary source. Hong Mai's book compiled a comprehensive collection of folktales from the Song dynasty with a specific emphasis on stories concerning shamans. Through these records, we will address the above questions and reconstruct the environment in which the folk shamans lived and the dangers they faced by practicing their profession during the Song dynasty.

This paper is divided into two parts. The first part addresses how shamans treated diseases and how people believed in shamanic healing. Shamans, in contrast to traditional Chinese medicine which uses medicines and acupuncture to treat illnesses, frequently used magic and religious ceremonies to treat illnesses. By the Song dynasty, the government had begun to oppose the practice of medicine by shamans and implemented regulations against their practices. These restrictions were later repealed.

However, shamanic doctors never completely vanished from society; they continued to treat diseases. The shamans' healing abilities have been recorded in various accounts. This initial section will focus on shamans' treatment of ailments as well as their sorcery and medicines.

In the second section, we will also look at another often-overlooked social purpose of shamans: rain prayer. This section will discuss two little-known shamanic practices, one involving fire and another using lizards to produce rain. While these accounts appear to be mystical stories, they may have been based on real or perceived experiences of these authors.

The major theme of this essay is how shamanism and shamans served the people even though it was a religion banned by the government. Although shamans were distained by the educated class who were immersed in Confucianism, they performed a variety of social duties. Did people intentionally seek out shamans to perform religious rites and those who believed in the spiritual nature of their mysterious powers? We will next examine the clash between folk religion and official court policy in this essay, namely how shamans are accepted and viewed by the general population in the face of government opposition.

SECTION A: CURING DISEASES

According to the research of James George Frazer (1854-1941), shamans were not only the forefathers of medics and surgeons, but they were also early scientists and inventors. As a result, ancient Chinese shamans had a close working connection with physicians. Even though the shaman and the doctor became two separate professions, inviting a shaman to cure illness was still a vital method for those who were afflicted by a disease. Since the Song government placed a strong emphasis on the advancement of medicine, shamans took on the function of doctors in society.[1] The use of shamans to cure diseases became increasingly important when people became afflicted with illnesses. As a result, shamans were frequently called upon to practice medicine during the Song dynasty when more conventional Chinese medical doctors were unable to heal the patient. The story The Great Mercy Shaman in Fuzhou (福州大悲巫) was recorded in *The Record of the Listener*:

> In Fuzhou, there was a shaman who used *huiji* incantations to perform rituals and effectively cure illnesses for people. As a result, he was known as the Great Compassion. A virgin from a normal family became pregnant unexpectedly. Her parents enquired as to the reason, but she had no response. They

---

[1] Wang, 2005, p. 560.

invited the shaman to help them with their daughter's treatment. When the shaman arrived at their home, he noticed a small boy stagger through the door, danced for a long time, and then jumped into the pool. This boy was the son of a wealthy neighbor, and he did not show up again until dusk. Another boy did the same thing the next day.[2] The fathers of these two families attacked the shaman and attempted to have him arrested by the government. "Wait a few seconds for me to finish my magic," said the shaman. "Your sons will show up unscathed."

Many people gathered around the pool to watch. A short time later, thousands of people were heard shouting in the pool, circling it. Two small boys emerged from the pool, and one of them tied a large carp with a rope. Another minor swung at the carp. The carp died when they landed. These two small boys remained calm and had no idea what had occurred. The shaman placed some bottles on the girl's stomach and used a stick to break them. The girl was not pregnant when these bottles broke. The shaman had investigated and concluded that a carp was cause of these difficulties.

巫，能持秽迹咒行法，为人治祟蛊甚验，俗呼为大悲。里民家处女忽怀孕，父母诘其故，初不知所以然。召巫考治之，才至，即有小儿盘辟入门，舞跃良久，径投舍前池中。此儿乃比邻富家子也，迨暮不复出。明日，别一儿又如是，两家之父相聚诟击巫，欲执以送官。巫曰："少缓我，容我尽术，汝子自出矣吗，无伤也。"观者踵至，四绕池边以待，移时，闻若千万人声起于池，众皆辟易。两儿自水中出，一以绳缚大鲤，一从后棰之。曳登岸，鲤已死，两儿扬扬如平常，略无所知觉。巫命累瓶覮于女腹上，举杖悉碎之，已而暴下，孕即失去。[3]

According to myths and stories from the Song, when people were afflicted by odd diseases, they would often prefer to consult shamans than seek conventional medical attention. Furthermore, shamans were not only popular among the common people, they were also consulted by the wealthier people as well, particularly the bureaucratic classes. This is illustrated by the story *Jiu Sheng Qi Gui* (九圣奇鬼).

---

[2] Translation by the author.
[3] Hong, 2006, p. 482.

Xue Jixuan [courtesy name Shilong] was Prime Minister Huiyan's son. In the second year of Longxing (1164 CE), his neighbor, Ms. Shen's mother became ill. Xue Jixuan visited her with his son and two nephews and invited a shaman to heal her and banish ghosts.

薛季宣,字士隆,左司郎中徽言之子也。
隆兴二年秋，比邻沈氏母病。宣[4]

Medicine in China reached a high level of sophistication during the Song dynasty. During the early years of the Song dynasty, for example, Emperor Taizu (927-976) authorized the local government to publish medical texts.[5] Why then did some people continue to believe that shamans could treat sicknesses when conventional doctors could not heal them? On the one hand, the Song dynasty was plagued by calamity after calamity. Even though the government provided medicines to sick individuals, it was unable to eradicate epidemics. When the epidemics became uncontrollable, government officials resorted to praying to the gods. The common people had a long-standing tradition of gathering plants to use in the preparation of medicines to ward off plagues. Take, for example, the *biwen* powder 避瘟丹, which was a treatment that was developed by ordinary people to treat plagues.[6] Although the Song dynasty's court prohibited citizens from engaging shamans and prohibited them from using their remedies, changing this custom proved impossible. Additionally, as a result of the government's and the medical community's inability to efficiently combat illnesses, the populace turned to alternate means such as shamans.

Shamans gained popularity, particularly among those suffering from debilitating diseases.[7] Common people were more likely to understand a shaman's explanation of the sickness and how to treat it compared to the more scientific explanation and practices by professional doctors. For instance, shamans frequently ascribed illness to harassment by ghosts— this was a simple explanation that convinced people that shamans were knowledgeable and capable of treating their diseases. Trained physicians, on the other hand used medical jargon and proposed more technical treatments that the average person did not comprehend, especially when the sickness was rare and serious. When the shaman suggested that he could treat the patient by subduing the ghost the patient's family often accepted the explanation. In one recorded example:

[4] Ibid., p. 364.
[5] Tian, 2017, p. 120.
[6] Wu, 2015, p. 175. The title of this article collection is "A Golden Millet Dream".
[7] Wang, 2005, p. 443.

A girl recently married had returned to her mother's house. When she cleaned her clothes at the well she experienced difficulty breathing. She returned to her husband's house and collapsed. Her family members arranged for her to be cured by a shaman. According to the shaman, the girl agitated the ghost of the female corpse in the well. As a result, the shaman utilized magic to create an image of four people clothed in purple clothing using paper. Subsequently, the shaman lit a light, fashioned a piece of red paper to resemble clothing, then poured wine and prepared food for the ghost's sacrifice. The woman regained consciousness later that night.

数日前，外间民女嫁人，归母家，至井上浣衣，忽闷绝不省。异归婿家，唤巫者治之，曰犯井中伏尸女伤鬼。其法用纸画紫衣四人，持烛笼，剪乾红纸作背子一领，具酒饭烧祭之。闻昨夕事毕，三更后，女病良愈。[8]

Apart from healing patients, shamans also safeguarded mothers during childbirth. Childbirth was often hazardous for woman during the Song dynasty and their family members would frequently seek the assistance of a shaman to keep their pregnant women safe.[9] Shamans employed different techniques to protect pregnant women. Among the most common protocol was to instruct pregnant women to consume rabbit brains. Shamans would put a rabbit's brain in between two pieces of tissue paper and beat the paper thirty to fifty times. When a woman had trouble in the parturition process, the shaman would make a talisman out of these two pieces of paper by drawing the words 'heaven' and 'birth' on them. The pregnant woman then ate the talisman with vinegar soup to ward off potential problems.

取腊月兔脑髓，涂于一张薄纸上，更用一张合拓，槌三五十下。每遇难生，有巫医者书符子，画'天生'两字，以醋汤下，极效。[10]

This identical method was documented in the medical book, *Boji Fang* (Comprehensive and Effective Prescriptions) written in 1047 by Wang Gun. The book contains several shamanist prescriptions. Wang Gun wrote of putting a rabbit's brain on a piece of tissue paper and making a talisman with this paper and writing 'birth' on it. It was specifically mentioned that this prescription should be prepared in January or February.

---

[8] Hong, 2006, p. 1712.
[9] Wang, 2005, p. 202.
[10] Hong, 2006, p. 184.

When the pregnant woman felt that the fetus moved frequently, she should eat the talisman with boiled lilac wine.

用腊月兔头一个，摊于纸上，均剪作符子，
于上面书'生'字一个，觉阵频动时，煎丁香酒调下。[11]

According to these records, people throughout the Song dynasty thought that shamans' talismans and prescriptions were effective in protecting pregnant women. The use of rabbit brains may have been related to rabbits' propensity for reproduction. Imitating animals was a frequent theme of shamanism. Shamanist remedies were often based on the assumption that people would assume some traits of that animal they consumed.[12] Although these ways of safeguarding pregnant women are considered illogical in modern times, the concepts were widespread throughout the Song dynasty. We have no data on whether these treatments succeeded in protecting pregnant women. However, *The Listener's Record* and *Boji Fang* reported the effectiveness of the techniques.

SECTION B: PRAYING FOR RAIN

Because people living in earlier times could not understand the causes of natural calamities that were beyond their control they assumed that a deity governed these events. To communicate with this god or gods, people invented various forms of sorcery (*fashu* 法术) to influence the forces of heaven. Various forms of magic existed throughout the Song dynasty and were associated with shamanism. One of the main practices of shamanism was performing special prayers to make it rain. Shamans occupied a prominent role during the Song dynasty in performing rain prayers.[13]

Setting small fires to pray for rain was a frequent practice among shamans throughout the Song dynasty. *The Record of the Listener* recounted how a shaman used fire to pray for rain.

Because of the severe drought, villagers decided to sacrifice lizards to pray for rain. The shaman rejected this approach and sat down swiftly on the firewood pile. The sun was scorching the following day around noon, and a large crowd gathered to watch him. When the fire ignited his beard, however, the heavens began to pour.

即坐积薪上。及明，烈日滋炽，万众族观，至炬以须。
如期，果大雨。[14]

---

[11] Wang, 2006, p. 67.
[12] Ibid., p. 125.
[13] Thompson, 1975, p. 201.
[14] Hong, 2006, p. 65.

The practice of praying for rain by setting fires has a long history in China. People in the ancient world used to sacrifice animals or people as a means to ask heaven for rain. Many bones and tortoise shells have been uncovered that were likely sacrifices in hopes it would satisfy heaven and bring rain. One story tells of a shaman who set himself on fire in order to appeal for rain. The narrative detailed another method of invoking rain: sacrificing lizards.

Sacrificing lizards to make it rain has a long history, much like the use of fire. According to Song Zhaolin's study, the Yangshao Cultural Site has ceramics decorated with frogs and lizards.[15] Furthermore, some bronzes from the Pre-Qin Period decorated with lizards have been discovered in Guangxi Province recently. In ancient times, pottery and bronzes were necessary props for the rain prayer ceremony.[16] This ceremony persisted throughout Song dynasty shamanism. The procedures for this ceremony are also detailed in *The Song's History*:

> The summer of 1068 was quite dry. Thus, the people sacrificed lizards for rain. They grabbed over a dozen lizards and placed them in a container; they then soaked them in leaves. Additionally, they selected twenty-eight males ranging in age from ten to thirteen. The lads were separated into two groups and were attired in green. Green jewels adorn their hands and faces. As they moved around the pot, the lads used willows to sprinkle water. The boys shouted: "Lizards, lizards! You have the ability to create clouds and fog. When it has rained, we will release you."

> 熙宁十四年，以夏旱，内出蜥蜴求雨法。
> 捕捉蜥蜴数十纳甕中，渍以杂木叶。择童男十三岁下，
> 十岁上者二十八人，分两番，衣青衣，以青饰面及手足。
> 人持柳枝沾水散洒，昼夜环绕。诵咒曰：蜥蜴蜥蜴，
> 兴云吐雾。雨令滂沱，令汝归去。

This ritual may have been influenced by Buddhist practices. Specifically, the Buddhist Bodhisattva Guanyin was known to sprinkle water with a willow branch, therefore, the young boys may have been instructed to emulate the Guanyin bodhisattva by also using willow sticks. Instead of using live lizards to pray for rain, some rituals substituted wooden lizards. For example, another custom mentioned in *Xu Bowuzhi* said:

[15] Song, 1987, p. 2.
[16] Ibid., p. 25.

If you want to pray for rain using lizards, you need first build a wood lizard. Little boys dressed in green attire would dance while holding bamboo in their hands and shout: "Lizards, lizards! You can create clouds and fog. We'll allow you back in if it starts raining cats and dogs."

蜥蜴祈雨法，作木蜥蜴，小童操青竹，衣青衣以舞。歌曰：'蜥蜴蜥蜴，吞云吐雾，雨令滂沱，令汝归去。

This ritual was recorded in which the boys circled a wood lizard with bamboo sticks in their hands, according to the observer's notes. Even though these methods were distinct from the previous record, they were both parts of a ceremony in which lizards were used to pray for rain. Why did people use lizards to beg for rain? Some lizards live in both water and land at different periods. Lizards can be seen on the ground, especially just before it rains. Therefore, ancient humans assumed that citing lizards meant that wet weather was coming.[17]

Conclusion

Although the Song government suppressed shamanism, this ancient practice persisted throughout the Song dynasty. *The Record of the Listener* was the major source documenting numerous folktales concerning shamanism and shamans during the Song dynasty. Hong Mai conducted research for his book for over nearly sixty years and each volume was published as soon as he completed it. As a result, *The Record of the Listener* became popular among modern readers throughout China.

What role did shamanism have in society? We learned from numerous primary and secondary sources that shamanism served three tasks in Song society: treating illnesses, praying for rain, and safeguarding women during the parturition process. Regarding the first function, the author reported that when individuals encountered unusual diseases, they would seek treatment from a shaman. Thus, despite the absurdity of some of their approaches, shamanism enriched Chinese medical history. Shamans also conducted two ancient rain-prayer ceremonies during the Song. Another important function fulfilled by shamans was protecting pregnant women with talismans and other protocols. This paper examined the development of shamanism throughout the Song dynasty. Shamanism evolved and survived in a highly complex context. Under these conditions although shamanism operated under more clandestine conditions it continued to play a vital role in Song society.

---

[17] Song, 1987, p. 3.

Bibliography

CAMPANY, R., & YAN WANG (2012). *Signs from the unseen realm: Buddhist miracle tales from early medieval China.* Honolulu: University of Hawai'i Press.

CAVANAUGH, W. (2009). *The myth of religious violence: Secular ideology and the roots of modern conflict.* Oxford: Oxford University Press.

DAVIS, E. (2001). *Society and the supernatural in Song China.* Honolulu: University of Hawai'i Press.

HONG, MAI (2006). *The record of the listener* (Yijian Zhi). Beijing: Zhonghua Shuju.

INGLIS, A. (2006). *Hong Mai's record of the listener and its Song dynasty context.* Albany, NY: SUNY Press.

KING, R. (1999). *Orientalism and religion: postcolonial theory, India and 'the mystic East'.* London: Routledge.

THOMPSON, L. (1975). *Chinese religion: An introduction.* Belmont, CA: Dickenson Publishing.

TIAN, JIANPING (2017). *Publishing history in the Song dynasty, Vol. 1.* Beijing: People's Press.

NONGBRI, B. (2013). *Before religion: a history of a modern concept.* New Haven: Yale University Press.

MEIR, S., & WELLER, R. (1996). *Unruly gods: Divinity and society in China.* Honolulu: University of Hawai'i Press.

SONG, ZHAOLIN (1987). *The worship of frog and rice agriculture.* Beijing: Zhonghuashuju Press.

THROWER, J. (1999). *Religion: the classical theories.* Edinburgh: Edinburgh University Press.

WANG, GUN (2006). *Boji Fang* (Comprehensive and effective prescriptions). Shanghai: Shanghai Science and Technology Publishing House.

WANG, ZHANGWEI (2005). *Between the state and society* (Zai Guojia Yu Shehui Zhijian). Beijing: Zhonghua Shuju.

WU, ZIMU (2015). 夢梁錄新校注 (Mengliang Luxin's Annotation). Chengdu: Bashu Publishing House.

228 Memorial Museum
Taipei, Taiwan

The February 28 Incident in Taiwan: A Milestone of Taiwan's Foundation for Democracy

by Paofong Cheng

Introduction

After China's Nationalists' party—the Guomintang (KMT)—lost the Chinese Civil War to Mao Zedong and the Chinese Communist Party, they retreated to Taiwan in 1949. Taiwan had been placed under the administrative control of the Republic of China since 1945. After two years, accusations of corruption and a failing economy sparked a local protest that was brutally quashed by the KMT government. The "February 28 Incident" (commonly called the "228 Incident") of 1947 led to nearly four decades of martial law that later became known as the "White Terror." The KMT censored any reference to or discussion of the 228 Incident during this period, and all dissent directed at the KMT and its rule was violently suppressed. However, since the lifting of martial law in 1987, this long-buried history has been discussed and commemorated through a variety of forums including films. This research aims to understand how the 228 Incident became a milestone of Taiwan's foundation of democracy. As Thomas Shadduck, a specialist in Taiwan affairs, has written:

> Though a vibrant and thriving democracy today, the Republic of China (Taiwan) was once a nation plagued with corruption, mass violence, and totalitarian rule. In Taiwan, the period immediately following the 228 Incident is known as the "White Terror" for the massive suppression, murder, and imprisonment of political dissidents, or anyone who the Kuomintang (KMT), known as Nationalists in English, perceived as a threat to its one-party rule. The Martial Law that was implemented in the aftermath of the Incident was not lifted until 1987.[1]

---

[1] Shattuck, 2020.

I. BACKGROUND

Guomintang's Retreat to Taiwan

Taiwan was incorporated as a province of mainland China by the Qing Empire in 1885. Then, under the Treaty of Shimonoseki of 1895 which was signed after Japan defeated China in the First Sino-Japanese War (1894-95), the Qing rulers ceded Formosa (Taiwan) to Japan in perpetuity. Japan ruled Taiwan as a colony until Japan's defeat in World War II in 1945. China's nationalist government, known as the Republic of China (ROC), led by the Guomintang, took control of Taiwan. In 1949, after losing control of mainland China in the Chinese Civil War, the KMT led by Chiang Kai-shek and over two million of his supporters relocated to Taiwan.

The KMT's retreat to Taiwan in 1949 was a lengthy and monumental undertaking that required more than a year with countless freight and air trips.[2]

Welcoming the Dawn of a New Era

Despite the yoke of Japanese colonial rule, the people of Taiwan retained a "motherland complex" (祖國情結) for China. For this reason, the news of Japan's surrender delighted the people of Taiwan, and the whole society welcome the arrival of the Nationalists. Many residents of Taiwan wanted to learn the Mandarin Chinese, mainland China's national language, especially after having been forced to learn Japanese and adopt Japanese culture during Japan's occupation. The Taiwan people warmly greeted the first group of Nationalist soldiers who arrived in Keelung, Taiwan. The national flag of the ROC was displayed everywhere; people lined the road to welcome the Nationalist army's arrival.

Chiang Kai-shek appointed the Governor of Fukien Province, Chen Yi, to be the Chief Executive of the administration of Taiwan. When Chen Yi arrived at Sungshan Airport in Taipei on October 24, 1945, throngs of well-wishers greeted him. The next day he officiated at the opening of the new government office, and he received the formal surrender of Japan's "Chinese Theater of War, Taiwan Province." The surrender documents were presented to Chen Yi by Lt. General Haruki Isayama, the Chief of Staff of Japan's Tenth Front Army who was stationed in Taiwan. Thereafter, October 25 was proclaimed as "Taiwan Retrocession Day." It began a new era for Taiwan.

A Disappointed Return to Rule by the Chinese Motherland

The greater the oppression of the Japanese occupation, the stronger the attachment Taiwan people felt toward the motherland. Ultimately, the

---

[2] Cheung, 2016.

greater the expectation, the more profound the disappointment. The people of Taiwan were naive to think that the representatives from the "motherland" would act and rule more virtuously than the Japanese. Their assumption was also that the culture of the motherland must be more advanced than that of Japan's.

However, when the people saw the Chinese army looking disheveled and wearing shabby uniforms, they were stunned and concerned. Even more disconcerting was the Chinese military's lack of discipline. This shattered the image that the Taiwanese had for the Chinese homeland and the joy of Japan's surrender suddenly became another nightmare. One colonial regime was over, just to be replaced by another colonial regime. The Taiwanese people were treated second-class citizens in the eyes of the new regime.

On the same day that he proclaimed "Taiwan Retrocession Day," Chinese General Ge Jingen gave a speech to the Taiwanese public. He said that the Taiwanese have not yet accepted true Chinese culture[3] and he considered them as second-class citizens. The behavior of the Chinese army scared the residents. Merchants closed their shops and the people stayed indoors.

Mainland China Exploited Formosa

Although World War II had ended in 1945, the civil war between the KMT and the Communist Party had resumed in China. The KMT did not consider Taiwan as an important center of the country's development. Instead, Taiwan became the most important source of logistical supplies for the KMT government. In addition to the outflow of materials, the government transferred funds to the mainland to support the KMT government. The Bank of Taiwan had to continuously print money which resulted in severe inflation in Taiwan after the war and depreciation of the Taiwan dollar. To stem hyperinflation, on June 15, 1949, the KMT replaced the former Taiwan dollar at a rate of 1 New Taiwan dollar for 40,000 of the old Taiwan dollars. The financial plunder carried out by the KMT in Taiwan resulted in a sharp decrease in the wealth of the people, and which wiped out the life savings of many Taiwanese. These policies deepened the Taiwanese people's anger with the KMT.

The new provincial government officials were corrupt; the soldiers lacked discipline and harassed the people, plundering whatever they wished to take. The economy was in ruins, the currency exchange rate in relation to the currency of mainland China was unreasonable, and the price of goods skyrocketed. The corruption and indifference of the Chinese army led to starvation and disease among Chinese POWs who had been held by

---

[3] Zhan, 1918.

the Japanese. As they had no hope of being officially repatriated to the mainland, these former prisoners had to fall back on their own resources and find their own way home. Many died creating further anger and resentment towards the government among returnees and their families.[4]

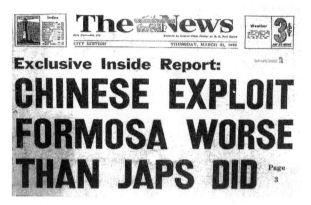

The Washington Daily News on March 21, 1946
Public domain.

II. THE UPRISING AND THE CRACKDOWN

The Cause of the February 28 Incident

There are Chinese sayings:

「不胜其怒」 "Anger is extreme and unbearable"
「人何以堪」 "How can one bear it!"

The KMT had pushed the Taiwanese to their limits and provided the people with reasons to fight for their rights. Their anger needed only a trigger to turn resentment into violence. The "tobacco event" that occurred the day before the 228 Incident provided that trigger.

The Tobacco Monopoly Bureau confiscated the contraband cigarettes that a women named Lin Chiang-mai was selling illegally and they took her money. During the arrest, one agent beat the women on the head with a pistol. A crowd gathered around the agents who attacked the woman and one agent fired into the crowd killing a man named Chen Wen-si. The next day (February 28, 1945, hence the name the "228 Incident"), a crowd of 2,000 Taiwanese occupied the Tobacco Monopoly Bureau to demand justice for the death of Chen Wen-si and compensation for the women's injuries. During the protest, some government offices were vandalized. The protests then spread to other cities in Taiwan to express the people's general resentment toward the Nationalists' rule.

---

[4] Chou, 2015, p. 311.

Violence and unrest continued for a week with the military attempting to keep order. There were many incidents of the army firing upon civilians. Protesters occupied Taiwan's radio station seeking to rally the citizens of the island to resist the government. A Committee of Taiwanese legislators, students, and professionals was formed on March 1, 1945. The Committee submitted a list of thirty-two demands to Chen Yi in which they stipulated that more Taiwanese be represented in the local government and that the people be guaranteed freedom of speech, a free press, and the right to organize, among others.

The incident had a serious impact on the coherence of Taiwanese society and the future development of the island's politics. This tragedy would become deeply rooted in the historical memory of Taiwanese people and Taiwanese society.[5]

Martial Law

「欲加之罪 何患無辭」
"He who has a mind to beat his dog
will easily find a stick."

Not long after the 228 Incident, the KMT government declared martial law which allowed the Nationalist army to enter Taipei to initiate a bloody crackdown, later known as the "White Terror." The suppression lasted four decades in various forms. The military and police conducted manhunts and assaults, including executions, arrests, and caused the disappearance of people who advocated resistance including elites, students, and ordinary citizens. It was not until 1987, when the government lifted the ban, that the 228 Incident became open for discussion. In fact, even now, 73 years later, the event is still under a historical cloud that Taiwan society cannot relinquish.

On March 9, 1947, Chen Yi declared martial law in Taipei and Keelung. The Nationalist army entered Taipei and marched through the streets firing as they went. The sound of gunfire continued all day and citizens were seized and killed. On March 10, Chiang Kai-shek issued a statement about the emergency in Taiwan citing Communist incitement as one of the reasons for the Incident. On the same day, Chen Yi ordered the disbanding of the Resolution Committees for the February 28 Incident and all other "illegal groups." Members of the citizen committees against the crackdown were targeted for liquidation in a campaign of arrests and summary executions.

In July 1987, the government of Taiwan announced the following measures:

---

[5] Memorial Foundation, 2019.

1. Lifting of martial law
2. Guarantees of individual rights
3. Lifting of censorship on news, books, and postal services
4. Greater freedom of movement including to mainland China.[6]

III. TAIWAN MOVES FORWARD
228 INCIDENT:
The First Spark that Ignited the Movement to Taiwanese Democracy

History cannot be forgotten, and a lesson must be learned. The 228 Incident in 1947 led to the imposition of martial law until 1987, ushering in the nearly forty-year reign of White Terror. Despite the government's heavy-handed rule, civil democratic movements such as the "Kaohsiung Formosa Incident" (高雄美麗島事件) continued to rise and fall. The Kaohsiung Formosa Incident, also known as the Meilidao Incident, was a crackdown on pro-democracy demonstrations in Kaohsiung, Taiwan. It took place on December 10, 1979, during Taiwan's martial law period. These incidents fueled the pro-democracy movement and portended the current era of democracy. Taiwan's people did not fully enjoy democratic self-government until the first legislative elections were held in 1992 and the first direct presidential election that occurred in 1996. The Democratic Progressive Party (DPP) formed in 1986 and its candidate, Chen Shui-bian, won the presidential election in 2000 thereby ending the KMT 55-year rule of Taiwan. The KMT returned to power in 2008 when Ma Ying-jeou won the election for president.

The Nationalist government originally announced the Constitution of the Republic of China on January 1, 1947, thereby proclaiming its intention to protect human rights. However, two months after the new constitution was issued, the Taiwanese people experienced a horrific massacre on February 28, which became a stain on the Nationalists' credibility during its initial constitutional period. The gap between the government's claims to protect human rights and its actions in Taiwan made a mockery of its constitution.

In 1987, the 228 Peace Day Promotion Association was established, breaking down the greatest political taboo in Taiwan's post-war history and prompting the government to disclose the truth of the tragic Incident. The hidden agony that had lurked in Taiwanese people's minds was gradually coming to the surface. It has been over 70 years since the outbreak of the February 28 Incident and more than thirty years since the lifting of martial law.[7]

---

[6] Chou, 2015, pp. 322-324.
[7] Memorial Foundation, 2019.

IV. Conclusion

Until democratization, the local majority "Taiwanese" people (about 85% on the island's population) felt oppressed under what they called the "White Terror" of the imposed rule of the KMT and its "mainlander" supporters who fled to Taiwan. Freedom does not fall from the sky. Those victims who sacrificed their lives in 228 or in other incidents sustained Taiwan's march toward democracy. Through the efforts of the generations, the historical tragedy of the 228 Incident has become a precious historical legacy of Taiwan. February 28 is now a national holiday for everyone to remember, honor, and acknowledge this history. The progress of a nation cannot be built on hate. We cannot change history, but we can learn from the lessons to make us wiser and more robust.

Bibliography

SHATTUCK, T. (2017 February 27). Taiwan's white terror: Remembering the 228 Incident. Foreign Policy Research Institute. https://www.fpri.org/article/2017/02/taiwans-white-terror-remembering-228-incident/

CHEUNG, HAN (2016 December 4). Taiwan in time: The great retreat. *Taipei Times* [on-line]. http://www.taipeitimes.com/News/feat/archives/2016/12/04/2003660529/1

CHOU, WAN-YAO (2015). *A new illustrated history of Taiwan*. Plackitt, C. & Casey, T. (Trans.). Taipei: SMC Publishing Inc.

MEMORIAL FOUNDATION OF 228 (2019 March 13). Special exhibition massacre of stations–Revisiting the February 28 Incident [on-line]. Taipei. https://www. 228.org.tw/en_exhibition-view.php?ID=13

ZHAN, WANQI 詹婉琪 (2018 August 14). After the end of the war: Taiwanese lingering "second-class citizen" label (終戰之後：台灣人揮之不去的「次等公民」標籤。天下雜誌: 獨立評論). *Commonwealth Magazine: Independent Review*. https://opinion.cw.com.tw/blog/profile/52/article/7178

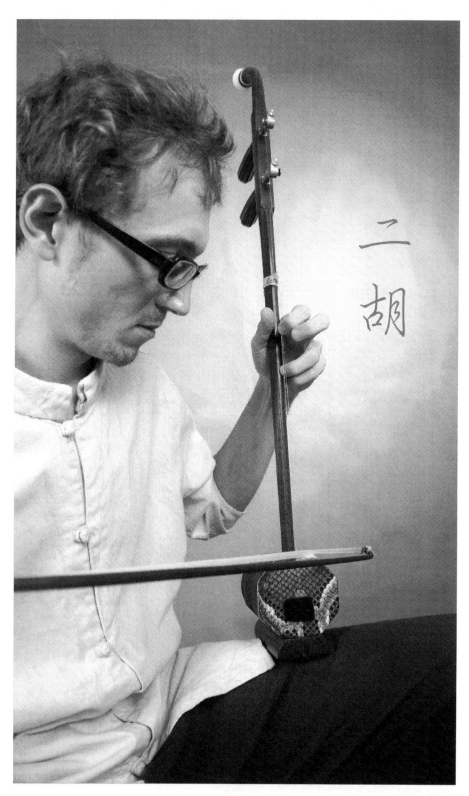

二
胡

Chapter 11

A Phenomenology of
Teaching Chinese Tones with an Erhu

A Case Study of a Chinese Language School in New Jersey

by Li Kang

Abstract

Among the many challenges for English speakers who are endeavoring to learn how to speak Chinese is how to produce the correct Chinese tones because English does not use tones to differentiate meanings. Even though there are only five tones (including a light tone), they affect the listening comprehension of Chinese words. This article uses a phenomenological approach to studying Chinese tones with an erhu, a Chinese traditional music instrument, in a language class in an American Chinese Sunday School. The analysis is based on this unique teaching experience. The results show that an erhu could be useful to introduce tones to heritage students when they are learning how to pronounce words using pinyin romanization.

Introduction

Problem: Many American students learning to speak Chinese find it difficult to produce the correct tones. Xiaonan Shen (1989) found that "American students do not have much difficulty learning Chinese phonemes. The difficulty lies in mastering the tone of Chinese." This problem regarding tones can result in a foreign accent when speaking Chinese. Tao Lin (1996: 19) points out: "The major reason for a foreign accent is [neither] consonant nor vowel, but tones and other language tiers that are higher than tones." Therefore, the tone is viewed as a "sensitive standard" for judging the proficiency of Chinese (Ren, 1984).

Therefore, it is necessary to pay great attention to teaching tones in a Chinese language class in America. The tone is a physical character of language and results from vibrations. Some researchers suggest students practice how to control their vocal cords (Wu & Hu, 2004). It might be an abstract concept for ordinary learners because they are not used to controlling their voices like trained singers. Can Chinese language teachers train students to become more attuned to tones as if they were musicians? Ren Yuan (1984), a Chinese language teacher at Beijing University, described a specific case in his article about a Romanian student in his Chinese class

189

in 1973. He found that this student acquired tones quickly from the start. He knew that this student had studied music and could play the piano. This example illustrated how a musical background can help students to learn tones. Other scholars have also considered this concept and some have devised ways to use music to teach students to learn to produce the tones of Chinese words.

As a Chinese teacher in America, I have been constantly searching for the best way to teach students to speak with correct tones. To find an innovative approach to this problem, I have experimented with using an erhu, a traditional Chinese instrument, to teach Chinese tones. I recorded this experience and will analyze it to address three questions: (1) can an erhu play the four Chinese tones? (2) if it can, how do you teach tones with an erhu in a class? and (3) how do students respond to this new teaching tool?

TEACHING TONES WITH MUSIC

Tones and Pitches

Every Chinese character has a tone, a linguistic feature dating to ancient China. The South and North dynasty scholars discovered this fact in the late 5th century. However, they described tones with words like "short and long, light and heavy, slow and quick, high and low," and Zhao Yuanren considered these descriptions not to be helpful (Cao, 2007).

In 1930, Zhao Yuanren designed a "tone-letter" system. He labeled each tone based on duration and pitch. He divided the range of pitch into 4 equal parts with a total of 5 points, numbered 1 through 5, corresponding to low, half-low, medium, half-high, and high, respectively (Zhao, 1980). The tones were simplified with time-pitch curves.

This system cannot precisely capture every pitch or measure its precise frequency. Still, it represents the tones used in most cases because the intervals of speech tones are expressed in relative intervals. Therefore, it is the most common way to describe the tones of different languages, including Mandarin. While it might sacrifice precision, it succeeds in making the tones more convenient, elegant, and musical. It is also more accessible to academic researchers and students.

There are four tones in Mandarin, named *yinping* (level tone), *yangping* (rising tone), *shangsheng* (falling and rising tone), and *qusheng* (falling tone), which are represented by four curves or patterns that are simplified versions of the "tone-letter" system that Zhao Yuanren designed—see diagram at right.

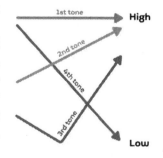

190

One of the purposes of the system for Romanizing Chinese characters known as pinyin was making the language easier to learn (Huang & Miao, 2002). These four curves represent the two key factors of tones: time and pitch. Duration and pitch are also two essential elements in music. Some researchers suggest that listening to music can help language learners, specifically when it comes to teaching tones.

LITERATURE REVIEW

This section will review studies in two areas: (1) teaching tones with music and (2) applying phenomenology to education.

Teaching Tones with Music

Music is beautiful, but it can also be complex. Tone and music share some characteristics, but the challenge for researchers is determining what kind of music is appropriate for teaching tones. Here are some suggestions from different researchers:

SHEET MUSIC. Researchers suggested using sheet music for teaching tones. For example, Yu Jiang (2007) says when a teacher is teaching a level tone, he or she could use the tone ā as an example. First, the teacher should pronounce ā and guide students to feel that this is articulated with a flat and high voice, draw a horizontal line at the top of the music sheet and tell students it represents level *yingping* ā tone. The teacher would repeat this method to introduce and chart á, ǎ, and à to students.

Many researchers view introducing sheet music as the first step to learning tones, but as for the next step, different researchers propose different options. For instance, Jiang Yiliang (1999) indicated that there is an exact correlation between music sheet and the tone-letter system. Therefore, the first step is transforming the tone-letter system into sheet music and introducing the letter's tone using a form of written music. Ren Yuan (1984) recommends that teachers draw five lines on the blackboard and paint four tones in different colors to represent different pitches.

Conductor: As an option, Yu Jiang suggests that the next step is for the teacher to become a passionate conductor. She believes that every tone has its emotion. For example, the falling tone sounds like being angry, and it could be expressed by the teacher's body language. A teacher could act like a passionate conductor because they both use their gestures to convey information.

Human Voice

Jiang Yiliang (1999) suggests an other option for the next step which is to encourage students to hum the four tones. He also suggests that students should keep humming as long as they can through high-flat and low-flat sounds. After humming, let the students remember their feeling on the vocal cord and practice four tones while replicating that feeling. However, this method only focuses on a single character rather than a structure with complete meaning. As a result, other researchers suggest singing more than one tone at one time. For instance, Jin Xiaoda (2014) proposes that students hum or sing and extend from one syllable to the next to simulate prosody, the rhythm of speech. In other words, they will imitate the tonal patterns of multi-word phrases or sentences. For example, students could imitate *"xīn zhí kǒu kuài,"* 心直口快 which is an idiom of four characters with four different tones meaning "straightforward" in English. Even though the two methods have different focuses, they both use the human voice to imitate tones.

Instrument. Ren Yuan suggests using instruments as the next step. He says that if it is possible to demonstrate with music after showing tones on the music sheet, it might be helpful for students to understand the differences between tones caused by the changes from different pitches and grasp the essence of tones (Ren, 1984). But what kinds of instruments should a teacher use?

Some people use a piano to intimate four tones, but it is only suitable to imitate *yinping*, the level tone, because the other tones change from one pitch to another pitch, and the piano has a specific array of sound based on its keys. It cannot make the sounds between keys. But a stringed instrument can articulate a glissando, smoothly sliding between pitches.

TEACHING TONES WITH A STRINGED INSTRUMENT. Researchers suggest that teachers could use a guitar as a stringed instrument to intimate tones because it is usually readily available to both students and teachers (Xiao & Zhang, 2010). Zhao Yuanren, the founder of the "tone-letter" system, used a *guqin*, an ancient Chinese instrument with seven strings to imitate the tonal variations of various Chinese dialects spoken in Beijing, Tianjin, Kaifeng, Wuchang, Chongqing Changsha, Nanjing, Suzhou, and Fuzhou dialects (Xiao & Zhang, 2010). This instrument can intimate the different tones that appear throughout various regions of China.

The *erhu* is similar to the guqin. It probably dates to the Tang dynasty, and it is one of the most common Chinese traditional instruments available (Qiao, 2000). Even though erhu only has two strings, it is still an appropriate tool to teach tones. Some scholars have already made a connection between this instrument and the tones of Chinese speech. Fang Xiang

(2011) considers stringed instruments as the best way to intimate tones, and he has done this with an erhu. So, does that mean it is possible to use it in a classroom to teach Chinese tones?

Phenomenology in Education

Edmund Husserl, one of the famous philosophers in 20th century, is known as the founder of phenomenology. He argued that phenomenology begins with the analysis of consciousness or experience. Phenomenology holds that learning implies perceiving, conceptualizing, experiencing, or understanding something differently (Bao, 1999). Since both phenomenology and education focus on the uniqueness of human beings, many researchers have applied phenomenology to education. For example, Pramiling (1995) explored the use of phenomenology in educational practice. Rueda and Mehan (1986), Stone and Reid (1993), and Klenk (1993) attempted to put phenomenology into special education (Jean C. Mcphail, 1995).

Bao (1999) applies Spiegelberg's "Seven Essential Steps" of phenomenology into teaching with a laptop:

1. Investigating particular phenomena
2. Investigating general essences
3. Apprehending essential relationships among essences
4. Watching modes of appearing
5. Exploring the constitution of phenomena in consciousness
6. Suspending belief in the existence of phenomena
7. Interpreting the meaning of phenomena.

I selected Spiegelberg's "Seven Essential Steps" as a way to analyze my primary source, a video recording capturing my experience of teaching Chinese tones in a language class in an American school, as well as my reflections on the experience.

FINDINGS

Investigating Particular Phenomena

I am a teacher in a language school located in New Jersey where I teach Chinese to third-grade students for 90 minutes each week. There are twelve students in my class, and they are around nine years old. All of them are heritage students and their parents can speak Chinese. The textbook is *New Shuangshuang Chinese* [新双双中文]. The first part of the textbook focuses on pinyin and the second part on characters. After covering the first part of the textbook, I spent one class reviewing pinyin and teaching Chinese tones with an erhu.

The classroom displays examples of Chinese culture such as calligraphy, paintings, and paper cuttings as well as teaching aids such as a map of China, illustrations of Chinese characters, and a graph of four tones.

I rearranged the students' chairs into four groups with a space in the center where I could perform, and I arranged to record a video to evaluate the classes. An edited clip is available on YouTube.[1] There are four segments in this video: (1) an introduction of the lesson including the tones, (2) a demonstration of two songs illustrating the contrast between a high and low pitch; (3) a demonstration on the four tones using the erhu, and (4) I discussed how using the wrong tone can confuse listening where you are trying to communicate in Chinese.

Segment 1

At the beginning of the class, I outlined the goals for the day's lesson and demonstrated how it is more likely for new learners to make tonal mistakes than make errors with pronouncing consonants or vowels. Such as "*jiāo ào*," which means arrogant, a word the students had already learned in a previous lesson. According to the recordings the students sent to me, they always pronounced the word as "*jiǎo ào*."

Segment 2

I demonstrated high and low pitches with recordings of two songs. One was Adele's Rolling in the Deep, and another was Jiangyang Zhuoma's Hongyan [降央卓玛，鸿雁]. Both singers were females. The first song is by an English singer known for her high pitch, and the second is a Chinese song at a lower pitch.

Segment 3

To show the relationship between the changes of pitches and the four tones, I played the four tones using the outer string of the erhu. I pronounced the four tones, ā, á, ǎ, à, while I played. At first, I intimated tones separately. I played the highest pitch and said ā; said á when changing pitch from low to high; ǎ when the pitch dipped from high to low and then back to high; and I expressed à when the pitch changes from low to high. Students did not react much until I played these four tones on the erhu. The instrument attracted the students' attention.

Segment 4

Next, I introduced five cases in which tones were misused. In the first case, I presented the word *kànshū* 看书 [to read a book] and *kǎnshù* 砍树

---

[1] Li Kang, "Play Four Tones with Erhu," Youtube: https://www.youtube.com/watch?v=bys9eR_5318.

[to cut down trees] and *dàrén* [lord] and *dǎrén* [beat up someone], and *qīngwěn* 请吻 [please kiss] and *qǐngwèn* 请问 [to ask].

Conclusion

This experiment showed that using an erhu can help young students to understand the tones in the Chinese spoken language, especially when used in conjunction with the use of graphs of tones and arm gestures. Using a musical instrument garners students' attention. While not sufficient unto itself this process introduces new language learners to the idea that Chinese tones are changes of pitches during the unit time. Listening to songs with different pitch styles can also supplement this lesson. It is also crucial to introduce the examples of potential errors to emphasize the importance of using tones. This is an important step in helping students to communicate.

Bibliography

BAO, XUE-MING (1999). *A phenomenology of teaching with laptop computers: A case study through the eyes of a trainer*. eRepository @ Seton Hall.

CAO, WEN (2007). The attributions of Mr. Zhao Yuanren's research on Chinese phonology and tones. *Chinese Teaching in the World*, No. 4: 75–85+3.

FANG, XIANG (2011). The practical ways of teaching Chinese tones to students from Europe and America—The key characteristics of the combing model for Chinese tones. *Modern Chinese*, No. 1: 127–133.

GUI, MINGCHAO, & JICHUN YANG (2003). Another discussion on the American English tone interference on American students when they are learning Chinese tones. *Journal of Yunnan Normal University*, No. 1: 38–43.

JIANG, YILIANG (1999). Music and Chinese phonetic teaching. *Chinese Language Learning*, No. 3: 38–41.

MCPHAIL, J. (1995). Phenomenology as philosophy and method: Applications to ways of doing special education, remedial and special education, *Hammill Institute on Disabilities, 16*(3): 159-165.

JIN, XIAODA (2014). Sing four tones, metrical feet, and tone ranges—A classroom practice on correcting Exotic accents of foreign students. *International Chinese Teaching and Research*, No. 4: 24-30+59.

LIN, TAO (1996). Phonetic research and teaching Chinese as a second language. *Chinese Teaching in the World*, No. 3: 18–20.

LIU, YI (1998). The analysis on Japanese and Korean students' Chinese tones. *Chinese Teaching in the World*, No. 1: 95–100.

QIAO, JIANZHONG (2000). An instrument and a century–A hundred-year review on erhu. *Music Research*, No. 1: 36–44.

REN, YUAN (1984). A talk about teaching Romanian students Chinese tones. *Language Teaching and Linguistic Studies*, No. 2: 81–90.

SHEN, XIAONAN (1989). American learn Chinese tones. *Chinese Teaching in the World*, No. 3: 158–168.

SONG, YIDAN (2006). The review of experiments on Chinese tones. *Linguistic Research*, No. 1: 41–45.

WANG, YOUMING (1998). A quantitative analysis on the way of Hungarian students marking Chinese double syllable. *Chinese Teaching in the World*, No. 2 : 91–98.

WANG, YOUMING (1998). Japanese students' problems on learning Chinese tones. *Journal of East China Normal University* No. 2: 95–96.

WANG, YUNJIA (1995). Discussing American students learning Chinese tones. *Language Teaching and Linguistic Studies*, No. 3: 126–140.

WANG, ANHONG (2006). The teaching discussion on the characteristics of Chinese tones. *Language Teaching and Linguistic Studies*, No. 3: 70–75.

WU, MENJI, & HU, MINGGUANG (2004). "The Reasons Why Vietnam Students Make Tones Mistakes When Speaking Chinese." *Chinese Teaching in the World*, No. 2 : 81–87+4.

XIAO, RENFEI, & ZHANG, FANG (2010). Two inspiration from a system of 'tone-letters' and a discussion on 'teaching Chinese tones.' *Journal of Language and Literature Studies*, No. 7: 66–68.

YU, JIANG (2007). A new teaching plan on teaching Chinese tones. *Language Teaching and Linguistic Studies,* No. 1: 77-81.

ZHANG, HONG (2006). The analysis on mistakes of light tone in double syllable made by Japanese students and their acquisition. *Journal of Yunnan Normal University*, No. 1: 46–48.

ZHAO, YUANREN (1980). A system of 'tone-letter.' *Fangyan* (Dialect), No. 2: 81–83.

Above: Yang Qingyu lived in Puli, Taiwan, where he taught the traditional Yang Taiji system. Below: Lin Shengxuan is one of Yang Qingyu's longtime students from Taipei. During a visit to Erie, Pennsylvania, Mr. Lin taught students a repetitive drill based on the "grasp sparrow's tail" sequence which included alternating sides. Photographs courtesy of M. DeMarco.

Chapter 12

Yang Taiji Practice Through the Eyes of Western Medical Health Guidelines

by Michael A. DeMarco

Introduction

According to Chinese consumer packaging labels and research reports—green tea, beer, peanuts, qigong, acupuncture, taijiquan, and "Long Life" brand cigarettes—all have a strong commonality. Each promises the benefits of greater strength and vigor, improvement in mental faculties, deeper spiritual awareness, and (of course) increased sexual prowess. In short, many Chinese exercise and dietary programs claim to offer a healthy, happy life with the longevity of the pine, tortoise, and crane.

The tendency of the Chinese to claim such benefits from so many of their products and activities raises valid questions concerning their acceptability as being truly conducive assets for a healthier lifestyle. This paper will focus on the unique art of Yang style taijiquan, usually referred to in abbreviated form simply as taiji. During the last few decades, there has been a rapid growth in taiji practice outside Asia, a growth largely linked to claims concerning its health nurturing qualities (Baer, 1997). To verify these claims, this paper will utilize the most recent health and fitness guidelines provided by leading research institutes. These guidelines can serve as criteria for analyzing and assessing Yang style taiji as an activity that we may consider in our research concerning the relationship between lifestyle and well-being. Therefore, this paper:

1) defines and lists the established guidelines for health and fitness;
2) describes what taiji is and how it is practiced; and
3) ascertains the role taiji may take in our lives according to the ideals set by the world's leading authorities on health and fitness.

Guidelines for Health and Fitness

According to the World Health Organization, "Health is defined as a state of complete physical, mental, social, and spiritual well-being, and not merely the absence of disease and infirmity." Dr. Nieman adds that "Physical fitness is a condition in which an individual has sufficient energy and vitality to accomplish daily tasks and active recreational pursuits without undue fatigue" (1998: 4).

A review was made of some of the published literature that focuses on the subject of health and physical fitness. The general guidelines derived from these works permit practical, clear-cut conclusions helpful in the assessment of any exercise program, including taiji. A synopsis of their findings is given in the following eight guidelines for a successful approach to adopting and maintaining a physically active lifestyle (U.S., 1996: 46, 47; Nieman, 1998: 17):

1) Be active!
2) exercise at least 30-minutes daily
   (this can be accumulated time);
3) participate in an exercise program of moderate intensity;
4) consider behavioral and attitudinal factors in selecting
   a program;
5) have support from family and friends;
6) select an activity open to males and females of varied ages,
   which has appeal to all;
7) eliminate "high-risk" behaviors;
8) select an activity that can be done life long.

The importance of these eight guidelines are obscured by their simplicity. A closer look at the meaning of each guideline and how they interrelate with each other represents an enormous amount of medical knowledge in a concise format. Therefore, we should not dismiss the guidelines because of their simplicity but come to understand the implications of each and their importance in our lives.

The rational for adopting the above guidelines, including the social and medical factors influencing such a decision, will be described after the following section describing the Yang taiji curriculum. Thus, the significance of both the modern medical guidelines for health and Yang taiji as an activity can be simultaneously presented in the concluding section.

Overview of the Taiji Curriculum

Chen Wangting (cir. 1597–1664) is credited as being the founder of the original Chen style taiji. As a garrison commander in Henan Province, Wangting absorbed many noted boxing styles of his day. He is said to have created boxing routines and associated exercises from which all other forms of taiji were derived (DeMarco, 1992: 14–15; Wallace, 1998; Gu, 1984: 1–12).

The Chen style was been passed on for numerous generations only within the Chen family clan and a direct lineage continues today (Huang, 1993: 51–54; Stubenbaum, 1994: 90–99). However, a Chen family servant named Yang Luchan (1799–1872) was taught by the 14th generation master, Chen Changxing (1771–1853). Yang was the first "outsider" to learn and popularize the system which is now associated with his family name and lineage (DeMarco, 1992: 20; Jou, 1988: 42–44; Wile, 1996: 3).

Like the evolution of painting styles, the original Chen style taiji differs from the Yang style for social and political reasons related to the history of Chinese boxing. As modern weaponry became common, the necessity for secrecy waned in the traditional boxing traditions. At the same time, the purpose and function of taiji changed to meet the times (Wile, 1996: 3–30).

The Yang style was adapted to public needs and some of the original movements were eliminated or changed. The routines came to be practiced in a slow, even tempo, and relaxed manner. Once taiji was available to the general public, rumors spread of how practicing the art helped many improve their health and the number of practitioners rapidly rose. As a result, Yang style taiji soon spread across China. Its popularity and fame as an exercise system continues to spread throughout the world (DeMarco, 1992: 20–24).

As a pure fighting system, the original Chen style was developed for facing life-and-death situations. This necessitated familiarity with assorted weaponry and open-hand fighting skills. Leading masters attempted to take under consideration every aspect of the human condition which would help the boxer emerge victorious in any conflict. The truths they learned about the human body, mind, and spirit remains important today, even though the original intent of their research has been overshadowed by the emergence of taiji as an appropriate activity adaptable to modern health care (Koh, 1981a).

Taiji has a fairly long history based on Chinese cultural traditions reaching back over a millennium (Koh, 1981b). However, it was not until the early twentieth century that Yang taiji became standardized under Yang Chengfu (1883–1936), the grandson of the founder Yang Luchan (Huang, 1993: 65–68; Wong, 1998: 204–205; Jou, 1988, 42–47). To this day, the leading representatives of the various taiji systems retain the traditional skills and knowledge associated with the original fighting arts, such as mastery of the straight sword, staff, and other weapons. But true masters of complete taiji systems are rare.

Today, many study taiji solely for health benefits and some dabble in self-defense aspects. As a result, Yang taiji is the most popular style and is often mistakenly looked upon only as an exercise for the elderly (Lim, 1996: 91). It appears this way because many teachers have only studied taiji for its health benefits and are unfamiliar with the complete system.

There are four aspects of taiji that should be noted. Taiji is a martial art, a holistic health exercise, an aesthetic dance-like art, and a form of moving meditation. Most students begin their taiji study because of an interest in one of these aspects. As a result, the traditional Yang style taijiquan curriculum focus on the following practices:

1) a solo routine,
2) two-person routines, and
3) taiji sword routines.

The Traditional Yang Style Solo Routine

Most students, even many taiji teachers, only practice the taiji solo routine. Traditionally, this routine consists of 108 martial movements which are arranged in a flowing sequence from beginning to end as a river current. There are forward, backward, sideways, and turning movements. The body moves harmoniously in a continuously even tempo which is slow enough to finely focus on being relaxed and balanced with every gesture (Jou, 1988; Huang, 1993; Wong, 1996).

Some taiji movements look poetically inspired with names like: "wave hands like clouds," "snake creeps downward," "rooster stands on one leg," and "embrace moon." Other movements are clearly martial in application, such as "lotus kick," deflect, push, roll-back, punch, and press.

For a beginning student, solo practice is characterized by tenseness, staccato movements, and off-balanced postures. To make the routine evolve into an exercise characterized by balance, smoothness, and relaxed grace can take many decades of continuous polishing through the forge of practice (DeMarco, 1997: 48–58).

In China, taiji practitioners usually meet daily at dawn amid the fresh air and tranquil surroundings of a lake, park, or river bank (Reynolds, 1982: 104–110). They often chat and stretch while waiting for others to arrive. When the teacher arrives, students organize to do the solo routine together in synchronized fashion. The routine takes from twenty to thirty minutes to perform, depending upon the tempo and exact number of movements included in the style. After the routine, the teacher will instruct beginners in new movements or offer tips to advanced students on how to improve a movement or offer insights into the deeper aspects of taiji's underlying philosophy (Horwitz, et. al., 1976: 15–25; Lehrhaupt, 1993, 61–69; DeMarco, 1997).

After class, students may depart for breakfast, work, school, or remain to socialize for a short time. They usually discuss taiji in between more personal discussions concerning family, work, or other matters.

Some beginning students find taiji too boring and soon quit. Others, who have the patience to get through this initial stage, may continue the daily routine for years on end. Because of changing personal schedules, many practitioners quit the group after learning the solo exercise and practice on their own (U.S., 1996: 46; Horwitz, et., 1976: 15–25; Lehrhaupt, 1993, 61–69). The stability of the group rests primarily on the teacher's talents and knowledge which allows the teacher to provide continuous instruction, guidance, and inspiration for maintaining the interest of each student. Unfortunately, many so-called "taiji teachers" do not know the complete system and students may eventually quit the group and often taiji practice altogether.

Part of the early morning taiji routine in a park in Xi'an, China.
Photograph courtesy of M. DeMarco.

The solo routine can be practiced daily for one's entire life and there will always be more to learn within its subtle complexities. A perceptive practitioner will receive instruction indirectly from the solo routine itself by continuously discovering ways of moving, thinking, and sensing that results from dedicated practice. The solo routine was designed for the practitioner to learn about himself, i.e., how the body and mind function together holistically (DeMarco, 1994). Thus, taiji is not just physical exercise. It is considered an "internal art" because of the importance placed on cultivating one's mental, emotional, and spiritual aspects. Since it is a "person" who does taiji, it is necessary to cultivate the whole person in order to make progress in mastering taiji.

Two-Person Taiji Routines & Taiji Sword Routines

The true martial arts have always dealt with personal combat. If taiji's solo routine was designed to allow the individual to "know himself," two-person routines were designed to allow him to "know others." What this actually means can be ascertained by a description of the practices involved.

There are three main two-person exercises associated with Yang taiji. The first, called "push-hands" (*tuishou*), is a two-person exercise based on fundamental martial applications aligned in the four cardinal directions. The movements are: ward-off, roll-back, press, and push (Chen, n.d.; Kuo, 1994: 33–42; Jou, 1988: 226–253; Davis & Mann, 1996: 55–56; Ma & Zee, 1990). Another duet practice is referred to as "four-corners" or "large rollback" (*dalu*) since it covers the four directions between the cardinal

Wu Hangxin and Jin Huiying practicing two-person sword routines in Hangzhou, China. Photograph courtesy of D. Mainfort.

points with movements called: elbow, split, pull-down, and shoulder-strike. Duets are practiced in fixed stances or with active stepping (Chen, n.d.; Smith, 1997: 56–69; Jou, 1988: 253–256).

There is another rare duet routine called *sanshou*, often translated as "free hands" or "dispersing hands," which may refer to the self-defense goal of meeting any confrontation in a relaxed, easy manner to defeat the opponent. This is more complex than dalu and tuishou, containing a lengthy arrangement of attack and counter movements (Yiu, 1981).

The taiji sword routines have similar movements as those found in the solo routine. In the traditional solo sword routine, the sword's weight and length allows the practitioner to sense how his own movements effect the sword. A duet routine allows each swordsman to extend his sensitivity through the blade in order to detect the movement of his partner.

The duet practices of tuishou, dalu, sanshou and the taiji sword are complementary to the solo routine. They enlarge the scope of taiji by bringing in a complex host of elements such as speed, movement, direction, and intention. All the routines should follow the fundamental taiji principles of relaxation, balanced movement, coupled with a developed sensitivity required to be aware of the "one's self" and "others" (Honda, 1995; Jacobson, 1997).

Two-person practices, such as *push-hands (tuishou),*
four-corners (dalu), and free hands (sanshou).
Illustrations courtesy of Oscar Ratti.

Assessing Yang Taiji as an Activity for Health

Eight guidelines for a successful approach to adopting and maintaining a physically active lifestyle were presented earlier in this paper. We can gain a better understanding of the role taiji may take in our lives by looking at these guidelines as a criteria for Yang taiji practice.

1) Be Active!

The National Institutes of Health concluded that "All ... should engage in regular physical activity at a level appropriate to their capacity, needs, and interest" (U.S., 1996: 41). They reached this conclusion in large part because inactivity is a major risk factor for cardiovascular disease (CVD), a leading cause of death. The activity chosen can greatly effect other CVD risk factors, including high blood pressure, lipid levels, and obesity. However, people who are not physically fit, such as those who are overweight, smoke, or have arthritic problems, may find many exercises to be too difficult or strenuous to do. The paradox is that they need to exercise, but feel that exercise is too grueling to carry on regularly.

Taiji is highly adaptable to the practitioner's state of health and fitness. The movements can be done in high or low postures, in narrow or wide stances. Practicing the movements in a slow, relaxed manner ensures that anyone who can walk can learn the traditional solo routine. As one gradually learns the routine, he gains strength and flexibility (Lai, 1995). There is an awareness of becoming gradually more fit and taking satisfaction in the progress made.

2) Exercise at Least Thirty-Minutes Daily

Inactivity is not only a major cause of cardiovascular disease, but bears heavily on other diseases, such as diabetes, osteoporosis, hypertension, and even some cancers (U.S., 1996: 43). A minimum of thirty minutes exercise is considered ample for reducing such illeffects (ACSM, n.d.: 163).

The traditional Yang style solo routine takes just about thirty minutes to perform. It can therefore be easily fit into a daily schedule with the practitioner knowing that the minimum exercise time is met.

The Yang taiji solo routine is a comprehensive approach to exercising, affecting the cardio-respiratory system, body composition, muscular strength, and joint flexibility (Koh, 1982; Lumsden, 1998; Powerful, 1996; Jacobson, et. al., 1997). Benefits can be measured even after a month or two of taiji practice. However, as the National Institutes of Health stresses,

"... physical activity must be performed regularly to maintain these effects" (U.S., 1996: 43; Nieman, 1998: 46).

Physical fitness is health and skill related. With the daily practice of taiji, skills are acquired which inspire the practitioner to not miss the exercise. As one acquires greater insights into the art, one's state of health also continually improves.

3) Participate in an Exercise Program of Moderate Intensity

High-intensity and fast moving sports are attractive to competitive athletes, but these activities pose dangerous to their health. Their motivating factors may be a quest for fame and excitement rather than for health and fitness. Those who are truly seeking an activity for their health should beware of any dangers associated with the sport or activity they may consider. Under proper instruction, taiji poses no risk to the practitioner.

"The majority of benefits of physical activity can be gained by performing moderate-intensity activities" (U.S., 1996: 43). Whether taiji's solo routine fits into the "moderate-intensity" range is questionable (Zhuo, et. at., 1984: 9). A cardio-respiratory rate at 50% VO_2max is recommended for general health (Nieman, 1998: 9; ACSM, n.d.: 158), but taiji's slow motion movements may not meet this criteria. More research is needed in this area to be certain. However, if the associated duet and swords routines are included in the assessment, then taiji would certainly meet this criteria as well. Because taiji practice falls in the low and moderately-intense category of exercise, there is little risk of injuring oneself during practice. There is also a stronger inclination for the individual to continue taiji practice on a regular basis.

4) Consider Behavioral and Attitudinal Factors in Selecting a Program

A big factor in selecting an activity for health and fitness is personality. The "behavioral and attitudinal factors that influence the motivation for and ability to sustain physical activity are strongly determined by social experiences, cultural background, and physical disability and health status. For example, perceptions of appropriate physical activity differ by gender, age, weight, maritial status, family roles and responsibilities, disability, and social class" (U.S., 1996: 46). Although these barriers may be found in some degree in taiji practice, the most foreboding barrier is that taiji may be too exotic to be easily assimilated. First, one must be aware of what taiji is and what it has to offer. This may then motivate one to learn the art.

It is recommended that an activity should be enjoyable, easily fit into one's daily schedule, should be of low financial or social cost, and should present a minimum of negative consequences, such as injury, peer pressure, and self-identity problems (U.S., 1996: 46). All of these recommendations concur with taiji practice, except that it is not easily accessible. Although there are more and more people claiming to teach taiji, most do not possess the appropriate experience or credentials. It is unfortunate that more competent teachers are not available; it is sad that charlatan posing as taiji instructors discredit the art and may actually harm their students through poor instruction.

5) Support from Family and Friends

The decision to start participating in a particular activity and the resolve to maintain a regular exercise schedule on a long-term basis greatly depends on the support, encouragement, and fellowship of others. This may be indirectly given by others who do not partake in the exercise itself, but direct support offered by fellow practitioners proves to be very significant for anyone who wishes to maintain a regular exercise activity.

Taiji is usually taught in pleasant natural surroundings conducive to the relaxed mode of the routine. The teacher-student relationship is important since the instructor serves as a example of a healthy lifestyle which should inspire and guide students in their own practice and lifestyle habits. This is further reinforced by like-minded individuals who have decided to make taiji part of their own lives (U.S., 1996: 46).

Taiji practitioners not only exercise together, but discuss what they learn through their practice and incorporate it into their lives as much as possible. For example, taiji theory tells us to "go with the flow" and be in harmony with the movement of others, even when their movements are aggressive. When we are confronted with daily problems at home or at work, we can utilize the same principles: be calm, patient, balanced, and work with the situation without making the problem worse. A novice practitioner soon learns that taiji is more than just physical exercise. It demands the integration of one's whole being, tying-in the physical with the mental and spiritual aspects as well. Teacher and fellow students come to represent a "taiji family" which encourages regular practice and a commitment to a lifestyle conducive to the ultimate health goals of taiji.

6) Select an Activity Open to Males and Females of Varied Ages and Appeals to All

Many exercises and leisure activities attract individuals of a particular age or gender. Taiji is usually taught in groups, but the foundation of its practice rests on the individual regardless of gender or age. A dedicated teacher will instruct on a one-on-one basis in order to develop the student as an individual artist with a unique personal makeup. It has been shown that any comprehensive physical fitness program must be individualized (Yan, 1995: 62–63).

Taiji can be practiced by anyone, but does it appeal to all? It does not, primarily because it is too exotic and its theory and practice is little understood by the general public (Honda, 1995). However, even without a clear understanding of what taiji is, people are attracted to it for one or more of its qualities as a martial art, a wholistic exercise, a moving meditation, and a dance-like art form. For anyone who has taken the time to watch taiji for a few hours, there is a good chance that they would be drawn into its practice for one of the reasons mentioned.

7) Eliminate "High-Risk" Behaviors

The fundamental objectives in practicing the taiji solo routine are to seek relaxation in every move and to execute the movements slowly in a steady flow of balanced form. When students begin to practice taiji seriously, they soon discover many tensions in their bodies. Often, even when performing the simplest movements, they feel tense and awkward. They find that it is not the movement itself which is difficult to master, but dealing with underlying conditions that distort the movements. Taiji may bring an initial awareness of underlying problems and thus a desire in the individual to eliminate these problems.

Improvements in taiji practice can be felt by the practitioner and noticed by other students. To make continual progress requires the student to look inward, to modify any factors which cause the taiji movements to be too tense or the postures to fall off-balance. As a result, the student is encouraged by the presence of teacher, classmates and the art of taiji itself to modify any high risk behaviors, such as smoking and poor diet. To reinforce such changes in behavior, involvement in taiji calls for an appropriate change in attitude which guarantees a better, healthier lifestyle than the present one. Taiji beckons one to be constantly aware in order to make continual improvements in lifestyle, for only in this way can one approach a masterful level in the art.

8) Select an Activity That Can Be Done Life Long

"A key ingredient to healthy aging, according to many gerontologists, is regular physical activity" (Nieman, 1998: 32). Taiji is noted for its suitability as an exercise for the elderly (Wolf, et. al. 1996, 1997b; Wolfson, et al., 1996; Schaller, K. 1996; Province, 1995). Its movements are slow and non-strenuous, yet invigorating to mind and body.

Taiji's suitability for the elderly does not mean it is unsuitable for younger generations, but many younger persons fail to see the value in taiji as an activity. Their temperaments are often too unruly and they usually do not have the patience to try taiji for a long enough time to actually feel the beneficial effects of the exercise.

Those attracted to taiji are usually adults in their thirties and older. The quest for relaxation is a primary motivation factor, but others come to taiji from other sports and activities that have caused them physical or mental injury. In general, taiji is looked at for its therapeutic benefits to mind, body, and spirit (Zhuo, 1982). The desire to obtain such benefits can start at any age. A look at the graceful aging of many noted taiji instructors illustrates that they often started taiji because of an illness, benefited from it, and so dedicated themselves to daily practice for the rest of their lives. Some centenarians continue to teach taiji on a daily basis to "youngsters" in their 70's, 80's, and 90's.

Summary

There is a strong agreement between the National Institute of Health's guidelines and the Yang taiji curriculum indicating that taiji meets the criteria as an activity that we may consider in our research concerning the relationship between lifestyle and well-being. However, we should look a little closer before making any final conclusion.

Guidelines numbered 1 thru 3 involve the participation in an activity of moderate intensity, hopefully on a daily basis. Regularity of practice is necessary to attain and/or maintain health. Through its own design and traditional method of instruction, taiji clearly meets these guidelines (Koh, 1981a: 15–17, 21).

Guideline number 4 considers behavioral and attitudinal factors in selecting an exercise or activity. Yang taiji is based on Daoist principles, which value spiritual and mental development along with the physical aspects. It is non-competitive and not as exciting as most mainstream sports. For these reasons, Yang taiji is fitting for some personalities, but certainly not all. Similarly, in respect to guideline 6, Yang taiji may be open to all, but it has a limited appeal because of its call for patient students who are able to find joy in the subtleties of the art.

The calming, relaxed practice of taiji attracts individuals who prefer or need this in their life. So, as encouraged in guideline number 5, taiji practitioners find an active support group from like-minded practitioners and others who may see the value in it but may not have the time or opportunity to be involved themselves.

"If you're one with
the Dao, to the end
of your days you'll
suffer no harm."
—*Laozi, in Henricks, 1989: 68*

Above character for Dao by taiji Master Yang Qingyu.

Activities conducive to a healthy lifestyle are given special attention in guideline 7. When we consider the theory and practice of Yang taiji, we find that, in addition to offering an encompassing system for health and fitness, its practice has a strong tendency to eliminate "high-risk" behaviors (U.S., 1996: 46). To make progress in doing taiji, it is necessary to look deeply into one's character development. Only when a practitioner does this can the movements reflect the tranquility, grace, and balance associated with the art. This concurs with an ancient Chinese proverb: "What is accomplished in the mind, is made known by the hand."

Guideline 8 requires that such an activity be suitable for long-term practice. Yang taiji body mechanics allow almost anyone to practice the art. The fact that it is noted for benefitting the elderly attests to its suitability for the aged as well as a therapeutic system (Nieman, 1998: 125; Yan, 1995: 61; Wolf, 1997a).

211

To assess Yang style taiji as a physical activity we must be aware that it is based on the Daoist yin-yang principle. It seeks to harmonize the body and mind, the internal with the external. Yang taiji involves the total person, working on all the body's systems. Because of its focus on relaxation, even when practiced with moderate intensity, the movements gently exercise the joints, develop balance, and calm the nerves.

From research regarding Yang taiji, we see that this unique art offers "health" in the complete sense as defined by the World Health Organization "as a state of complete physical, mental, social, and spiritual well-being." It is unfortunate that such an artistic gem remains hidden behind cultural barriers which color our receptivity to the exotic.

Note: An earlier version of this article was published in M. DeMarco, (Ed.), (1998), *Journal of Asian Martial Arts, 7*(4), 22-35.

Bibliography

AMERICAN COLLEGE OF SPORTS MEDICINE [ACSM]. (n.d.). *ACSM's guidelines.* pp. 153–176.

BACKLETTER (1996, June). Powerful evidence that the martial art tai chi can help frail patients with osteoporosis. *Backletter, 11*(6), 63.

BAER, K. (1997, July). A movement toward t'ai chi. *Harvard Health Letter, 22*(9), 6.

CHEN, Y. (n.d.). *T'ai-chi ch'uan: Its effects and practical applications.* Hong Kong: n.p.

DAVIS, D., & MANN, L. (1996). Conservator of the taiji classics: An interview with Benjamin Pang Jeng Lo. *Journal of Asian Martial Arts, 5*(4), 46–67.

DEMARCO, M. (1992). The origin and evolution of taijiquan. *Journal of Asian Martial Arts, 1*(1), 8–25.

DEMARCO, M. (1994). The necessity for softness in taijiquan. *Journal of Asian Martial Arts, 3*(3), 92–103.

DEMARCO, M. (1997). Taijiquan as an experiential way for discovering Daoism. *Journal of Asian Martial Arts, 6*(3), 48–59.

GU, L. (1984). The origin, evolution and development of shadow boxing. In Zhaohua Publishing House (Compilers), *Chen style taijiquan* (pp. 1–12). Hong Kong: Hai Feng Publishing Company.

HENRICKS, R., (Trans.). (1989). *Lao-tzu te-tao ching.* New York: Ballantine Books.

Honda, C. (1995 February). Cultural diversity: Tai chi chuan and Laban Movement Analysis. *Journal of Physical Education, 66*(2), 38.

Horwitz, T., Kimmelman, S., & Lui, H. (1976). *T'ai chi ch'uan: The techniques of power.* Chicago: Chicago Review Press.

Huang, A. (1993). *Complete tai-chi: The definitive guide to physical and emotional self-improvement.* Rutland, VT: Charles E. Tuttle Co.

Jacobson, B., Chen, H., et al. (1997, February). The effect of t'ai chi chuan training on balance, kinesthetic sense, and strength. *Perceptual & Motor Skills, 84*(1), 27.

Jou, T. (1981). *The tao of tai-chi chuan: Way to rejuvenation.* Warwick, NY: Tai Chi Foundation.

Koh, T. (1981a). Tai chi chuan. *American Journal of Chinese Medicine, 9*(1), 15–22.

Koh, T. (1981b). Chinese medicine and martial arts. *American Journal of Chinese Medicine, 9*(3), 181–186.

Koh, T. (1982). Tai chi and ankylosing spondylitis—A personal experience. *American Journal of Chinese Medicine, 10*(1–4), 59–61.

Koh, L. (1994). *The t'ai chi boxing chronicle.* (Guttmann, Trans.). Berkeley, CA: North Atlantic Books.

Lai, J., et. al, (1995, November). Two-year trends in cardiorespiratory function among older tai chi chuan practitioners and sedentary subjects. *Journal of the American Geriatric Society, 43*(11).

Lehrhaupt, L. (1992). Taijiquan: Learning how to learn. *Journal of Asian Martial Arts, 2*(1), 60–69.

Lim, P. (1992). The combative elements of Yang taijiquan. *Journal of Asian Martial Arts, 5*(3), 90–99.

Lumsden, D., (1998, February). T'ai chi for osteoarthritis: An introduction for primary care physicians. *Geriatrics 53*(2).

Ma, Y., & Zee, W. (1990). *Wu style taijiquan push-hands (tuishou).* Hong Kong: Shanghai Book Co.

Nieman, D. (1998). *The exercise-health connection.* Champaign, IL: Human Kinetics.

Reynolds, D. (1982). *The quiet therapies: Japanese pathways to personal growth.* Honolulu: University of Hawaii Press.

Schaller, K. (1996, October). Tai chi chih: An exercise option for older adults. *Journal of Gerontol Nursing, 22*(10), 12–17.

Smith, R. (1994). Dalu and some tigers. *Journal of Asian Martial Arts, 6*(2), 56–69.

Stubenbaum, D. (1994). An encounter with Chen Xiaowang: The continued growth of Chen taijiquan. *Journal of Asian Martial Arts, 3*(1), 90–99.

U.S. DEPARTMENT OF HEALTH AND HUMAN SERVICES (1996). *Physical activity and health: A report of the Surgeon General.* Atlanta: U.S. Department of Health and Human Services, Centers for Disease Control and Prevention, National Center for Chronic Disease Prevention and Health Promotion.

WALLACE, A. (1998). Internal training: The foundation for Chen taiji's fighting skills and health promotion. *Journal of Asian Martial Arts, 7*(1), 58–89.

WILE, D. (1996). *Lost t'ai-chi classics from the late Ch'ing dynasty.* Albany, NY: State University of New York Press.

WOLF, S., ET AL. (1993, March). The Atlanta FICSIT study: Two exercise interventions to reduce frailty in elders. *Journal of the American Geriatric Society, 41*(3), 329–332.

WOLF, S., ET AL. (1996, May). Reducing frailty and falls in older persons: an investigation of tai chi and computerized balance training. Atlanta FICSIT Group. Frailty and Injuries: Cooperative Studies of Intervention Techniques. *Journal of the American Geriatric Society, 44*(5), 489–497.

WOLF, S., ET AL. (1997a). Exploring the basis for tai chi chuan as a therapeutic exercise approach. *Arch Physical Medical Rehabilitation, 78*(8), 886–892.

WOLF, S., ET AL. (1997b). The effect of tai chi quan and computerized balance training on postural stability in older subjects. Atlanta FICSIT Group. Frailty and Injuries: Cooperative Studies on Intervention Techniques. *Physical Therapy, 77,* 371–381.

WOLFSON, L., ET AL. (1996, May). Balance and strength training in older adults: intervention gains and tai chi maintenance. *Journal of the American Geriatric Society, 44*(5), 498–506.

WONG, K. (1996). *The complete book of tai chi chuan: A comprehensive guide to the principles and practice.* Rockport, MA: Element Books, Inc.

YAN, J. (1995, November/December) The health and fitness benefits of tai chi. *JOPERD, 66*(9), 61.

YIU, K. (1981). *Tui shou and san shou in t'ai chi ch'üan.* Hong Kong: Self Published.

ZHUO, D., SHEPHARD, R., PLYLEY, M., & DAVIS, G. (1984). Cardiorespiratory and metabolic responses during tai chi chuan exercise. *Canadian Journal of Applied Sport Science, 9*(1), 7–10.

ZHUO, D. (1982). Preventive geriatrics: An overview from traditional Chinese medicine. *American Journal of Chinese Medicine, 10*(1–4), 32–39.

Appendix

A List of
Professor Edwin Pak-wah Leung's Publications

ENGLISH PUBLICATIONS

Books/Monographs

1. AUTHOR (2016). *The quasi-war in East Asia: China's dispute with Japan over the Ryukyu (Liuqiu) Islands and its global implications.* Paramus, NJ: Homa and Sekey Books.
2. CO-EDITOR (2015). *Global modernization review: New discoveries and theories revisited.* Singapore: World Scientific.
3. CO-AUTHOR (2013). *Historical dictionary of the Chinese Civil War*, 2nd edition. Lanham, MD: Scarecrow Press.
4. AUTHOR (2011). *Managing China's modernization: Perspectives on diplomacy, politics, education, and ethnicity.* Paramus, NJ: Homa and Sekey Books.
5. AUTHOR (2010). *The A to Z of the Chinese civil war.* Lanham, MD: Scarecrow Press.
6. AUTHOR (2006). *Essentials of modern Chinese history.* Piscataway, NJ: Research and Education Association,
7. EDITOR (2002). *Political leaders of modern China.* New York: Greenwood Press,
8. AUTHOR (2002). *Historical dictionary of the Chinese civil war.* Lanham: Scarecrow Press,
9. EDITOR-IN-CHIEF (2001). *Our New York experience.* Hong Kong: Cosmos Books.
10. CO-EDITOR (1997). Papers of the International Conference on the 50th Anniversary of the War of Resistance. Taipei: Academia Historica.
11. CO-EDITOR (1995). *Modern China in transition: Studies in honor of Immanuel C.Y. Hsu.* Claremont, CA: Regina Books.
12. EDITOR (1992). *Historical dictionary of revolutionary China, 1839-1976.* New York: Greenwood Press. (CHOICE Outstanding Academic Book of 1992).
13. AUTHOR (1989). *Adaptability of the Chinese immigrant students: Issues of language and culture.* Montclair, NJ: Global Learning Inc.
14. EDITOR (1988 October). *China and the West: Studies in education, nationalism, and diplomacy, Special volume of Asian Profile*, 16.5
15. EDITOR (1981/82 Winter). *Ethnic compartmentalization and autonomy in the People's Republic of China.* Special volume of Chinese Law and Government, XIV.4

Articles

1. (2011). Prelude to the Diaoyutai Dispute: Chinese-Japanese controversy over the Liuqiu Islands as seen from an international system-change perspective. In Yufan Hao and Bill Chou (Eds.), *China's Policies on its Borders and the International Implications.* Singapore: World Scientific, pp. 117-136.

2. (2009). Liuqiu Islands. In David Pong (Ed.), *Encyclopedia of Modern China.* Detroit: Gale Gengafe Learning, p. 522.

3. Co-AUTHOR (1994 Fall/Winter). Developing China's market economy, *Business Opportunities Journal*, p. 50.

4. (1994). Li Hung-chang and the Liu-ch'iu (Ryukyu) controversy, 1871-1881. In Kwang-ching Liu and Samuel Chu (Eds.), *Li Hung-chang and China's Early Modernization.* Armonk, NY: M.E. Sharpe, pp. 162-175.

5. (1993). Transition from de-ethnicization to re-ethnicization: The re-emergence of Chinese ethnic identity and the birth of a new culture in Hong Kong prior to 1997. In *Hong Kong in transition.* Hong Kong: One Country Two Systems Economic Research Institute, pp. 594-603.

6. (1990, May). Book Review: Pat Howard, Breaking the iron rice bowl: Prospect for communism in China's countryside. *Asian thought and society: An International Review 15*(44), pp. 333-334.

7. (1989). Chiang Kai-shek, 1897-1975. In *Read more about it: An encyclopedia of information sources on historical figures and events.* Ann Arbor: The Pierian Press, pp. 112-113.

8. (1988 October). China's decision to send students to the West: the making of a 'revolutionary' policy. In Edwin Pak-wah Leung (Ed.), *China and the West: Studies in education, nationalism and diplomacy, special volume of Asian Profile 16*(5), pp. 391-400.

9. (1988 October). The making of the Chinese Yankees: School life of the Chinese educational mission students. In Edwin Pak-wah Leung (Ed.), *China and the West: Studies in education, nationalism and Diplomacy*, special volume of *Asian Profile 16*(5), pp. 401-412.

10. (1988 October). The first Chinese college graduate in America: Yung Wing and his educational experiences. In Edwin Pak-wah Leung (Ed.) *China and the West: Studies in Education, Nationalism and Diplomacy*, special volume of *Asian Profile 16*(5), pp. 453-458.

11. (1987). Central authority vs. regional autonomy: The Inner Mongolian autonomous movement and the Chinese response, 1925-1947. *Journal of Oriental Studies 25*(1), 49-62.

12. (1986 December). From prohibition to protection: Ch'ing government's changing policy toward Chinese emigration. *Asian Profile 14*(6), 485-491.

13. (1986). Educating China's minority nationalities: Integration through ethnicization, *Proceedings of the 8th International Symposium on Asian*

Studies Vol. II, pp. 309-310.

14. (1986 December). Book review: Jane Leonard, Wei Yuan and China's rediscovery of the maritime world. *China Quarterly* 108, pp. 736-737.

15. (1986 May). Book review: Kay Ray Chong, Americans and Chinese reform and revolution, 1898-1992: The role of private citizens in diplomacy. *Pacific Historical Review*, pp. 328-329.

16. Co-author (1985). Chiang Kai-shek. In *Funk and Wagnalls New Encyclopedia*, *Vol. 6*, pp. 110-111.

17. (1984 June). Book review: Michael Hunt, The making of a special relationship: The United States and China to 1914. *China Quarterly* 98, pp. 367-368.

18. (1984). Education of the early Chinese students in America. In Jenny Lim (Ed.), *The Chinese American Experience*. San Francisco: The Chinese Historical Society of America and the Chinese Culture Foundation, pp. 203-210.

19. (1984). To Americanize China: The career of Yung Wing, Proceedings of the Sixth International Symposium on Asian Studies, Hong Kong, pp. 257-267.

20. (1983 April). The quasi-war in East Asia: Japan's expedition to Taiwan and the Ryukyu controversy. *Modern Asian Studies 17*(2), pp. 257-281.

21. (1983 Spring). The quest for an education in America: Chinese students' legal battle and the Supreme Court's decision. *The Courier: Journal of International Affairs II*(2), pp. 22-26.

22. (1983 Spring). China's national minorities, *Endeavors* (Seton Hall University) *I*(1), pp. 19-20.

23. (1983 December). China's quest from the West: the Chinese educational mission to the United States, 1872-1881. *Asian Profile 11*(6), pp. 527-534.

24. (1979 August). Review article: The politics of Chinese communism during the Kiangsi Period. *Asian Profile 7*(4), pp. 389-393.

25. (1979). General Ulysses S. Grant and the Sino-Japanese dispute over the Ryukyu Islands. *Proceedings of the First International Symposium on Asian Studies, Vol. II*, pp. 421-449.

26. (1973 May). Book review: Michael Gasster, Chinese intellectuals and the Revolution of 1911: The birth of modern Chinese radicalism. *History Journal 2*, pp. 25-28.

CHINESE PUBLICATIONS

Books/Monographs

1. (2021). 《東風再起時: 我半世紀的美國學術與文化之旅》, 香港: 三聯出版社。

2. (2021).《近代中國外交巨變與中西交流》，澳門：啟蒙時代出版社。
3. (2014).《世界現代化報告：首屆世界現代化論文集》（合編），
　　北京：科學出版社。
4. (2010).《中大人在美東》（合編），香港：天地出版社。
5. (2010).《正義的天使張純如》，武漢：湖北人民出版社。
6. (2008).《全球化下中西文化的交流：回顧與前瞻》，澳門：
　　澳門理工學院。
7. (2006).《近代中國在世界的崛起》，武漢：武漢大學出版社。
8. (2003).《複製成功的魔法》，香港：匯訊出版有限公司。
9. (2001).《中大人在紐約──香港中文大學美東校友會千禧文集》
　　（合編），香港：天地圖書有限公司。
10. (2000).《順逆境自強》（合著），香港：天地圖書有限公司。
11. (1999).《國際商業貿易》（浙江大學/香港理工大學國際企業
　　培訓中心），香港：香港理工大學。
12. (1998).《經濟環境》（浙江大學/香港理工大學國際企業培訓
　　中心），香港：香港理工大學。
13. (1997).《抗戰勝利五十周年國際研討會論文集》（合編），
　　臺北：國史館。
14. (1991).《近代中國外交的巨變──外交制度與中外關係的研究》，
　　臺北：臺灣商務印書館。
15. (1990).《近代中國外交的巨變──外交制度與中外關係變化的
　　研究》，香港：商務印書館。

Articles/Essays

1. (2015).《印象·武漢：三十載文化之旅》，余濟美、張雙慶編：
　　《文化生態之旅》，香港：香港中文大學聯合書院，第619-625頁。
2. (2013).《龍在海外的身影：走訪美國的華人與文化》，余濟美、
　　張雙慶編：《行走的愉悅》，香港：香港中文大學聯合書院，
　　第689-600頁。
3. (2008).《翱翔美洲的春夏秋冬》，張雙慶、危令敦編：《情思滿
　　江山 天地入沉吟》，香港：香港中文大學聯合書院，
　　第428-439頁。
4. (2004).《臺灣事件的真相與中日琉球爭端的翻案》，李金強等編：
　　《我武維揚：近代中國海軍史新編》，香港：香港海防博物
　　館，第222-231頁。
5. (2003).《璀璨多姿的中國多元文化》，《李文斯頓中文學校二十
　　周年校慶特刊》。
6. (2002).《華人的全球意識──中西文化整合的反思》，《人文論
　　叢》年卷，第125-129頁。
7. (2002).《一個香港人在北京──北大講學隨想》，《海外香港協
　　會會刊》。
8. (2001).《學術大觀園隨想》，梁伯華等主編：《中大人在紐約》，
　　香港：天地圖書有限公司。

9. (2001, 12月).《九一一的文明衝突震撼》，《中大校友》第28期。

10. (1999).《容閎的西學與中國的現代化》，吳汶萊主編：《容閎與中國近代化》，珠海：珠海出版社，第307-322頁。

11. (1995).《李鴻章和琉球爭端，1871-1881年》，劉廣京、朱昌崚合編：《李鴻章評傳》，陳絳譯校，上海：上海古籍出版社，第198-214頁。

12. (1994).《中國首批官費留學生：廣東的"留美幼童"》，鄭良樹主編：《潮州學國際研討會論文集》（下冊），廣州：暨南大學出版社，第763-774頁。

13. (1994, 11月).《教授夢·我的夢》，《中大美東校友通訊》創刊號。

14. (1989, 10月).《歐美學者對容閎與留美幼童研究的成果》，《社會科學動態》，第39-41頁。

15. (1989).《中外學者對"留美幼童"研究的成果》，《六十年來中國近代史研究》（下冊），臺北：中央研究院近代史研究所，第719-729頁。

16. (1988, 9月).《學人專訪——郭穎頤教授》（合著），《漢學研究通訊》卷七第三期，第148-152頁。

17. (1987).《臺灣事件與琉球問題的關係》，黃康顯主編：《近代臺灣的社會發展與民族意識》，香港：香港大學校外課程部，第237-251頁。

18. (1985).《容閎的西學與洋務》，《中國文化研究所學報》（香港中文大學）第十六卷，第43-52頁。

19. (1985).《歷史論文的寫作（整理王德昭教授演講）》，《王德昭教授史學論集》，香港：《王德昭教授史學論集》編輯委員會，第52-58頁。

20. (1983, 5月).《王德昭教授與近代中國史研究》，《中報月刊》總第40期，第88-89頁。

21. (1985, 11月).《悼念德昭師》，《史潮》新刊號第八期。

22. (1973, 5月).《書評：Michael Gasster, Chinese intellectuals and the Revolution of 1911: The birth of modern Chinese radicalism》，《歷史學報》第二期。

23. (1985, 1月).《辛亥革命與新軍——關於革命份子獲取軍力的途徑與辛亥革命成敗之關係》，《史潮》第八期，第1-3頁。

24. (1971, 10月).《洋務運動期間滿清外交政策轉變的審權》，《史潮》第七期，第7-24頁。

25. (1971, 6月).《追求中國現代化——談近代中國知識份子的思想傾向》，《聯合學生報》第55期。

26. (1970, 8月).《論中國的傳統政體——中外學者對中國傳統政體是否專制的論爭》，《史潮》第五、六期合刊，第16-21、35頁

Index

Made in the USA
Middletown, DE
07 April 2024

52498367R10133